T0323032

Sustaining Tanzania's Economic Development

UNU World Institute for Development Economics Research (UNU-WIDER) was established by the United Nations University as its first research and training centre and started work in Helsinki, Finland, in 1985. The mandate of the institute is to undertake applied research and policy analysis on structural changes affecting developing and transitional economies, to provide a forum for the advocacy of policies leading to robust, equitable, and environmentally sustainable growth, and to promote capacity strengthening and training in the field of economic and social policy-making. Its work is carried out by staff researchers and visiting scholars in Helsinki and via networks of collaborating scholars and institutions around the world.

United Nations University World Institute for
Development Economics Research
(UNU-WIDER)
Katajanokanlaituri 6B, 00160 Helsinki,
Finland
www.wider.unu.edu

Sustaining Tanzania's Economic Development

A Firm and Household Perspective

Edited by

OLIVER MORRISSEY
JOSEPH SEMBOJA
AND
MAUREEN WERE

*Study prepared by the United Nations University World Institute
for Development Economics Research (UNU-WIDER)*

OXFORD
UNIVERSITY PRESS

Great Clarendon Street, Oxford, OX2 6DP,
United Kingdom

Oxford University Press is a department of the University of Oxford.
It furthers the University's objective of excellence in research, scholarship,
and education by publishing worldwide. Oxford is a registered trade mark of
Oxford University Press in the UK and in certain other countries

Published in the United States of America by Oxford University Press
198 Madison Avenue, New York, NY 10016, United States of America

British Library Cataloguing in Publication Data

Data available

Library of Congress Control Number: 2023943840

ISBN 9780192885746

DOI: 10.1093/oso/9780192885746.001.0001

Printed and bound by
CPI Group (UK) Ltd, Croydon, CR0 4YY

Links to third party websites are provided by Oxford in good faith and
for information only. Oxford disclaims any responsibility for the materials
contained in any third-party website referenced in this work.

Foreword

In early 2019, in partnership with the Institute of African Leadership for Sustainable Development, more known as the UONGOZI Institute, in Dar es Salaam, UNU-WIDER conceived and launched a large collaborative research project—Sustainable Development Solutions for Tanzania—aimed at informing the development and implementation of policies towards economic transformation and sustainable development in Tanzania and the region.

The sizeable project marshalled Tanzanian, regional, and international researchers to focus on macroeconomic perspectives, domestic resource mobilization, extractives, industrialization, sustainable livelihoods, with gender as a cross-cutting issue giving a dimensional nuance. A value-added within the life of the research project was the capacity-building initiatives at UONGOZI, which included research mentorships, internships at UNU-WIDER, and tailor-made training research workshops.

Some of the founding research questions for the project were: What are the public debt dynamics in Tanzania? What are the implications of tax-benefit policies for development in Tanzania? What kind of incentives and policies are needed for mobilizing revenue from the large informal sector? What is the environmental and socio-economic impact of the extractive sector in Tanzania? What are the linkages between small- and medium-scale enterprises and large enterprises? How do households diversify their income? What are the implications of climate change on livelihoods? What constrains women's participation in the productive formal sector?

Weaving together the threads of the research findings into a coherent body of work, a cornerstone of the project was to provide stakeholders with a platform for research and policy discussions on Tanzania and the region generally, and bridge the discussions to the regional and international development debate on the Sustainable Development Goals (SDGs). In addition to engagement in Tanzania, UNU-WIDER disseminates research outputs more widely through various publications. A single-book volume could not include all the various research outputs while remaining coherent and of manageable length, so this book takes a narrow focus covering studies on firms and households. This in-depth book before the reader is solid testimony to the aims of the project.

I sincerely thank the editors—Oliver Morrissey, Joseph Semboja, and Maureen Were—for their leadership in the book project.

The research project was undertaken with special financial support of the Ministry for Foreign Affairs of Finland, for which all parties are most grateful.

UNU-WIDER gratefully acknowledges the support and financial contribution to its work programme by the Institute's core donors of the governments of Finland and Sweden. Without this vital funding our research and policy advisory work would be impossible.

Kunal Sen
Director UNU-WIDER
Helsinki, September 2023

Acknowledgements

In February 2020, UNU-WIDER and UONGOZI Institute organized a review workshop in Dar es Salaam in which early versions of the chapters were presented. At the workshop authors received comments and suggestions from participants and reviewers to help hone their drafts, and further comments on substance were provided by the book's trio of editors to allow finalization of the chapters. The editors and contributors are grateful to all who provided comments, and to the management and staff of UNU-WIDER and UONGOZI Institute for organizing the workshop—which was held just before the global extent of the COVID-19 pandemic hit—and ensuring successful completion of the collaborative research.

The editors want to thank the publications and communications staff at UNU-WIDER—especially Lorraine Telfer-Taivainen for her continuous guidance and expert support through the process of preparing the volume. We are grateful to the team at Oxford University Press, in particular Adam Swallow for advice and guidance, and their reviewers for useful comments on the proposal.

In addition, the editors wish to thank the Ministry for Foreign Affairs of Finland for supporting the project and research work.

Oliver Morrissey, Joseph Semboja, and Maureen Were
September 2023

Contents

List of figures

List of tables

List of abbreviations

ACT	Agricultural Council of Tanzania
AfCFTA	African Continental Free Trade Area
AGOA	African Growth and Opportunity Act
ASIP	Annual Survey of Industrial Production
ATM	automated teller machine
AW	agricultural wage
CET	Common External Tariff
CIP	Census of Industrial Production
CMT	cut, make, and trim
CPI	consumer price index
CRE	Central Registry of Establishment
DBRs	*Doing Business Reports*
DFS	digital financial services
DR	duty remission
EAC	East African Community
EPZ	export processing zone
FDI	foreign direct investment
FE	fixed effects
FOB	free on board, full package service
FTA	free trade area
FYDP	Five-Year Development Plan
GCI	global competitiveness index
GDP	gross domestic product
GSMA	Global Systems for Mobile Association
GVC	global value chain
HI	Herfindahl index
HS	Herfindahl-Simpson
ID	income diversification
IFC	International Finance Corporation
IGC	International Growth Centre
ILO	International Labour Organization
IMF	International Monetary Fund
ISIC	International Standard Industrial Classification
ISO	International Organization for Standardization
ITC	International Trade Centre
IV	Instrumental Variables
K&K	khanga and kitenge
KBLP	The Kilombero Business Linkage Project

KHDS	Kagera Health and Development Survey
KSCL	Kilombero Sugar Company Limited
LIC	low-income country
LSMS	Living Standards Measurement Study
MECI	measuring export competitiveness index
MFN	most favoured nation
MNE	multinational enterprise
MSMEs	micro, small, and medium-sized enterprises
NAS	non-agricultural self-employment
NAW	non-agricultural wage
NVC	national value chain
OBM	own brand manufacturer
ODM	original design manufacturer
OECD	Organisation for Economic Co-operation and Development
PTA	Preferential Trade Agreement
R&D	research and development
RCA	revealed comparative advantage
RE	random effects
RER	real exchange rate
ROO	relaxed rules of origin
RTA	regional trade agreement
RVC	regional value chain
SADC	Southern African Development Community
SDG	Sustainable Development Goal
SEZ	special economic zone
SITC	standard international trade classification
SMEs	small and medium-sized enterprises
SSA	sub-Saharan Africa
ST&I	science, technology, and innovation
STEM	science, technology, engineering, and mathematics
STISA-2024	Science, Technology, and Innovation Strategy for Africa 2024
T&A	textiles and apparel
TBL	Tanzania Breweries Limited
TCF	third-country fabric
TFL	Tanga Fresh Limited
TFLSS	Tanzania Firm-Level Skills Survey
TNPS	Tanzania National Panel Survey
UN	United Nations
UNCTAD	United Nations Conference on Trade and Development
UNIDO	United Nations Industrial Development Organization
UNU-WIDER	United Nations University World Institute for Development Economics Research
UV	unit value
VAT	value-added tax

VC	value chain
WDI	World Development Indicator
WITS	World Integrated Trade Solution
WRAP	Worldwide Responsible Accredited Production
WTO	World Trade Organization

Notes on contributors

Antonio Andreoni is professor of development economics at the Department of Economics of SOAS University of London. He is also a visiting professor of the South African Research Chair in Industrial Development, University of Johannesburg and UCL Institute for Innovation and Public Purpose. He has published extensively on industrial development, structural transformation, and the political economy of industrial policy, including in Eastern and Southern Africa. Among his books, *Structural Transformation in South Africa* (Oxford University Press 2021) and *From Financialisation to Innovation in UK Big Pharma* (Cambridge University Press 2022). Antonio is an editor of the *European Journal of Development Research*.

Laura Barasa is an economist specializing in development economics. She is a lecturer in the Department of Economics and Development Studies at the University of Nairobi, where she teaches econometrics and statistics. Laura has published in leading journals such as *Research Policy*. She is a European Investment Bank—Global Development Network (EIB-GDN) fellow, experienced in impact financing of innovative African start-ups.

Julian Boys is an economics researcher and consultant, currently working at Vivid Economics. He specializes in sustainable development, industrial and trade policy design and implementation, political economy analysis, regional integration and upgrading in global and regional value chains. He completed his PhD in economics at SOAS, University of London, and has previously been an economic advisor to the governments of Haiti and the United Kingdom as well as to international organizations, donors, social businesses, and NGOs.

Marco Carreras is a post-doctoral fellow at the Institute of Development Studies (IDS). His main research interests include innovation, the role of development banks, and corporate taxation. Marco holds a PhD in science, technology, and innovation (ST&I) from the Science Policy Research Unit (SPRU) at the University of Sussex and two MScs, one in economics from the University of Bologna and one in development economics from the University of Sussex.

André Castro is a PhD candidate at the University of Bonn, Center for Development Research. His research interests lie in the fields of agricultural and development economics, with a particular focus on the challenges and opportunities of the agro-processing sector in East Africa.

Ralitza Dimova is an associate professor at the Global Development Institute, University of Manchester. Her primary area of research is population economics, mainly in the context of West Africa and the Middle East and North Africa. She is particularly interested in the implications of intra-household decision-making and social norms for labour market outcomes and food security. Her recent and ongoing field work involves behavioural field experiments.

Daniele Guariso is a research associate at the Alan Turing Institute, working on the ESRC-funded project Agent Computing and AI to Achieve the 2030 Agenda. His main research interests lie in machine learning, network analysis, and computational methods in political economy and development economics. Daniele holds a PhD in economics from the University of Sussex, and has worked as a consultant for IDS, IGC, and other organizations.

Sandra Kristine Halvorsen is a senior advisor for data management at Norwegian Church Aid. Her research focuses on livelihoods, household dynamics, and women's empowerment in East Africa.

Caroline Israel is a researcher at the Institute of African Leadership for Sustainable Development (UONGOZI Institute). Her main areas of research are leadership, gender, and business management.

Rumman Khan is a lecturer in economics and econometrics at Keele University. He obtained his PhD from the University of Nottingham in 2017, the thesis was entitled 'Essays in Poverty and Household Analysis in Africa'. His research interests are broadly within the area of economic development in sub-Saharan Africa, with a particular focus on applied microeconometric analysis of household welfare and livelihoods using nationally representative surveys.

Josaphat Kweka is a founder and lead research associate/consultant of Talanta International, an advisory and research firm based in Tanzania, and a senior research associate with ESRF and REPOA. With twenty-six years of professional experience, he has extensive knowledge of the Tanzanian and East African economies, and strong competency in undertaking development policy research. He has worked and published on a wide range of development policy issues, including tourism economics, industrialization, SMEs, special economic zones, trade and regional integration.

Roseline Misati is a researcher at the Central Bank of Kenya. She has previously worked with different government ministries, as well as the Kenya Institute for Public Policy Research and Analysis. She has also served as a guest lecturer at the University of Nairobi and as a senior researcher in the African Institute for Remittances. She has published widely in the fields of development economics, monetary policy, trade and financial development.

Oliver Morrissey is a professor of development economics and Director of CREDIT, School of Economics, University of Nottingham, and a managing co-editor of the *Journal of Development Studies*. His primary research interests lie in aid policy (especially fiscal effects and conditionality), trade policy reform (including impacts on agriculture and on households), taxation, agricultural production, and labour markets, all with a focus on sub-Saharan Africa. He has published numerous articles in international journals, co-edited eight books and contributed to over fifty edited volumes.

Kethi Ngoka is a researcher at the Central Bank of Kenya. She has also worked at the Kenya Resident Representative Office of the International Monetary Fund as the country economist, and served as a guest lecturer at the Kenya School of Monetary Studies. She has published in the field of monetary policy, trade, exchange rates, and financial development.

Milla Nyyssölä is a research associate at UNU-WIDER and the focal point of the Tanzania country programme: Sustainable Development Solutions for Tanzania—strengthening research to achieve SDGs. She is also chief researcher at the Labour Institute for Economic Research, LABORE. Her research focuses on the microeconomics of development with a focus on livelihoods, gender, and social policies. She also has a background in studying aid effectiveness, conditional cash transfer programmes, and poverty measurement.

Maureen Odongo is a macroeconomist at the Central Bank of Kenya. Her research interests lie in international finance and macroeconomics, including exchange rates, trade and investment, monetary policy, gender, and public debt.

Amrita Saha is a research fellow at the Institute of Development Studies (IDS). Her work with international organizations and development agencies focuses on trade policy, agriculture, innovation, and political economy questions in development. She holds a PhD in economics from the University of Sussex. She has published in various development journals, including in the *European Journal of Political Economy, Economics and Politics, Food Policy*, and *Applied Economics*.

Joseph Semboja is the founding chief executive of the Institute of African Leadership for Sustainable Development—the UONGOZI Institute. An unprecedented organization in Tanzania, the UONGOZI institute focuses on executive education, policy dialogue, and research. Professor Semboja has in-depth knowledge of socio-economic development within Tanzania, as well as aspects of leadership, particularly within the public service, where he has published several articles and books. His career has spanned socio-economic research, senior management, and advising on the development, implementation, and analysis of major strategic policy and reform in Tanzania. In addition, Professor Semboja led the Tanzanian socio-economic research body REPOA for fifteen years.

Kunal Sen is director of UNU-WIDER and a professor of development economics at the University of Manchester. He has over three decades of experience in academic and applied development economics research, and has carried out extensive work on international finance, the political economy determinants of inclusive growth, the dynamics of poverty, social exclusion, female labour-force participation, and the informal sector in developing economies. His research has focused on India, East Asia, and sub-Saharan Africa.

Fadhili Sooi is an economist and research analyst at Talanta International. His professional areas of research interests include macroeconomics modelling, natural resources economics, and industrial economics. He has worked on a number of policy development areas including international trade, industrial competitiveness, financial inclusion, special economic zones, regional integration, and technical and vocational education and training. His expertise in policy research includes survey data analysis, econometrics, policy review, as well as project monitoring and evaluation.

Maureen Were is a senior economist at the Research Department of the Central Bank of Kenya (CBK). She spearheaded the work in this book while working as a UNU-WIDER researcher responsible for the collaborative research with the Institute of African Leadership for Sustainable Development (UONGOZI Institute) in Tanzania, 2018–21. She has a wealth of experience in economic policy, research, macroeconomic modelling, and teaching. Some of her awards include the Mo Ibrahim Leadership Fellowship award won in 2013. Before joining the CBK in 2008, she previously worked at the Kenya Institute for Public Policy Research and Analysis (KIPPRA) as a policy analyst and taught economics at Egerton University. She has authored several articles in refereed journals, working papers, and book chapters. Her research interests include macroeconomics, financial inclusion, trade and gender perspectives to development in Africa.

1

Firms and households in Tanzania's development

Oliver Morrissey, Joseph Semboja, and Maureen Were

1.1 Introduction

The contributions in this book address the sustainability of firms and households in Tanzania, taking retrospective and prospective perspectives. How successful have firms and households been in building resilience to sustain their growth and development—considering competitiveness and productivity for firms, and income or welfare for households? Has the ability to navigate successfully through shocks and a changing economic environment improved over the past two decades (since about 2000)? What are the lessons for managing and recovering from shocks, including the current shock of the global COVID-19 pandemic? The focus is on the achievements of firms and households, with a mainstreaming concept of the strategies adopted and how these relate to an ability to manage shocks and the implications for sustainability. Export competitiveness, innovation, and developing linkages contribute to the resilience and sustainability of firms, whereas income diversification and financial inclusion promote the resilience and sustainability of households. The volume is not about the broader national or community sustainable development agenda of meeting needs and improving human development without diminishing the development prospects of future generations. We do not address an integrated approach incorporating social, economic, political, and environmental concerns for a national development strategy.

The volume is not about the conventional broad perspective of sustainable development and not intended to assess national sustainable development strategies, although the themes addressed relate to some of the Sustainable Development Goals (SDGs) of the United Nations (UN 2015). This is not to deny the importance of national strategies, if only as statements of intent; indeed, Tanzania has had a series of national development plans for decades. Incorporating and planning for the SDGs revived the practice of preparing national development plans for almost all countries, so that by 2018 some 134 countries had such plans, more than double the number in 2006 (Chimhowu et al. 2019). This new approach to 'national development planning is largely a practice-led paradigm with a body of knowledge, concepts and practices that relate both to state responses to economic

Oliver Morrissey, Joseph Semboja, and Maureen Were, *Firms and households in Tanzania's development*. In: *Sustaining Tanzania's Economic Development*. Edited by: Oliver Morrissey, Joseph Semboja, and Maureen Were, Oxford University Press. © UNU-WIDER (2024). DOI: 10.1093/oso/9780192885746.003.0001 globalization and to how they plan to implement Agenda 2030 for Sustainable Development' (Chimhowu et al. 2019: 77). We do not assess Tanzania's development plans, although the topics covered contribute to issues to be addressed in implementing aspects of the plans.

The concept of sustainable development originated at the 1992 Earth Summit and, as the environment community were primarily concerned with stewardship of the ecosystem, 'sustainable development was identified with mainly environmental objectives' (Scholz 2015: 2). Managing natural resources and reducing adverse impacts on biodiversity and the environment became increasingly important global issues so that the environment was included in discussions of trade and global finance, and by 2000 climate change was firmly on the development agenda. The concern became institutionalized within the United Nations (UN), in part because sustainable development is 'a seductive notion, implying that we can have ecological protection, economic growth, social justice and international equity [all together]' (Brown 2002: 219). The SDGs represented a culmination of incorporating development and environmental concerns to provide a broader global conception of sustainable development: the 2030 Agenda (UN 2015) explicitly recognized 'the immediate link between improving and ensuring human welfare and the need to maintain the capacity of the planet to provide environmental services' (Scholz 2015: 4).

The scope of the SDGs and associated broad concept of sustainable development goes far beyond what can be addressed here, and we do not assess Tanzania's achievements against the multiple goals and numerous targets. Nonetheless, given the comprehensive nature of the SDGs, it is unsurprising that the issues addressed in this volume are relevant to some of the seventeen Goals, notably Goals 8 (includes growth and employment) and 9 (includes industry and innovation), gender equality (Goal 5), poverty reduction (Goal 1), and to a lesser extent Goal 17 (global partnerships include trade policies). The aims of promoting inclusive and sustainable industrialization and fostering innovation under Goal 9, with targets to increase the share of industry in employment and GDP, reflect the development aspirations of developing countries including Tanzania. Although, in certain respects, industrialization conflicts with other SDGs concerned with reducing emissions and environmental sustainability, much of the focus is on manufacturing, and certain targets are relevant to this volume (Rippen et al. 2015: 59–60):

Target 9.3: increase the access of small-scale industrial and other enterprises, in particular in developing countries, to financial services, including affordable credit, and their integration into value chains and markets.

Target 9.4: upgrade infrastructure and retrofit industries to make them sustainable, with increased resource-use efficiency and greater adoption of clean and environmentally sound technologies and industrial processes.

Chapters address issues related to the welfare of households, including employ-ment and financial inclusion, and performance of firms, including value chains, linkages, and innovation, especially for small and medium enterprises (SMEs). The focus is on the analysis of development experiences in Tanzania since 2000, considering perspectives of business (trade and firms) and households, to offer insights informing Tanzania's path to sustainable development. The chapters cover: competitiveness and value chains as determinants of trade performance; the importance of technology, innovation, linkages, and value chains for firms; trends in household income diversification and rural livelihoods; and improvements in financial inclusion, particularly through digital financial innovations such as mobile money services. Chapters incorporate gender and regional, including urban–rural, differences.

The information contained in this volume contributes to the design and imple-mentation of policies relating to improving the business environment and enhanc-ing households' welfare and access to income-earning opportunities. The volume is intended as a complement to existing studies of Tanzania. Previous research and policy analysis addressed poverty and macroeconomic performance, as out-lined in Section 1.2, but less attention has been given to analysis at the firm and household level. For example, whereas Adam et al. (2017) focuses mostly on macroeconomic and sector issues, Potts (2019) focuses on the sustainability of development and poverty reduction—most of the chapters provide a historical overview, with a focus on longitudinal surveys for poverty analysis and the agri-cultural sector. By addressing the firm and household level, this volume intends to address this information gap and complement existing studies of Tanzania.

The chapters in the volume describe aspects of the economy in the 2000s, up to about 2018, after almost two decades of economic reform efforts. There is no detailed assessment of the impact of the COVID-19 pandemic, as the research was completed before this shock occurred, although some implications are considered. Despite this, the chapters in this volume offer insight on the trajectory of the Tanza-nian economy when the pandemic hit, and the constraints identified in the studies will shape recovery and development options in the post-pandemic environment. While the research is specific to Tanzania, there are implications for the sustain-ability of development in other developing countries, at least in sub-Saharan Africa (SSA).

1.2 Context: Tanzanian performance since 2000

Economic performance in Tanzania since 2000 has been good by SSA standards—real GDP growth rate averaged over 5 per cent a year since 2010. This has contributed to a reduction in poverty, although the extent depends on the source of data. Using the World Bank *Povcal* US$1.90 a day measure, headcount poverty fell from 72 per cent to 49 per cent between 1991 and 2011, equivalent to a reduction of almost 2 per cent per annum. Although poverty declined, given the increase in population almost half of the population remained below the US$1.90 a day level in 2018 (World Bank 2019: 3). In contrast, using the national poverty line, the Tanzania Household Budget Surveys suggest that consumption poverty fell from 39 per cent in 1991/92 to 28 per cent in 2011/12 (United Republic of Tanzania [URT] 2014). There were improvements on all measures: basic needs poverty fell from 34 per cent in 2007 to 28 per cent in 2012 and 26 per cent in 2018, while extreme poverty fell from 12 per cent in 2007 to 10 per cent in 2012 and 8 per cent in 2018 (World Bank 2019: 7). The slowdown in the rate of poverty reduction since 2012 is cause for concern given the 'signs of an increasingly weak response of poverty to economic growth' (Aikaeli et al. 2021: 1872), even if partly explained by the tendency of GDP per capita growth to be faster than average consumption growth (World Bank 2019: 19).[1] Nevertheless, by SSA standards, Tanzania achieved reasonable growth and poverty reduction. Following the two decades of sustained growth, Tanzania formally graduated from low-income country to lower-middle-income country status in July 2020.

The performance of the economy since 2000 reflects the impact of sustained economic reform efforts initiated from the 1980s, with encouragement and sometimes pressure from development partners, although the relationship with some, especially the IMF and World Bank, was often difficult (Edwards 2014). Significant reforms were implemented from the early 1990s in the areas of trade (reducing tariffs, removing import restrictions, and providing export incentives), exchange rates (moving to a market-oriented regime), macroeconomic and public financial management, and gradual privatization (Edwards 2012: 40–2). Kessey et al. (2017) highlight the importance of greater central bank (Bank of Tanzania) independence from the mid-1990s. As monetary policy was less constrained by the need to finance fiscal deficits, the Bank of Tanzania's ability to manage inflation and interest rates strengthened and contributed to maintaining macroeconomic stability (certainly compared to the 1980s). Ndulu and Mwase (2017: 31) attribute better macroeconomic performance to a combination of institutional and policy stability, improved human capital indicators and favourable changes in the external environment. These laid the groundwork for a more stable growing economy, although major challenges persisted due to the slow structural economic transformation and limited achievement of sustainable livelihoods (consistent with slow consumption growth, especially in rural areas).

Perhaps the most important trade policy event in the period was the (re)establishment of the East African Community (EAC) with Kenya and Uganda on 7 July 2000 (Burundi, Rwanda, and South Sudan joined later, and the

---

[1] The two are not directly comparable as GDP and consumption measures are adjusted for inflation in different ways and growth in non-household components of GDP (such as government and investment) was faster than consumption growth.

Democratic Republic of Congo in 2022). The most obvious effect of the EAC is the Common External Tariff (CET) that came into force in January 2005 with a simplified structure of tariffs at rates of 0 per cent, 10 per cent, or 25 per cent (although the average was below existing tariffs in Tanzania, 40 per cent of tariff lines were at the higher rate). As Tanzania had relatively high tariffs compared to its partners, this represented significant trade liberalization—the mean average tariff fell from 15.1 per cent in 2000 to 12.9 per cent (Morrissey and Jones 2009: 39). Data from the World Trade Organization (WTO) show that this understates the tariff reductions for most manufactures, whilst agriculture commodities continued to face an average tariff of 17 per cent and some foods faced high tariffs (WTO 2007: 18–19), such as rice (75 per cent), milk (60 per cent), and maize (50 per cent). Agreeing the CET required compromise as the three countries had conflicting interests (Uganda's tariffs increased); in general, tariffs on imported inputs were reduced while protection was maintained for products produced in the EAC, especially in agriculture. This was expected to provide a boost for intra-regional trade, and for producers reliant on imported inputs (including of capital goods), although there was less success in agreeing common consistent non-tariff measures.

While typically justified as protecting domestic producers, tariffs impose a cost on consumers, especially where food imports from outside EAC are subject to tariffs. There is evidence that reductions in tariffs on food imports over 1991–2007 benefited Tanzanian households, especially in urban areas: lower food prices due to tariff reductions are of more benefit to urban households, who are more likely to consume imported food, compared to the rural poor who consume locally produced food (Leyaro et al. 2010: 446). This suggests, conversely, that the costs of higher food tariffs (prices) for urban consumers were not offset by benefits to the rural producer population, consistent with a general bias against agriculture (or policies that did not incentivize increases in agricultural production and productivity).

Government policies on agriculture focused on production have not been successful (Edwards 2014), especially in expanding production of food crops. Gollin and Goyal (2017) observe that farmers have the ability to grow the grains desired by local consumers. Consequently, they argue for promoting rural–urban links and agri-processing to create domestic value chains to meet growing urban food demand, potentially displacing food imports (especially of rice and wheat for urban consumption). In this way, promoting agriculture goes hand-in-hand with promoting local manufacturing. Although agriculture is important for rural livelihoods it has not been a source of income growth. Poverty rates are highest in farm households and lowest among households headed by wage employees engaged in non-agricultural businesses as a main source of income; non-farm employment appears to be a route out of poverty (World Bank 2015: 25–6).

Agricultural products and fishing have accounted for a large share of exports, although trade (export duties) and exchange rate policy (typically overvalued) and the operation of marketing boards have been unfavourable to agriculture since the 1970s. Liberalization in the 1990s did not eliminate the bias against all agricultural exports. By the early 2000s implicit taxation remained high for cotton and tea, although it was eliminated for coffee and sisal; for food crops, taxation of maize was eliminated and rice and wheat were effectively subsidized (Morrissey and Leyaro 2009: 319). Ineffective policy support notwithstanding, agriculture remained the dominant sector in the economy—export crops alone, if value of linkages with other firms through production and marketing are included, were more important than manufacturing for demand, employment and income in 2000 (World Bank 2001). Despite the growth of services and to a lesser extent manufacturing, agriculture is still the major sector. Gollin and Goyal (2017) note that agriculture accounted for almost 30 per cent of GDP, a third of exports (mostly tobacco and coffee) and nearly three-fourths of employment by 2012, but suffers from low productivity (output per worker) and low growth rates in productivity and yields.

The share of employment in the agriculture sector—the sector with the lowest average labour productivity—has been declining so the sector 'has not played an important role in job creation: the net increase in agricultural employment accounted for only 11 per cent of the total increase in employment between 2002 and 2012; almost 90 per cent of the jobs created over this ten-year period were in the non-agriculture sector' (Ellis et al. 2018: 297–8), mainly by the micro and small firms in the informal economy. The agriculture sector has not performed to potential—income growth is lower, and poverty vulnerability higher, in rural compared to urban households (Aikaeli et al. 2021)—perhaps one reason why agriculture was not viewed as a dynamic sector for growth. Although Tanzania is resource-rich, efforts to promote commodity-based industrialization in the mining sector such as through backward linkages from gold mining have also not been successful (UNCTAD 2022). This is partly due to low competitiveness of local firms given high import costs of services and inputs to smelting and refining activities (Mjimba 2011).

There is a prevalent view in development that industrial policy could develop sub-sectors 'of industry with the potential for both high levels of productivity [and] high rates of productivity growth' (Weiss 2015: 135). Tanzania followed this view and proposed policy reforms to support improvements in industrial performance (Morrissey and Leyaro 2015). At first this involved state ownership, widespread in Tanzania up to the 1990s, especially for the largest firms. State-owned enterprises probably accounted for over a fifth of medium and large manufacturing firms even in the mid-1990s and were more likely to be exporters than private firms, perhaps because they were larger and often in agri-processing (Grenier et al. 1999). Following more than a decade of privatization, fewer than 10 per cent of manufacturing firms were state-owned by the mid-2000s (URT 2009). Most manufacturing firms are micro, small and medium enterprises (MSMEs), family-owned and with less than ten or even five employees, and employment in manufacturing 'accounts for less than 5 per cent of the total labour force, with the largest 40 manufacturing companies employing 36 per cent of all manufacturing labour' (UNIDO and URT 2012: 17).

The manufacturing sector is concentrated in Dar es Salaam and to a lesser extent Arusha, and based on low-value-added, low-technology activities. Manufacturing value added (MVA) only exceeded 10 per cent of GDP (half of this accounted for by the food and beverages sector) after 2010, below the level in Mozambique, Kenya, and Malawi (UNIDO and URT 2012: 35), although MVA per capita increased by more than a quarter between 2007 and 2012 (UNIDO 2014: 87). McMillan et al. (2017) note that manufacturing grew rapidly between 2000 and 2010, albeit from a very low base, and many MSME firms (such as in furniture and textiles) have higher output per worker than the manufacturing average. These firms have potential for job creation and could be supported through targeted policies such as supporting clusters in export processing zones (EPZs), incentives (such as grants), and improving trade logistics. This is relevant given the slow rate of employment growth in manufacturing, reflecting the predominance of MSMEs, even if improvements in the trade and exchange rate regimes and the more stable macroeconomic environment help to increase competitiveness (UNIDO and URT 2012: 19). There only appear to be a few reasonably dynamic sectors: garments and textiles are a source of employment growth in new companies, as is the food sector (but older companies continue to be the largest employers). At the regional level, intra-African backward integration in regional value chains is also low—less than 8 per cent of the manufacturing value added—and regional value chains have not developed sufficiently to effectively facilitate gainful integration into the global value chains (GVCs) (Abreha et al. 2021; UNCTAD 2022).

Whereas trade reforms, including reducing export duties and tariffs, improves price incentives for exporters, Tanzania also introduced a number of measures to promote manufacturing exports, including tariff-free imports of capital equipment and inputs used in export production. In 2002, mainland Tanzania established a manufacturing EPZ with some tax exemptions to encourage sectors including agri-processing, textiles, and garments (Zanzibar has a longer-established scheme, mostly for garments and fish processing), attracting over US$80 million in investment by 2005 (WTO 2007: A2-159–162). This can begin to address one limitation in industrial policy: evidence shows that attracting foreign investment and technology is important to develop new industrial activities (Weiss 2015: 147) but this an area in which Tanzania has had at best limited success. Measures have also been implemented to improve transport and logistics and reduce trade costs, notably investment in increasing the efficiency of the port of Dar es Salaam. Investment in trade facilitation (reducing trade costs) is important for competitiveness, although Kunaka et al. (2017) caution against over-investing in capital-intensive ports and roads given the limited potential to create employment. While trade and exchange rate reforms and a more stable macroeconomic environment facilitate manufacturing growth, there has been a failure to achieve the structural transformation to supplant the importance of the agriculture sector. Consequently, the major constraints facing manufacturing firms have changed little over the past few decades (Wangwe et al. 2014). The low quality of transport and utilities infrastructure increases costs and discourages investment, especially given the difficulty of access to credit. These themes are taken up in a number of chapters in the book.

Access to credit and expanding financial inclusion is seen as a vital route to improving household welfare (and potentially supporting MSMEs, at least the smallest with low financing requirements); the success of mobile money in Kenya is held up as an example (Jack and Suri 2014). The process of economic liberalization and privatization of the state-owned banks from 1996 has been associated with financial development and a steady reduction in financial exclusion, from 54 per cent in 2006 to 27 per cent in 2013, with more than half of the adult population using mobile financial services (Mwamba et al. 2017: 286). All the major telecommunications companies in Tanzania offer mobile money services, making it easier for businesses—most importantly MSMEs—to send and receive payments (Ellis et al. 2018). Riley (2018) demonstrates the benefits of financial inclusion, comparing households who receive remittances through mobile money to households without access to mobile money in villages experiencing a rainfall shock between 2009 and 2013. She finds that households using mobile money are able to increase consumption (by up to 10 per cent) when they experience an income shock, whereas households without access to mobile money experience a reduction in consumption (about 6 per cent following a rainfall shock).

The spread of mobile money, financial innovation, and deregulation permitting entry of non-traditional players and mobile network operators, dramatically increased access to financial services. For example, use of banking services increased from 9 per cent to 14 per cent between 2006–13, but use of non-bank financial services (including microfinance and mobile money) grew from 2 per cent to 43.5 per cent over the same period (Mwamba et al. 2017: 279–80). That notwithstanding, Tanzania still lags behind Kenya in financial inclusion and the gender gap has not improved substantially.

1.3 Outline of the book

This book focuses on firm-level and household-level analysis with a view to examine challenges, opportunities, and policy insights that are relevant for informing Tanzania's path to sustainable development. There are eight chapters covering, inter alia, firm performance, trade linkages and the growth of SMEs, income diversification at the household level, and gender gaps in firm innovation and financial inclusion. Employment growth in manufacturing as part of structural transformation is essential to increase the wage share in labour income. Greater engagement in international trade offers one route to a growing manufacturing sector. However, the SMEs in Tanzania have limited involvement in regional and global value chains so it is important to address how firms can enter value chains and which sectors have the greatest potential. Growth, increasing the employment and value added of firms, and financial inclusion support increasing household incomes to achieve sustainable development and livelihoods.

Four chapters address export diversification and competitiveness, especially the role of participation in value chains for the growth of Tanzania's manufacturing exports. Chapter 2 (Kweka and Sooi) investigates how the growth of small and medium enterprises (SMEs) can be enhanced by creating linkages with large firms, especially through international trade. The SMEs sector is dominated by very small firms mostly in the informal sector with a very low survival rates (hence not sustainable), with over half the SMEs in domestic trade and a third in services (the sectors with low capital requirements). Given the lack of good data on firm networks, indirect measures of linkages are used—exporting, including access to GVCs, and importing inputs support a relationship with foreign firms that are likely to be large; technology sharing requires networks; and being in more concentrated sectors indicates the degree of competition with large firms. The analysis identifies the role of linkages with larger firms, or more generally engagement with foreign firms, for sustaining SMEs.

Chapter 3 (Boys and Andreoni) considers the differential effects of engaging in national, regional, or global value chains on the ability for upgrading in the textiles and apparel sectors, using data from a firm survey, semi-structured interviews, and official sources. Does participating in GVCs offer the greatest potential for upgrading, or do regional and national value chains (RVCs and NVCs) provide similar opportunities to increase competitiveness and upgrade into higher-value activities (and facilitate subsequent entry into potentially more lucrative GVCs)? Upgrading is a strategy for sustainable growth but may be enhanced or constrained by details in trade agreements, such as Rules of Origin requirements, that affect incentives and the ability of firms to expand and sustain growth. The chapter considers industrial and trade policies at the national, regional, and global levels, to assess the extent to which they enable firms to benefit from different value chains.

Chapter 4 (Saha, Bueno Rezende de Castro, Carreras, and Guariso) also addresses textiles and apparel firms with export potential through GVCs but focuses on the role of imported technology for improving productivity and absorptive capacity. Trade-linked technological change has the potential to improve firm performance if available technologies and best practices can be adopted to increase production efficiency and move into higher-value-added activities. The chapter employs primary and secondary survey data and qualitative information from semi-structured interviews to examine the role of absorptive capacity in firm productivity. Echoing earlier themes, the study considers the role of linkages between firms and local networks for improving access to technology and labour with appropriate skills to increase productivity. The chapter also considers the effect of differences across geographical clusters on the types of local linkages. This incorporates the role of industrial clusters in the context of how agglomeration 'enhances efficiency and reduces costs, but also facilitates the ability of firms with limited endowments to specialise and spread risks' (Nadvi 2015: 117).

Chapter 5 (Misati and Ngoka) examines the determinants of manufacturing competitiveness and export performance, distinguishing chemicals and manufactured products, and revealed comparative advantage (RCA) using panel data for the period 1997–2018. Classifying manufacturing exports according to skill and technology intensity, they show that technology-intensive manufacturing is still at a low level but there has been some increase in the share of medium-technology and skilled labour-intensive manufactures, such as fabricated metals and chemicals. Improvements in the RCA index and export performance since the late 1990s are observed for fabricated metal products, essential oils, textiles, and non-metallic mineral manufactures, while some sectors have benefited from GVCs (textiles, garments, and footwear). In investigating the determinants of performance, the analysis considers the role of labour productivity, imported inputs, tariffs faced in export markets and a GVC participation measure in addition to institutional and economic environment indicators.

Chapter 6 (Barasa) addresses innovation directly through a focus on gender differences in adopting new or improved products or processes by firms—are female entrepreneurs more or less innovative? This relates to the 'new' view of industrial policy that emphasizes the central role of innovation (new products and processes) as a driver of development (Weiss 2015: 136), with the focus on technology. Using data on 403 firms from the 2015 Tanzania Firm-Level Skills Survey, the analysis decomposes the determinants of innovation for male- and female-owned or managed firms by endowments (firm characteristics) and coefficients (gender differences in the effect of an endowment). The aim is to identify the factors that support innovation, and whether these differ between male- and female-owned firms, in order to derive (gendered) strategies to promote innovation and improve competitiveness. Gender gaps undermine the sustainable growth of female-owned enterprises as they imply that human capital is underutilized or misallocated, and if female entrepreneurs are disadvantaged, it is likely physical capital is also underutilized (for example, if they face more difficulties accessing credit). The chapter addresses the importance of greater female participation in private sector development to achieve the SDGs of gender equality and women's empowerment, innovation, and socio-economic inclusion for all.

Sustained growth of firms is important for households through creating employment opportunities and wage growth. Chapter 7 (Khan and Morrissey) uses three waves of Tanzanian National Panel Surveys (2008/09, 2010/11, and 2012/13, with 3,676 households in at least two waves) to explore the effect of income diversification on household welfare (in terms of expenditure on food consumption). Income diversification is captured by the number and types of sources of income for household labour in agriculture (farming), non-agricultural self-employment, agricultural wage and non-agricultural wage employment. Does the effect on household welfare differ according to the type of labour, such as between diversification into non-agricultural wage versus self-employment, how important is the expansion of off-farm employment, and are there gender differences?

On a related theme, Chapter 8 (Dimova, Halvorsen, Nyyssölä, and Sen) investigates the drivers of livelihood diversification for a panel of rural households in Tanzania over 1991–94, addressing the literature on whether income diversification is a means of survival or a means of accumulation. Income diversification is measured by the shares of different sources of household income. The determinants of income diversification for households in Kagera in the 1990s are used to predict diversification in 2004 and then compared with actual values observed for the same households in 2004. In this way the factors that determine diversification are identified and validated. The chapter contributes to understanding the role of diversification for sustained household development allowing for initial endowments that make it difficult to reduce inequality and considering the role of infrastructure improvements (supporting mobility and market access) and entry into new income-generation activities.

Tanzania, like many African countries, has seen significant expansion in mobile money services. Chapter 9 (Were, Odongo, and Israel) examines the access to and use of such digital financial services in increasing financial inclusion with a focus on gender differences. While financial inclusion increased to 65 per cent of adults in 2017 from 58 per cent in 2013, there was a gender gap of 9.4 percentage points against females in access to formal financial services. Using FinScope Tanzania survey data for 2017, the analysis shows that women (especially married women) are less likely to access mobile phone and bank-based financial services compared to men. Furthermore, women are less likely to save and borrow compared with men. The study identifies various factors—such as education, income, marital status, employment—that influence access to mobile money and banking services to suggest strategies to increase financial inclusion and support sustained increase in household welfare, accounting for gender differences in preferences.

The final chapter draws together the policy implications to identify the challenges and opportunities in ensuring the sustainability of development in Tanzania, in light of the regional and global effects of the COVID-19 pandemic.

References

Abreha K. G., W. Kassa, E. K. K. Lartey, T. A. Mengistae, S. Owusu, A. G. Zeufack (2021). *Industrialization in Sub-Saharan Africa: Seizing Opportunities in Global Value Chains*. Africa Development Forum. Washington, DC: World Bank.

Adam, C., P. Collier, and B. Ndulu (eds) (2017). *Tanzania: The Path to Prosperity*. Oxford: Oxford University Press https://doi.org/10.1093/acprof:oso/9780198704812.001.0001

Aikaeli, J., D. Garcés-Urzainqui, and K. Mdadila (2021). 'Understanding Poverty Dynamics and Vulnerability in Tanzania: 2012–2018'. *Review of Development Economics*, 25(1): 869–94, https://doi.org/10.1111/rode.12829.

Brown, K. (2002). 'Environment, Biodiversity and Sustainable Development: International Issues'. In C. Kirkpatrick, R. Clarke, and C. Polidano (eds), *Handbook on Development Policy and Management* (pp. 213–20). Cheltenham: Edward Elgar.

Chimhowu, A., D. Hulme, and L. Munro (2019). 'The 'New' National Development Planning and Global Development Goals: Processes and Partnerships'. *World Development*, 120: 76–89, https://doi.org/10.1016/j.worlddev.2019.03.013

Edwards, S. (2014). *Toxic Aid: Economic Collapse and Recovery in Tanzania*. Oxford: Oxford University Press.

Edwards, S. (2012). 'Is Tanzania a Success Story? A Long-term Analysis'. Mimeo, Anderson Graduate School of Management, University of California Los Angeles. Also a chapter in S. Edwards, S. Johnson, and D. Weil (eds) (2015) *African Successes* (Vol. I): *Government and Institutions*. Chicago: University of Chicago Press.

Ellis, M., M. McMillan, and J. Silver (2018). 'Employment and Productivity Growth in Tanzania's Service Sector'. In R. S. Newfarmer, J. Page, and F. Tarp (eds), *Industries without Smokestacks: Industrialization in Africa Reconsidered*. Oxford: Oxford University Press.

Gollin, D., and R. Goyal (2017). 'Agricultural Transformation in Tanzania: Linking Rural to Urban through Domestic Value Chains'. In C. Adam, P. Collier, and B. Ndulu (eds), *Tanzania: The Path to Prosperity*. Oxford: Oxford University Press.

Grenier, L., A. McKay, and O. Morrissey (1999). 'Exporting, Ownership and Confidence in Tanzanian Enterprises'. *The World Economy*, 22(7): 995–1011.

Jack, W., and T. Suri (2014). 'Risk Sharing and Transactions Costs: Evidence from Kenya's Mobile Money Revolution'. *American Economic Review*, 104 (1): 183–223.

Kessy, P. J., S. A. O'Connell, and J. Nyella (2017). 'Monetary Policy in Tanzania: Accomplishments and the Road Ahead'. In C. Adam, P. Collier, and B. Ndulu (eds), *Tanzania: The Path to Prosperity*. Oxford: Oxford University Press.

Kunaka, C., O. Hartmann, G. Raballand, and R. Shamte (2017). 'Trade, Logistics Infrastructure, and Regional Integration'. In C. Adam, P. Collier, and B. Ndulu (eds), *Tanzania: The Path to Prosperity*. Oxford: Oxford University Press.

Leyaro, V., O. Morrissey, and T. Owens (2010). 'Food Prices, Tax Reforms and Consumer Welfare in Tanzania 1990–2007'. *International Tax and Public Finance*, 17(4): 430–50.

McMillan, M., J. Page, and S. Wangwe (2017). 'Unlocking Tanzania's Manufacturing Potential'. In C. Adam, P. Collier, and B. Ndulu (eds), *Tanzania: The Path to Prosperity*. Oxford: Oxford University Press.

Mjimba, V. (2011). 'The Nature and Determinants of Linkages in Emerging Minerals Commodity Sectors: A Case Study of Gold Mining in [the United Republic of] Tanzania'. Discussion Paper 7. Making the Most of Commodities Programme. Milton Keynes: Open University.

Morrissey, O., and C. Jones (2009). 'Missed Opportunities: The WTO Trade Policy Review for the East African Community'. *The World Economy Global Trade Policy 2008*, 31(9): 1409–32.

Morrissey, O., and V. Leyaro (2009). 'Distortions to Agricultural Incentives in Tanzania'. In K. Anderson and W. Masters (eds), *Distortions to Agricultural Incentives in Africa* (pp. 307–28). Washington DC: World Bank.

Morrissey, O., and V. Leyaro (2015). 'Industrial Development in Tanzania: Reforms, Performance, and Issues'. In M. Tribe and J. Weiss (eds) *Routledge Handbook of Industry and Development* (pp. 382–97). London: Routledge.

Mwamba, N., N. Massawe, and K. Komba (2017). 'Financial Sector Development and Financial Inclusion'. In C. Adam, P. Collier, and B. Ndulu (eds), *Tanzania: The Path to Prosperity*. Oxford: Oxford University Press.

Nadvi, K. (2015). 'What Role for Small Enterprises? Industrial Clusters, Industrial Policy and Poverty Reduction'. In M. Tribe and J. Weiss (eds) *Routledge Handbook of Industry and Development* (pp. 116–34). London: Routledge.

Ndulu, B., and N. Mwase (2017). 'The Building Blocks towards Tanzania's Prosperity: Lessons from Looking Back and the Way Forward'. In C. Adam, P. Collier, and B. Ndulu (eds), *Tanzania: The Path to Prosperity*. Oxford: Oxford University Press.

Potts, D. (ed.) (2019). *Tanzanian Development: A Comparative Perspective*. Oxford: James Currey.

Riley, E. (2018). 'Mobile Money and Risk Sharing against Village Shocks'. *Journal of Development Economics*, 135: 43–58.

Rippin, N., T. Altenburg, and A. Pegels (2015). 'Goal 9: Build Resilient Infrastructure, Promote Inclusive and Sustainable Industrialisation and Foster Innovation'. In M. Loewe and N. Rippin (eds), *Translating an Ambitious Vision into Global Transformation: The 2030 Agenda for Sustainable Development*, Discussion Paper 7/2015. Bonn: German Development Institute (www.die-gdi.de).

Scholz, I. (2015). 'Introduction: A Universal Agenda for Sustainable Development and Global Co-operation'. In M. Loewe and N. Rippin (eds), *Translating an Ambitious Vision into Global Transformation: The 2030 Agenda for Sustainable Development*, Discussion Paper 7/2015, Bonn: German Development Institute (www.die-gdi.de).

UN (2015). *Transforming our World: The 2030 Agenda for Sustainable Development*, draft to be adopted by the UN General Assembly in its session on 25–27 September. New York: United Nations, https://sustainabledevelopment.un.org/content/documents/7891Transforming%20Our%20World.pdf

UNCTAD (2022). *The Economic Development in Africa Report 2022: Rethinking the Foundations of Export Diversification in Africa—The Catalytic Role of Business and Financial Services*. Geneva: United Nations Conference on Trade and Development (UNCTAD).

UNIDO (2014). 'Growth and Distribution Pattern of World Manufacturing Output: A Statistical Profile'. Working Paper 02/2014. Vienna: UNIDO.

UNIDO and URT (2012). *Tanzania Industrial Competitiveness Report 2012*. Vienna: United Nations Industrial Development Organization. Dar es Salaam: Ministry of Industry and Trade and President's Office Planning Commission of the United Republic of Tanzania (URT).

URT (2009). 'Annual Survey of Industrial Production (ASIP) Statistical Report. Dar-es-Salaam: Ministry of Industry and Trade, United Republic of Tanzania (URT).

URT (2014). *Household Budget Survey Main Report, 2011/12*. Dar es Salaam: National Bureau of Statistics, United Republic of Tanzania (URT).

Wangwe, S., D. Mmari, J. Aikaeli, N. Rutatina, T. Mboghoina, and A. Kinyondo (2014). 'The Performance of the Manufacturing Sector in Tanzania: Challenges and the Way Forward'. WIDER Working Paper 2014/085. Helsinki: UNU-WIDER.

Weiss, J. (2015). 'Industrial Policy: Back on the Agenda'. In M. Tribe and J. Weiss (eds) *Routledge Handbook of Industry and Development* (pp. 135–50). London: Routledge.

World Bank (2001). *Tanzania at the Turn of the Century: From Reforms to Sustained Growth and Poverty Reduction*. Washington, DC: Government of Tanzania and World Bank.

World Bank (2015). *Tanzania Mainland Poverty Assessment*. Washington, DC: World Bank. http://www.worldbank.org/content/dam/Worldbank/document/Africa/Tanzania/Report/tanzania-poverty-assessment-05.2015.pdf

World Bank (2019). *Tanzania Mainland Poverty Assessment: Executive Summary*. Washington, DC: World Bank.

WTO (2007). *Trade Policy Review for East African Community 2006*. Geneva: Bernan Associates for the World Trade Organization.

2

Linkages with large firms and growth of SMEs in Tanzania

Josaphat Kweka and Fadhili Sooi

2.1 Background and motivation

Globally, small and medium-sized enterprises (SMEs)[1] have increasingly been recognized by policy actors as important drivers of economic growth. In parallel, research on SME growth dynamics and their indispensable role in the economies of various nations has become an important field of study. Some of the key issues covered in SME studies include the role of SMEs in productivity increase (Diao et al. 2018); enhanced access to credit (Atieno 2009; Sibanda et al. 2018); human capital investment (Pauli 2015); the impact of technology and innovation (Subrahmanya et al. 2010); and the role of the government and business environment (OECD 2018). The underlying motivation in most studies is the recognition that SMEs are significant drivers of entrepreneurship, job creation, and innovation (e.g. Katua 2014; OECD 2018). Owing to the structure of the economy, policy, and institutional environment, the importance of SMEs differs across countries. For instance, Diao et al. (2018; 2019) found that the bulk of employment growth between 2008 and 2012 in Tanzania was accounted for by small firms in the informal sector and contributed more than one percentage point to economy-wide labour productivity growth in that period. Estimates by the International Labour Organization (ILO) show that the SME sector accounts for more than one-third of total gross domestic product (GDP) in emerging and developing economies, while globally, employment by SMEs more than doubled from 79 million in 2003 to 156 million in 2016 (ILO 2017). Consequently, policy actors across the world have increased policy attention towards SMEs as an engine for inclusive growth and development (Tewari et al. 2013).[2]

---

[1] The definition of SME varies across countries according to conceptual treatment of the informal sector and small business (Kweka and Fox 2011). This study uses the SME definition adopted by the micro, small, and medium enterprise (MSME) policy of 2002 (URT 2002), which is micro (1–4 employees), small (5–49 employees), medium (50–99 employees), and large (100+ employees), although the focus is on enterprises with 10+ workers.

[2] We acknowledge support from UNU-WIDER and UONGOZI Institute that made this work a reality. We greatly appreciate the helpful comments and guidance from the book's editors, and also

Josaphat Kweka and Fadhili Sooi, *Linkages with large firms and growth of SMEs in Tanzania*. In: *Sustaining Tanzania's Economic Development*. Edited by: Oliver Morrissey, Joseph Semboja, and Maureen Were, Oxford University Press.
© UNU-WIDER (2024). DOI: 10.1093/oso/9780192885746.003.0002

Despite their important role in the economy, SMEs in developing countries face a myriad of challenges that dampen their potential for growth. The challenges range from inadequate working capital and lack of access to markets, credit, and technology, to poor work premises and a generally unfavourable policy environment. Clearly, efforts to address these challenges have been limited because the majority of SMEs operate in the informal sector, which constrains their abilities to link with formal large enterprises. Recent literature on SME growth dynamics identifies linkages with large firms as some of the enablers of SME development and competitiveness (Barbin 2017; Francisco and Canare 2018) and finds that large firms can help small firms to grow and break into national and global markets (Hussain 2000; OECD 2005).

This study assesses the extent and determinants of linkages between SMEs and large firms in Tanzania and to what degree such linkages are an important driver of SME growth performance. Tanzania is an interesting case to examine this question for a number of contextual reasons. First, the country is endowed with enormous natural resources (e.g. mining, natural gas, expansive land, wildlife) that have been important factors for attracting investment (including foreign direct investment [FDI] by multinational enterprises [MNEs]). While FDI inflows have fuelled growth (especially the natural resource sectors such as mining, oil, and gas), a question is raised about the extent at which such growth is inclusive. Consequently, the government is strongly advocating for the need to strengthen linkages between MNEs/FDIs and local firms as one of the means to achieve inclusive growth. The SME policy (currently under review) focuses strongly on promoting linkages with large firms (URT 2016) and is considered an important pillar for the country's ongoing industrialization drive.

Despite the good policy intentions, the challenge remains that the majority of the domestic enterprise sector is largely characterized by a massive informal sector, which, despite being a notable source of jobs for the majority of youth entering the labour market, is limited in terms of ability to transform and tap the opportunities from economic growth. The recent analysis by Diao et al. (2018) shows that small informal firms account for the bulk of employment growth in the last decade and that a small subset of these firms experienced productivity growth that was higher than in the formal/large manufacturing sector. Clearly, it will be useful to understand whether and to what extent linkages with large firms can catalyse further growth of such firms, and which policy actions are critical for facilitating them.

Despite the numerous contributions offered by SMEs in developing countries, they are consistently faced with mitigating factors limiting their sustainability (Kwarteng et al. 2019; Qalati et al. 2021). These challenges may limit SMEs ability to grow such that a sudden crisis puts them at high risk of collapse or may

Milla Nyyssölä and Kati Hirvonen. Any errors or matters of interpretations should be the responsibility of the authors alone and should not be attributed to UNU-WIDER or UONGOZI Institute.

lead to SME closure completely and ultimately make their development unsustainable. Since the 2008/09 global economic crisis, various governments in both developed and developing countries have paid serious attention to SMEs because of the critical role they play in poverty reduction, job creation, and social cohesion (Qalati et al. 2021). Indeed, ensuring that SMEs development is sustainable is important because it ensures their sustainable contribution to the overall economy development. As noted earlier, linkages with large firms can help SMEs mitigate the challenges they face and become competitive. Creating linkages with large firms can potentially help SMEs become sustainable through adopting improved practices and technology from large firms and increased market opportunities. Some linkage programmes discussed in Section 2.4.4 have aimed to create sustainable businesses as part of their intended outcomes. Although there are no empirical studies relating firm linkages to sustainability, one can agree that sustainability is more likely gained when there is firm growth, increased competitiveness, and increased productivity.

In this chapter, we analyse SME linkages with large firms in Tanzania in order to examine the extent at which they enhance growth performance of small firms. Specifically, we (a) identify the types and extent of linkages between SMEs and large firms; (b) examine the factors that determine linkages between SMEs and large firms; and (c) estimate the impact of linkages on the growth performance of SMEs. Section 4.2 discusses the relevant literature. Section 4.3 outlines the approach and methodology for analysis, the results of which are presented and discussed in Section 4.4. Section 4.5 concludes and outlines some implications for policy.

2.2 Literature review

Although a recent strand of literature identified linkages with large firms as possible contributors to the growth of SMEs, there is a dearth of empirical evidence (Francisco and Canare 2018). Most of the reviewed studies on linkages between SMEs and large firms are mainly descriptive. The approaches used in the studies differ—ranging from a combination of descriptive and empirical analyses for country case studies, sectors, or a particular issue on the linkage between small and large firms (for a summary of the main findings of the empirical studies see Appendix A in Kweka and Sooi 2020). Topics covered include how the linkages can help spur SME growth by addressing different challenges (Musundi and Ogollah 2014), determinants and nature of linkages (Jamieson et al. 2012), costs and benefits of linkages (Francisco and Canare 2018), or identification of different types of linkages (Barbin 2017). A number of studies document the impact of linkages on SME growth, distinguishing patterns across sectors such as construction (Ishengoma and Lokina 2013), financial (Atieno 2009), agriculture and tourism (Hussain 2000), and furniture (Sibanda et al. 2018).

A number of studies are devoted to reviewing linkage programmes or initiatives. For example, Quak (2019) provides a useful review of a number of case studies at sector, country, and project level, ranging from lead firm–SME linkages in the Philippines, FDI and SMEs in Vietnam, the brewery industry in Africa, an aluminium smelter in Mozambique, and a project to link smallholder farmers with large processing businesses in Latin America. The Organisation for Economic Co-operation and Development (OECD 2018) summarizes different initiatives by country governments to foster linkages, including through subsidies to enhance the capabilities of local SMEs. Economies often cited in this regard are Singapore, Ireland, Chinese Taipei, and Malaysia. Based on a case study of several industries, Bekefi (2006) provides useful lessons from a review of initiatives for building linkages between small and large firms in Tanzania.

Pant et al. (2018) used meta-analysis to review the lead firms–SME linkage initiatives and noted that SMEs are increasingly involved as the supplier of niche products for lead firms. Furthermore, the study found evidence that the impact of top-down, privately led linkage initiatives is mainly seen in increasing quality and organizational capacity in creating efficient supply chains compared to the (often bottom-up) publicly led linkage initiatives whose objectives (hence impact) have mainly included job creation, policy reforms, and investments.

In general, empirical evidence shows that linkages with large firms exist, albeit weaker compared to linkages among large or small firms. More importantly, almost all studies conclude that small–large firm linkage plays an important role in SME growth.

2.3 Methodology

Various methods have been used in different studies to assess firm linkages, subject to data availability and reliability. Ideally, one would pursue linkage analysis using primary survey data. This could provide a powerful means to conduct qualitative and descriptive analysis and a more accurate picture of the types and extent of formal relationships between firms on the ground. As primary data collection was not feasible, we rely on the available Annual Survey of Industrial Production (ASIP) for the empirical analysis. This limits the scope of the study but is supplemented with insights from secondary information on programmes and initiatives by various actors engaged in promoting linkages in Tanzania.

2.3.1 Conceptual framework

Firm linkage refers to relationships and interactions between firms. These can be in the form of trade (buying and selling), information sharing, and competition (firm entrance into the market causing another firm to improve capacity or go out of business) (Francisco and Canare 2018). Most empirical studies (including the current one) analyse linkages between SMEs and large firms based on the pioneering work of Dunning (1992), in which four types of linkages are measured, namely:

- *Linkages with competitors*, where a large firm may raise standards in the economy, thus forcing SMEs to improve their method of production, distribution, and marketing.
- *Backward linkages with suppliers (SMEs)*, where large firms source their goods or services from SMEs and, in doing so, create opportunities for them. Such linkages may range from arm's-length transactions to deep inter-firm and long-term relationships.
- *Forward linkages with customers*, where large firms supply their output to SMEs including SMEs buying capital from large firms, SMEs selling merchandise produced by large firms, and SMEs insourcing auditing or other services from large firms.
- *Linkages with technology partners and other spillover effects*, where large firms supply technology and collaborate with SMEs in undertaking innovation or technological change.

We use the approach by Javorcik (2004), Blalock and Gertler (2008), and Sánchez-Martín et al. (2015) to measure forward and backward linkages. A forward linkage between two firms is measured as the proportion of total sales by one firm to another, while a backward linkage is the percentage of inputs (out of total inputs) of one firm obtained from another firm. As noted in Section 2.3.2, a limitation of ASIP is that it does not include data on the size of firms that any firms purchase from or sells to, so we use information on international trade (importing and exporting) to proxy links with large (foreign) firms. Following Francisco and Canare (2018), competition linkage is measured by the number of SMEs competing with large firms while technology linkage is measured by the number of SMEs that have formed a joint venture or strategic alliance with large firms in which they share technology and innovation.

Because we measure a linkage to analyse its role in SME growth, it is important to clarify how we intend to measure SME performance. The literature classifies methods of estimating SME growth into subjective and objective methods. The former assesses the individual's (the owner) satisfaction on the business outcome while the latter is based on financial and non-financial indicators (Hassan and Hart 2016). Financial indicators include sales, profits, and market shares while non-financial indicators include employment growth (Delmar et al. 2003). We use sales and employment to measure SME performance.

2.3.2 Empirical model and estimation

The empirical analysis involve estimation of two models, one to estimate the determinants of linkages between SMEs and large firms and the second model to assess the contribution of linkages to observed performance of SMEs. Following Mohammed and Beshir (2019), we use the following to estimate the determinants of linkages:

$$L_{it} = \emptyset + \Sigma_{t=1}^{m} \Sigma_{i=1}^{n} \alpha Z_{it} + \varepsilon_{it} \qquad (1)$$

Where L_{it} is a categorical dependent variable with values representing whether or not enterprise i participates in the linkage (forward, backward, technology, or competition linkage) at time t; $\emptyset$ is the constant term; Z_{it} is a vector of independent variables (firm characteristics, such as size, owner sector, training) as used in the literature; and α is a vector of parameters. The independent variables include firm experience in years (*lexper*) and total production (*ltotprod*), both in logs; and a number of binary variables such as training (*train*), business association membership (*association*), exporting (*export*), raw materials shortage (*raw*), capacity under-utilization (*capacity*), location in special economic zones (*SEZ*), and foreign ownership (*foreign*). The binary variables are coded 0 for negative values (No) and 1 for positive values (Yes), except capacity = 1 if operating below 80 per cent capacity.

While measurement of independent variables is straightforward, our data set is limited in the extent we can use it to measure forward and backward linkages. The ASIP panel data covering years 2008–16 is the most recent available firm-level survey data on Tanzania, covering establishments with ten or more employees. It provides firm-level information including production, sales, nature of activities, and costs but the data on sales and purchases by firms to/from other domestic firms (required for backward and forward linkages) is not available. Given these limitations, we improvised a measure of forward and backward linkages by creating a proxy of SME export and import relationships as follows. To measure a forward linkage (*forward*), we created a dummy variable with value 1 if the firm (SME) exports any of its products and 0 otherwise (the firm does not export). To measure a backward linkage (*backward*), we created a dummy variable with value 1 if the firm imports any of its inputs and 0 otherwise (the firm does not import).[3] Using exports and imports as proxies for forward/backward linkages means that, in effect, we are analysing the propensity to export or import. We did use the

---

[3] Exporting SMEs engage with more sophisticated foreign firms and learn skills and techniques, so such SMEs are more likely to supply sophisticated buyers (De Loecker 2007), which are mostly large firms. On the other hand, importing SMEs are able to source sophisticated inputs and are therefore more productive (Bas and Strauss-Kahn 2014), and this makes them more likely to buy from large firms.

limited measure of linkages in the data and the results were generally similar but statistically weaker.

The ASIP data contained sufficient information for measuring the other two dependent variables (technology and competition). Technology linkage (*tech*) is measured as a dummy variable with values equal to 1 if the firm has either cooperated with (or received) technology and production services from public technology intermediaries (e.g. Tanzania Automotive Technology Centre, Tanzania Bureau Standards) or has partnered with private companies in research and development (R&D) activities and 0 otherwise. Finally, the competition linkage (*compet*) was constructed as follows. First, we generated a measure for the proportion of large to small and medium-sized firms based on industrial subsectors across each firm. Then we calculated the average value of this measure across all firms in all sectors so that we generated a dummy variable (*compet*) with value 1 if the measure was equal to or higher than the calculated average and 0 if the measure was lower than average. Essentially, SMEs in subsectors with many large firms (with higher-than-average measure) participate in a competition linkage while those in subsectors with few large firms do not (less than average)[4].

Estimation uses the random effects (RE) logit for determinants because using fixed effects (FE) is not feasible given that most binary linkage variables are fixed: if a firm participated in linkages in all years the linkage measure is time-invariant, and the FE estimator will drop that observation. Inference and estimation are limited by the nature of the available data, as RE does not address the challenge of omitted variables so estimates may be biased.

The effect of linkages on SME performance is estimated with a semi-logarithmic model:

$$Ln\ Y_{it} = \gamma + \Sigma_{t=1}^{m}\Sigma_{i=1}^{n}\alpha X_{it} + \Sigma_{t=1}^{m}\Sigma_{i=1}^{n}\beta N_{it} + \varepsilon_{it} \qquad (2)$$

Where Y_{it} is the indicator for SME performance (sales or employment); X_{it} is a vector of linkage variables (backward, forward, competition, and technology linkages), all of which are binary variables with values 0 for not participating in the linkage and 1 for participating in the linkage; N_{it} is a vector of other factors determining the growth of SMEs including business association membership (*association*), providing training (*train*), foreign ownership (*foreign*), private ownership (*private*), log years of experience (*lexper*), log of value added (*lVA*) and log of capital value (*lK*); γ is the constant term; and ε_{it} is the random error term. Again, the RE estimator is employed.

---

[4] In effect, *compet* = 1 is a firm size composition measure. Although not an ideal measure of competition linkage, it reflects the extent to which SMEs coexist with large firms. In terms of performance, it captures differences of SMEs in sectors with relatively more compared to fewer large firms.

2.4 Results and discussion

The first subsection reports the measures of the extent of SME linkages in the industrial sector, based on estimating the total and annual number and percentage of SMEs that participated in each type of linkage. Discussion on the extent of linkages is brief to focus more on determinants of linkage and their role in SME performance (more detail and analysis of trends is available in Kweka and Sooi 2020). As noted, the analysis does not necessarily measure the linkage with domestic firms because the forward/backward proxies capture linkages with foreign firms (that are likely to be large relative to other Tanzanian firms).

2.4.1 Extent of linkages

The proportion of SMEs with linkages to large firms is highest for technology (38 per cent), followed by competition (19 per cent, indicating the proportion in sectors with relatively more large firms), while very few SMEs export output (5 per cent) for forward, or import inputs (8 per cent) for backward, linkages (Kweka and Sooi 2020: Figure 1). Overall, it appears that only a few SMEs participate in linkages with large firms, with the exception of technology, although they may participate in linkages with other SMEs. This result is not peculiar for Tanzania, as it corresponds with findings from other studies showing that relatively few linkages between SMEs and large firms exist (Jamieson et al. 2012; Musundi and Ogollah 2014; Francisco and Canare 2018). Interestingly, the number of large firms participating in linkages with other large firms is greater, including over 30 per cent exporting or importing and over 50 per cent for technology (Kweka and Sooi 2020: Figure 2), supporting the view that linkages occur more when firms are of a similar size. As established in the literature, large firms are more likely to export and import. Results also suggest a tendency for large firms to cluster in certain subsectors (indicated by competition linkages for 43 per cent of large firms).

2.4.2 Determinants of linkages between SMEs and large firms

Because the policy objective is to promote linkages between small and large firms, analysis of determinants of linkages will be informative for policy in identifying ways to increase participation of firms. The RE estimates reported in Table 2.1 are consistent with the descriptive statistics. Significant factors increasing firms' participation in technology linkage (column 1) are total production (relatively larger firms), association (networks), training (labour quality), experience (older firms), and location in a SEZ. Factors increasing the likelihood of a firm

Table 2.1 Determinants of firm linkages in the industrial sector

Variable	1.RE Tech	2.RE Backward	3.RE Forward	4.RE Compet	5.RE Total	6.POLS Supply	7.POLS Purchases
raw	0.038	−0.004	−0.002	0.008	0.012	−0.041	−0.029
	(−0.021)	(−0.006)	(−0.002)	(−0.004)	(0.023)	(0.021)	(0.055)
ltotprod	0.044***	0.016***	0.006**	0.005**	0.054***	0.960***	0.880***
	(−0.007)	(−0.003)	(−0.002)	(−0.001)	(0.007)	(0.008)	(0.021)
train	0.121***	0.008	0.004	0.014**	0.160***	0.041	0.079
	(−0.023)	(−0.006)	(−0.002)	(−0.005)	(0.024)	(0.021)	(0.057)
lexper	0.044***	−0.001	0.001	0.002	0.044***	−0.017	−0.067*
	(−0.011)	(−0.003)	(−0.001)	(−0.002)	(0.011)	(0.009)	(0.027)
association	0.225***	0.014*	0.005	0.005	0.235***	0.036	−0.168**
	(−0.024)	(−0.007)	(−0.003)	(−0.005)	(0.023)	(0.025)	(0.064)
export	0.024	0.028**		0.020*			
	(−0.048)	(−0.010)		(−0.009)			
foreign	−0.048	0.036***	0.013*	0.067***	0.249***	−0.162*	−0.565**
	(−0.045)	(−0.009)	(−0.006)	(−0.017)	(0.055)	(0.063)	(0.186)
private	0.020	0.038*	0.003	−0.010	0.023	0.045	0.117
	(−0.043)	(−0.018)	(−0.006)	(−0.009)	(0.046)	(0.047)	(0.112)
SEZ	0.138***	−0.006	0.001	0.008	0.158***	−0.008	0.210**
	(−0.027)	(−0.007)	(−0.003)	(−0.006)	(0.030)	(0.028)	(0.071)
Constant	−18.06***	−47.22***	−42.11***	−30.03***	0.93***	0.692***	−0.737
	(−2.86)	(−6.88)	(−7.05)	(−4.75)	(2.54)	(0.141)	(0.379)
N	4,094	3,729	4,001	3,878	4,094	3,968	3,123

Notes: RE indicates the RE logit estimator and POLS is pooled OLS. All regressions include region dummies; an unreported 2016 dummy is negative and significant for column 3. Sector dummies, with mining the omitted category are unreported: manufacturing dummy significant for columns 6 (negative) and 7 (positive); electricity sector dummy significant for columns 1 and 5 (negative) and 7 (positive); water sector dummy negative and significant for column 6. Standard errors in parentheses, significant at * $p<0.1$; ** $p<0.05$; *** $p<0.001$.
Source: Authors' calculations based on ASIP data, 2008–16 (URT 2018). More detail in Kweka and Sooi (2020: Tables 3 and 6).

to participate in backward linkages (importing) are again total production and association membership, but also foreign ownership and private ownership (the only case where this is significant). Only two factors are significant determinants of forward linkage (exporting), total production and foreign ownership. Three factors increase the likelihood of competition linkages, being in sectors with an above-average share of large firms—total production, training, and exporting, all consistent with relatively larger SMEs.

Regressions included dummies for region, sector, and year. Sector dummies were insignificant for linkages except that SMEs in the electricity sector are less likely to participate in technology linkage compared to SMEs in the mining sector. All regressions had large, negative, and significant constants, consistent with omitted variables that appear to be associated with not having linkages (recall that we could not account for fixed effects given the features of the data). Alternative estimators yielded broadly similar results (Kweka and Sooi 2020: Table 3).

Column 5 presents estimates of determinants of having any linkage using *total linkage* as the dependent variable (1 if the SME participated in any type of linkage and 0 otherwise). The results show that all the factors associated with any specific linkage (except private ownership) are significant. In general, while factors such as total production, foreign ownership, association, and training were significant determinants in more than one type of linkage, others such as being located in an SEZ and firm's age (experience) appeared only in the technology linkage, while private ownership only in the backward linkage. Our results are similar to those in Mohamed and Beshir (2019), except that shortage of raw material (*raw*) is insignificant in our case.

As noted earlier, using exporting and importing as proxies for forward and backward linkages is less ideal as there are SMEs that are linked with large firms but not necessarily exporting or importing. Furthermore, using exporting and importing implies that we are capturing SMEs that have linkage with foreign firms rather than local firms. To partially address this challenge, we use (the log value of) local sales (*supply*) and local purchases (*purchases*) made by SMEs as proxies for integration with domestic firms (forward and backward linkages respectively). These measures are only indicative; *supply* includes sales to final domestic consumers and neither measure captures the size aspects of the linkage. Results are in the final two columns of Table 2.1. Total production is a significant determinant of both forward and backward linkages and is the only factor significant and positive for both, consistent with relatively larger SMEs being more integrated. It is interesting to note that foreign ownership is significant and negative for both in contrast to being positive and significant for the trade measures of forward and backward linkages. Foreign-owned firms are more likely to be integrated with global value chains and this appears to displace local linkages (or reduces the value of them). Location in an SEZ is significantly associated with higher local purchases (but not with importing, column 2), suggesting the SEZ are encouraging adding value to local supplies. Older firms (*experience*) appear to purchase less locally, although this is only weakly significant—as age is not significant for imports, or sales, this may be capturing relatively small older firms. Alternative estimators yielded broadly similar results (Kweka and Sooi 2020: Table 4).

Although not reported, there are differences according to the sector of activity (compared to mining), indicating that the extent of linkages is influenced by the nature of industrial activities, in line with the finding in Quak (2019) that SME linkages with large firms have different patterns across sectors. Specifically, manufacturing firms have higher purchases but lower sales, consistent with being more domestically integrated but smaller on average than mining firms. Table 2.2 reports results of regressions for determinants of linkages focusing only on the manufacturing sector (comparable to columns 1–4 of Table 2.1). While there is no

Table 2.2 Linkages in the manufacturing sector

Variable	1.RE Tech	2.RE Backward	3.RE Forward	4.RE Compet
raw	0.054*	−0.004	−0.001	−0.003
	(−0.022)	(−0.009)	(−0.004)	(−0.013)
ltotprod	0.051***	0.024***	0.009***	0.004
	(−0.008)	(−0.004)	(−0.002)	(−0.004)
train	0.098***	0.017	0.005	0.051*
	(−0.022)	(−0.009)	(−0.003)	(−0.020)
lexper	0.043***	−0.003	0.001	0.009
	(−0.011)	(−0.005)	(−0.002)	(−0.007)
association	0.195***	0.018	0.006	0.035
	(−0.027)	(−0.011)	(−0.004)	(−0.019)
export	−0.004	0.037*		0.046
	(−0.052)	(−0.015)		(−0.033)
capacity	0.015	0.027**	0.004	0.007
	(−0.020)	(−0.010)	(−0.004)	(−0.012)
foreign	−0.059	0.041**	0.022***	0.228***
	(−0.045)	(−0.014)	(−0.007)	(−0.061)
SEZ	0.119***	−0.004	0.001	−0.001
	(−0.027)	(−0.012)	(−0.004)	(−0.017)
Constant	−12.08***	−36.26***	−52.19***	−31.2***
	(−1.79)	(−5.92)	(−9.11)	(−0.57)
N	3197	2891	3197	2471

Notes: RE indicates the RE logit estimator. All regressions including region dummies; private included but never significant. Dummies identified certain manufacturing sub-sectors less likely to have linkages, especially for importing, as food products, wood and wood products, non-metallic mineral products, and furniture. Standard errors in parentheses, significant at * $p<0.1$; ** $p<0.05$; *** $p<0.001$.
Source: Authors' calculations based on ASIP data (2008–16) (URT 2018). More detail in Kweka and Sooi (2020: Table 4).

change in the signs of coefficients, significance alters. A shortage of raw materials is significant in increasing the probability of technology linkage, perhaps indicating that manufacturing firms seek advice to make better use of (or gain access to) raw materials. In backward linkage, association has now become insignificant while capacity (operating below 80 per cent capacity) is significant and positive. The positive relationship between capacity and backward linkage (SMEs that import) is consistent with SMEs constrained by a shortage of domestic inputs, even if the latter is insignificant. Almost a third of SMEs that import (participate in backward linkage) operate below 80 per cent capacity, compared to 27 per cent for SMEs that do not import. While production and exporting were significant determinants of competition linkage in Table 2.1, these are insignificant for the manufacturing sector—production (relative size) remains very significant for all other linkages (and exporting is weakly significant for backward linkages).

2.4.3 Relationship between linkage participation and SME performance

The effect of linkages on performance is assessed by estimating the relationship between linkages and two performance measures, log total employment (*lemploy*) and log total sales (*lsales*), including SME characteristics, using both pooled OLS and RE (as mentioned earlier, fixed effects is inappropriate for the data). Data limitations prevent the construction of growth measures (variables such as association, SEZ, and technology linkage are available only for 2015 and 2016 while some firms only entered the survey in 2016) so employment and sales are in levels to measure SME performance. Results of determinants of SME performance are in Table 2.3—the first two columns show pooled and the final two RE results. Results are quite consistent for the estimators, albeit with some differences between employment and sales. Forward linkages, value added (*lVA*), capital (*lK*), association, and training are consistently associated with better performance on both measures. Competition and technology linkages are associated with higher sales (but not consistently employment) while backward linkages are associated with higher employment (but not sales). Underutilized capacity is associated with lower sales, as could be expected, but insignificant for employment, whereas foreign-owned firms seem to have higher employment (consistent with expectations, if perhaps surprising that they don't also have higher sales). Manufacturing firms have lower employment compared to mining (not reported), consistent with having smaller firms. Fixed effects estimates provided fewer significant results, consistent with the limitations of the data structure (Kweka and Sooi 2020: Table 5).

Overall, we observe that the importance of SME-large firm linkages differs depending on the measure of performance (sales or employment). Backward linkage (importing) is associated with employment only whereas forward linkage (exporting) is associated with employment and sales. Technology and competition linkages are only consistently important for sales, similar to the argument of Francisco and Canare (2018) that SMEs enjoy benefits such as improved productivity through competition with and learning from large firms. The current status of SME–large firm linkage is weak, but potential exists for strengthening it given its beneficial impact on the growth performance of SMEs. The next section considers successful cases of linkage initiatives from which to draw lessons for future support.

2.4.4 Are there successful linkage cases to learn from?

A review of experiences for Tanzania shows that there have only been a few initiatives by development actors to promote linkage between SMEs and large firms,

Table 2.3 Determinants of SME performance in the industrial sector

Variable	1.POLS lemploy	2.POLS lsales	3.RE lemploy	4.RE lsales
forward	0.214***	0.338**	0.142**	0.256*
	(−0.061)	(−0.113)	(−0.052)	(−0.117)
backward	0.229***	0.189	0.197*	0.193
	(−0.059)	(−0.101)	(−0.078)	(−0.101)
tech	0.045	0.239***	0.051	0.235***
	(−0.028)	(−0.051)	(−0.030)	(−0.054)
compet	0.0647	0.251***	0.0951*	0.232**
	(−0.040)	(−0.073)	(−0.044)	(−0.078)
association	0.122***	0.161**	0.122***	0.154*
	(−0.029)	(−0.056)	(−0.029)	(−0.063)
train	0.123***	0.117*	0.0951**	0.144**
	(−0.028)	(−0.051)	(−0.031)	(−0.054)
lVA	0.079***	0.744***	0.061***	0.750***
	(−0.009)	(−0.018)	(−0.009)	(−0.020)
lK	0.037***	0.073***	0.025***	0.059***
	(−0.007)	(−0.014)	(−0.006)	(−0.015)
capacity	−0.040	−0.145**	−0.060*	−0.133**
	(−0.024)	(−0.047)	(−0.024)	(−0.051)
foreign	0.149*	0.009	0.214***	0.064
	(−0.062)	(−0.117)	(−0.061)	(−0.115)
lexper	0.025*	−0.008	0.012	−0.001
	(−0.011)	(−0.021)	(−0.013)	(−0.022)
Cons	1.799***	3.676***	2.057***	3.778***
	(−0.132)	(−0.266)	(−0.136)	(−0.300)
N	1,741	1,715	1,741	1,715

Notes: RE indicates the RE logit estimator and POLS is pooled OLS. All regressions including region dummies. Other unreported variables included: manufacturing dummy significant for columns 1 and 4 (negative); electricity sector dummy never significant; water sector dummy negative and significant for column 1. Standard errors in parentheses, significant at * $p<0.1$; ** $p<0.05$; *** $p<0.001$.
Source: Authors' calculations based on ASIP data (2008–16) (URT 2018). More detail in Kweka and Sooi (2020: Table 5).

mainly as part of government and donor programmes. Although some appear to have had an impact on SME growth performance, these are isolated cases with limited if any replication. Tanzania Breweries Ltd. is the only large firm, of which we are aware, that has taken initiatives to assist SMEs in establishing linkages; the majority of large firms consider SMEs unsuitable or unprepared for entering such relationships given the challenges of informality and weak capacity. For instance, a UNIDO survey in 2010 found that only a few large firms (including foreign) were engaged in subcontracting local suppliers (forward linkage) and many declined to purchase from a local supplier because of poor quality (Oyen and Gedi 2013). The following cases are examples of past initiatives.

Case 1: UNCTAD-ITC Empretec linkage programme

In 2013, UNIDO in collaboration with the International Trade Centre (ITC) established a business linkage programme as part of Empretec, a flagship capacity-building programme for promoting entrepreneurship and SMEs to facilitate inclusive growth. The programme aimed at facilitating new linkages and deepening existing partnerships between MNEs/large companies and SMEs to enhance the latter's sustainability. A workshop conducted in 2015 to discuss progress and challenges facing the programme highlighted that SME suppliers for hotels were not aware of the required standards for supplying high-end hotels. Furthermore, local suppliers face competition from low-price imported products. High-end hotels prefer to engage with registered businesses, suggesting informality as the barrier for SMEs towards building linkages (UNCTAD 2015).

The initiative included technical assistance interventions to establish and consolidate business linkages between agricultural producers, large processors, and the tourism industry. One beneficiary of the programme has been the dairy farmers who supply milk to Tanga Fresh Limited (TFL), a company that processes and supplies milk all over Tanzania. Through the Tanzania Investment Centre/UNCTAD linkage programme, 565 TFL dairy farmers have been provided with training on good agricultural practices and entrepreneurship and helped to form linkages with tourist hotels in Arusha, Zanzibar, and Dar es Salaam (UNCTAD 2015). A subsequent evaluation on a sample of 126 dairy farmers showed that there was a considerable increase in milk supply, where those who received entrepreneurship training more than doubled their supplies between 2014 and 2015 (Table 2.4).

An important lesson from the programme is the usefulness of consolidating resources from various donor programmes/agencies to avoid multiplicity

Table 2.4 Impact assessment of UNCTAD's business linkage programme

Group of milk suppliers	Volume of milk supplied (per cent change over previous year)		
	2013	2014	2015
1. Farmers who received both Empretec and Farming as a Business (FaaB) training	8%	35%	110%
2. Farmers who received Empretec training only	9.3%	39%	50%
3. Farmers who received FaaB training only	5%	39%	49%
4. Farmers observing good practices from neighbours	4%	25%	30%
5. Control group	6%	10%	14%

Source: Authors' calculations based on UN (2017) data.

and leverage the specific technical competency of the participating actors. In this case, UNCTAD leveraged resources from Tanzania's government, ITC, and UNIDO. In particular, UNCTAD and ITC addressed the downstream with farmer groups, while UNIDO worked on the upstream with processors and government agencies on upgrading SME compliance with standards, developing marketing strategies, and accessing different markets. A review of the project evaluation shows that UNIDO's initiatives in arranging trade fairs and exhibitions, upgrading products, assistance in obtaining hazard analysis critical control point and International Organization for Standardization (ISO) certification, and providing technical assistance for SMEs have enhanced market linkages with large firms.

Case 2: The Kilombero Business Linkage Project (KBLP)

This is a 2002 initiative between Kilombero Sugar Company Limited (KSCL), International Finance Corporation (IFC), and the Africa Project Development Facility. The KSCL envisioned becoming a low-cost producer of sugar in Tanzania, but its suppliers (SMEs) faced impediments including skill deficiencies, lack of finance, poor outgrower infrastructure, lack of basic social services, and lack of support services, which limited cane-farmer expansion. Bekefi (2006) shows the project led to significant impact. Through KBLP, the SMEs were provided with finance, loan guarantees, and training on business skills. As a result, markets became more accessible through infrastructure improvement and improved capacities of the organizations that represented the SMEs. The number of outgrower farms almost doubled (from 2,760 to 5,000) in the first two years of the project while annual cane-harvest tonnage increased by 42.5 per cent, while the financial inputs of the project to the local community increased from TZS7–8 billion to TZS11 billion during the first year of the project.

Case 3: Tanzania Breweries Limited (TBL) and Kioo Ltd

As a producer and distributor of malt beer, non-alcoholic malt beverages, and alcoholic fruit beverages in Tanzania, in the late 1990s TBL saw the opportunity to source its inputs locally at lower costs and build local capacity. Initially, the company imported almost all inputs because local suppliers had neither the competence nor capacity to provide a regular supply of the required quality and quantity. TBL invested in upgrading capacity of potential local suppliers (glass, barley, and label suppliers), and these companies became important suppliers for TBL. For instance, Kioo Ltd. used to manufacture bottles, but the standards were poor with a high breakage rate. TBL assured it would buy all bottles produced by Kioo Ltd. if they were of the required quality and sent a South African engineer to assist with a production-system upgrade. By 2006, Kioo Ltd. had grown into a primary glass manufacturer, supplying 100 per cent of TBL bottles as well as producing for Coca-Cola and Pepsi in Tanzania (Bekefi 2006).

Other successful country cases provide lessons for Tanzania. For example, clustering in SEZs facilitated linkages between the Mauritius textile and knitwear subsectors, so that local firms supplied woollen yarn that had previously been imported (Hussain 2000). The weak nature of the SME sector means that the government and large firms need to show more commitment to support linkages. In Vietnam, Unilever assisted small business partners to upgrade their technology and comply with international standards, and introduced new products tailored to local tastes and suppliers. By 2001, contract manufacturing formed 48 per cent of the volume produced by Unilever in Vietnam and local enterprises supplied 40 per cent and 80 per cent of Unilever raw materials and packaging, respectively (Ruffing 2006). Support for training helps upgrade the labour force to equip SMEs with the knowledge, skills, and capacity to participate in the linkages (Ruffing 2006). Successful initiatives to enhance linkages between SMEs and large firms depend on the measures taken to upgrade SME capacity and the role of the government as a facilitator. The Tanzania experience shows that the demand-driven initiatives by large firms are more successful than the supply-driven initiatives of public programmes (including donor agencies), although the latter can play a useful role in capacity building and access to information, which appears critical for SME preparedness to enter the linkage relationships.

2.5 Conclusion and policy implications

Using firm-level industrial survey data, this chapter investigated the extent, determinants, and role of linkages between small and large firms on the performance of SMEs in Tanzania, addressing the following questions: What are the types and extent of linkages between SMEs and large firms? Which factors determine the extent of linkages between SMEs and large firms? What is the impact of linkages on SME performance? While addressing the questions is challenging because of a lack of appropriate data, but some clear findings emerge.

First, while important, the extent of linkages between SMEs and large firms is low compared to the linkages among large or small firms. The extent varies according to the types of linkages. The most common for SMEs appear to be in technology (almost 40 per cent) and this can play an important role in upgrading and improved capacity utilization, potentially enabling SMEs to become suppliers to larger firms. About a fifth of SMEs have competition linkages, measured by being in sectors with an above-average share of large firms—these SMEs will benefit from the need to remain competitive with larger firms, perhaps by producing niche products in the subsector. Fewer than a tenth of SMEs have backward (importing) or forward (exporting) linkages; although data restrict our measures to trade linkages with foreign (probably large) firms, it is likely that relatively few SMEs also have supply or purchase linkages with large firms. The manufacturing sector appears to have a much higher number of SMEs participating in linkages compared to other industrial sectors (water, energy, and mining).

While size (the level of production) and foreign ownership appear to be significant factors influencing all linkages, the significance of other determinants varies depending on the types of linkages. Technology linkage appears to be higher for older firms and among firms that provide training, are members of industry associations, and those located in a SEZ. Backward and forward linkages (with foreign firms) are also associated with size and membership in industry associations, and with foreign ownership (exporting SMEs are also more likely to have backward linkages, implying they import inputs). Size, training, exporting, and foreign ownership are associated with competition linkage, suggesting these are the characteristics of SMEs better able to coexist in a subsector with large firms. Although not significant in the sample of all SMEs, in the manufacturing sector shortage of raw materials encourages technology linkages and capacity under-utilization encourages backward linkages, reflecting manufacturing activities that require intermediate inputs.

The final part of the analysis assessed the role of linkages in SME performance, measured in terms of sales and employment levels. The findings show that linkages with large firms contribute to the higher performance of SMEs through such benefits as improved productivity, competition, and learning, and expansion of markets. In this way, linkages can contribute to sustained growth and a more resilient SME sector. However, specific types of linkages appear to play a more significant role on different aspects of firm performance. Whereas backward linkage is associated with higher employment growth, forward linkage is associated with higher sales growth.

2.5.1 Policy implications

These findings have several implications for industrial policy. Most importantly, the weak firm linkages evident in Tanzania compromise the potential to promote inclusive growth and underscore the role of the government as an enabler of linkages. That is, the government ought to step up efforts to build capacity of SMEs and facilitate an environment for nurturing their linkages with large firms. The challenge is how such interventions could be implemented. We recommend the government to:

i. *Encourage large firms to engage in partnerships with small firms.* Linkages with small firms are more likely and effective when the initiative comes from a large firm (demand side). There are failures where large firms have not been successful in engaging with SMEs, perhaps due to a perception that SMEs do not have the capacity to meet their requirements and a lack of information about opportunities and how to identify eligible SMEs. The government could identify the kinds of policy conditions or requirements needed to nurture or facilitate such linkages by leveraging enforcement of the existing policies and regulations (e.g. local content policy, disseminating information on standards).

ii. *Promote linkages with foreign firms to help the growth of SMEs and eventually support internal linkages.* The findings show that backward and forward linkages are relatively weak in Tanzania's SME sector. The question is how the government could catalyse such linkages. Because these linkages were measured using import and export proxies, they primarily reflect weak foreign (trade) linkage capacity. The government could provide incentives to strategic sectors, such as tourism and garments, in which SMEs have potential to supply to and source from large firms, including foreign firms. There is evidence that large firms prefer to work with registered SMEs so the government should aim to reduce the costs of registration and provide incentives, such as by making registration a condition of access to enhanced business services and support.

iii. *Support SME upgrading for partnerships with large firms.* Given the inherent resource constraints and accountability challenges, it is not possible for the government to support all SMEs to upgrade. The government could provide fiscal (tax deductions) or other forms of incentives for SMEs to engage in capacity-building initiatives and for large firms or training institutions to provide support. For instance, they could establish a rebate scheme in which large firms involved in upgrading SMEs to meet their linkage requirements are allowed to deduct/claim back a certain proportion of the skills development levy.

iv. *Strengthen R&D (technology) activities in the productive sectors.* Technology linkages are the most common and contribute to higher sales. This signifies a benefit for the government to strengthen R&D (technology) activities in the productive sectors of the economy. One option is to increase support to the R&D institutions, such as reinstating the R&D units that were almost mandatory in all productive sectors in the past. Another way is for the government to support SMEs in technology acquisition as one of the mechanisms for promoting their relationships with large firms.

The impacts of COVID-19 on Tanzania were initially felt from March 2020 particularly on economic activities linked to the external sector, especially tourism, manufacturing, and transport (URT 2020). A study by The Launchpad (2020) and Maarifa Hub on the impact of COVID-19 on SMEs found that 97 per cent of the firms cut production and the impacts were more severe for SMEs than for large firms. In March 2020, the Agricultural Council of Tanzania (ACT) undertook a rapid assessment of the agriculture sector, finding that horticulture, fish processing, cashews, and beef are the hardest hit subsectors. All are important for exports and the impact included an 80 per cent fall in production and a complete collapse in exports. The world price of cashew declined by 30 per cent between December 2019 and March 2020. The closure of Emirates flights that used to transport over 100 tons of beef (worth approximately US$500,000) per month badly affected the beef industry. Other value chain impacts include undersupply of agricultural inputs (ACT 2020); this would have reduced production and supply to agri-processing firms.

Tanzania experienced a less adverse impact on businesses than neighbours owing to the approach taken by the government in dealing with the pandemic. There was no major lockdown and the government implemented measures to mitigate the negative effects of the pandemic including reducing the discount rate, lowering the minimum reserve requirement ratio, incentivizing the restructuring of loans for severally affected borrowers, relaxing limits on mobile money users, and expediting domestic payment arrears and VAT refunds, giving specific priority to the SME sector (Masubo 2020).

The negative effect of COVID-19 will have reduced the desire and ability of SMEs to participate in linkages as some firms halted operations and all are now focusing on recovery. As Tanzania is recovering from the pandemic, there needs to be continued assistance to SMEs including improving the business environment by reducing the overall costs of starting, registering, and operating a business and supporting the sector's capacity to respond to disrupted international markets. This will help enhance the capacity of SMEs to participate in linkages. Given the differential impacts of COVID-19 on SMEs and large firms, the onus is now more on the latter to encourage linkages. The government can assist by helping large firms identify viable SMEs to partner with while also providing the support to help with SMEs recovery.

References

ACT (2020). 'Assessment of the Impact of COVID-19 on the Agriculture Sector in Tanzania'. Unpublished report. Dar es Salaam: Agriculture Council of Tanzania.

Atieno, R. (2009). 'Linkages, Access to Finance and the Performance of Small-Scale Enterprises in Kenya'. Working Paper 2009/06. Helsinki: UNU-WIDER.

Barbin, E. (2017). 'The Dynamics of SME-Large Business Linkages: Findings from Six Cases'. RSN-PCC Working Paper 17-008. Manila: Asian Institute of Management.

Bas, M., and V. Strauss-Kahn (2014). 'Does Importing More Inputs Raise Exports? Firm-Level Evidence from France'. *Review of World Economics*, 150(2): 241–75.

Bekefi, T. (2006). 'Tanzania: Lessons in Building Linkages for Competitive and Responsible Entrepreneurship'. Cambridge, MA: UNIDO and Kennedy School of Government, Harvard University.

Blalock, G., and P. J. Gertler (2008). 'Welfare Gains from Foreign Direct Investment through Technology Transfer to Local Suppliers'. *Journal of International Economics*, 74(2): 402–21.

Delmar, F., P. Davidsson, and W. Gartner (2003). 'Arriving at the High-Growth Firm'. *Journal of Business Venturing*, 18: 189–216.

Diao, X., J. Kweka, and M. McMillan (2018). 'Small Firms, Structural Change and Labor Productivity Growth in Africa: Evidence from Tanzania'. *World Development*, 105: 400–15.

Diao X., J. Kweka, and M. McMillan (2019). 'Economic Transformation in Africa from the Bottom Up: New Evidence from Tanzania'. In C. Monga and J. Y. Lin (eds), *The Oxford Handbook of Structural Transformation*. Oxford: Oxford University Press, 619–31.

Dunning, J. H. (1992). *Multinational Enterprises and the Global Economy*. Boston, MA: Addison-Wesley.

Francisco, J., and T. Canare (2018). 'Linkages between SMEs and Large Firms: Findings from a Survey in the Philippines'. *International Journal of Small and Medium Enterprises and Business Sustainability*, 3(3): 20–52.

Hassan, R.S., and M. Hart (2016). 'The Determinants of Small Firm Growth: An Empirical Study on Egypt'. *The Business & Management Review*, 7(2): 41.

Hussain, M. (2000). 'Linkages between SMEs and Large Industries for Increased Markets and Trade: An African Perspective'. Abidjan: African Development Bank.

ILO (2017). 'World Employment and Social Outlook 2017: Sustainable Enterprises and Jobs: Formal Enterprises and Decent Work'. Geneva: International Labour Office.

Ishengoma, E., and R. Lokina (2013). 'The Role of Linkages in Determining Informal and Small Firms' Performance: The Case of the Construction Industry in Tanzania'. *Tanzania Economic Review*, 3: 34–58.

Jamieson, D., S. Fettiplace, C. York, E. Lambourne, P. Braidford, and I. Stone (2012). *Large Businesses and SMEs: Exploring How SMEs Interact with Large Businesses*. Princeton, NJ: ORC International.

Javorcik, B. S. (2004). 'Does Foreign Direct Investment Increase the Productivity of Domestic Firms? In Search of Spillovers through Backward Linkages'. *American Economic Review*, 94(3): 605–27. https://doi.org/10.1257/0002828041464605

Katua, N. T. (2014). 'The Role of SMEs in Employment Creation and Economic Growth in Selected Countries'. *International Journal of Education and Research*, 2(12): 461–72.

Kwarteng, M. A., A. B. Jibril, F. Nwaiwu, M. Pilik, and M. Ali (2019, May). 'Internet-Based Channel Orientation for Domesticated Services Firm: Some Drivers and Consequences'. In *International Working Conference on Transfer and Diffusion of IT* (pp. 90–103). Cham: Springer International Publishing.

Kweka, J., and L. Fox (2011). 'The Household Enterprise Sector in Tanzania: Why It Matters and Who Cares'. Washington, DC: World Bank. https://doi.org/10.1596/1813-9450-5882

Kweka, J. P., and F. Sooi (2020). 'Partnership for Inclusive Growth: Can Linkages with Large Firms Spur the Growth of SMEs in Tanzania?' (No. 2020/102). WIDER Working Paper.

The LaunchPad (2020). 'Economic Impact on Entrepreneurs, Startups, Small and Medium Enterprises in Tanzania'. April. https://carolndosi.medium.com/covid19tzrealities-the-economic-impact-on-entrepreneurs-startups-small-and-medium-enterprises-8bc45eb26c79

De Loecker, J. (2007). 'Do Exports Generate Higher Productivity? Evidence from Slovenia'. *Journal of International Economics*, 73: 69–98.

Masubo, V. (2020). 'COVID-19 in Tanzania: Is business as usual response enough? International Growth Center'. https://www.theigc.org

Mohammed, S., and H. Beshir (2019). 'Determinants of Business Linkage between Medium-Small and Large Business Enterprises in Manufacturing Sector: The Case of Kombolcha City'. *Journal of Economics and Sustainable Development*, 10: 74–92.

Musundi, A. S., and K. Ogollah (2014). 'Challenges Facing Business Linkages between Small and Medium Enterprises and Mobile Telephone Companies in Kenya'. *European Journal of Business Management*, 1(11): 298–318.

OECD (2005). 'Encouraging Linkages between Small and Medium Sized Companies and Multinational Enterprises: An Overview of Good Policy Practice by the OECD Investment Committee'. Paris: OECD.

OECD (2018). 'Strengthening SMEs and Entrepreneurship for Productivity and Inclusive Growth'. OECD 2018 Ministerial Conference on SMEs, 22–23 February 2018, Mexico City.

Oyen, L. V., and L. Gedi (2013). 'Tanzania SME Development Policy 2003: Ten Years After'. Vienna: UNIDO.

Pant, A. A., B. E. Lapres, E. Olafsen, L. Ronchi, and P. A. Cook (2018). 'Partnership for Growth: Linking Large Firms and Agro-Processing SMEs—A Guidance Note for Policymakers'. No. 125941. Washington, DC: World Bank.

Pauli, U. (2015). 'SMEs Growth and Human Capital Investments (the Case of Poland)'. *Studia Universitatis Babes Bolyai-Negotia*, 60(4): 5–22.

Qalati, S. A., W. Li, N. Ahmed, M. A. Mirani, and A. Khan (2021). 'Examining the Factors Affecting SME Performance: The Mediating Role of Social Media Adoption'. *Sustainability (Switzerland)*, 13(1), 1–24.

Quak, E. (2019). 'The Impact of Creating Backward and Forward Linkages between Lead Firms and SMEs in Conflict Settings'. K4D Helpdesk Report. Brighton, UK: IDS.

Ruffing, L. (2006). 'Deepening Development through Business Linkages'. Washington, DC: UN.

Sánchez-Martín, M. E., J. De Piniés, and K. Antoine (2015). 'Measuring the Determinants of Backward Linkages from FDI in Developing Economies: Is It a Matter of Size'? Washington, DC: World Bank. https://doi.org/10.1596/1813-9450-7185

Sibanda, K., P. Hove-Sibanda, and H. Shava (2018). 'The Impact of SME Access to Finance and Performance on Exporting Behaviour at Firm Level: A Case of Furniture Manufacturing SMEs in Zimbabwe'. *Acta Commercii*, 18(1): 1–13. https://doi.org/10.4102/ac.v18i1.554

Subrahmanya, M. B., M. Mathirajan, and K. N. Krishnaswamy (2010). 'Importance of Technological Innovation for SME Growth Evidence from India'. Working Paper 2010/03. Helsinki: UNU-WIDER.

Tewari, P. S., D. Skilling, P. Kumar, and Z. Wu (2013). 'Competitive Small and Medium Enterprises: A Diagnostic to Help Design Smart SME Policy'. Washington, DC: World Bank.

UN (2017). 'Tanzania United Nations Trade Cluster Programme'. Washington, DC: United Nations.

UNCTAD (2015). 'Strengthening Tourism Market Linkages for Tanzania Producers and Processors: A Workshop Report'. Dar es Salaam: United Nations Conference on Trade and Development.

URT (2002). *Small and Medium Enterprise Development Policy 2002.* Dar es Salaam: Ministry of Industry and Trade.

URT (2016). *National Five-Year Development Plan 2016/17–2020/21.* Dar es Salaam: Planning Commission.

URT (2018). *Annual Survey of Industrial Production (ASIP) Data.* Dar es Salaam: National Bureau of Statistics.

URT (2020). *Annual Report 2019/20.* Dar es Salaam: Bank of Tanzania.

3

Upgrading and multi-scalar industrial policy in the Tanzanian textile and apparel sector value chain

Julian Boys and Antonio Andreoni

3.1 Introduction

Resilient industrialization in front-runner and latecomer countries in Europe and Asia involved the development of various strategic manufacturing sectors in turn, among them textiles and apparel (T&A) (Reinert 2007). Changes in the global production system in recent decades, particularly its increased organization into global value chains (GVCs) and the co-evolution of international trade policy regimes, have raised questions about the potential of T&A contributing to sustained structural transformation in low-income countries (LICs) today (Staritz 2011). With heightened uncertainty in global markets and a renewed push towards regional integration in Africa, there is hope that regional value chains (RVCs) within the continent and national value chains (NVCs) can more sustainably support firm competitiveness and productivity growth (Pickles et al. 2015; Morris et al. 2016). This chapter investigates how *value chain directionality*—orientation to NVCs, RVCs, or GVCs—and accompanying policies at the national, regional, and global levels—hence *multi-scalar* industrial policies—affect productive upgrading and development outcomes, with reference to T&A in Tanzania. The concept of 'value chain directionality' builds on seminal contributions emphasizing the different 'learning effects' of exports to different directions (Amsden 1986) as well as more recent work on the significance of input origin for productive outcomes (Amighini and Sanfilippo 2014; Boys and Andreoni 2023a).

After independence, Tanzanian policy makers prioritized an 'NVC approach' to developing a domestic T&A industry, emulating the industrialization strategies of front runners by using import substitution to create mass employment and backward linkages to agriculture, where cotton had been introduced under colonial rule (Kabissa 2014). Liberalization and privatization followed from the late 1980s, but overall, the industry has failed to act as an engine of resilient growth

Julian Boys and Antonio Andreoni, *Upgrading and multi-scalar industrial policy in the Tanzanian textile and apparel sector value chain*. In: *Sustaining Tanzania's Economic Development*. Edited by: Oliver Morrissey, Joseph Semboja, and Maureen Were, Oxford University Press. © UNU-WIDER (2024). DOI: 10.1093/oso/9780192885746.003.0003 and underperformed relative to regional competitors like Kenya and Ethiopia, despite Tanzania's preferential access to high-income markets and favourable foreign direct investment (FDI) incentives promoting integration into GVCs (Msami and Wangwe 2016; URT 2016). Nevertheless, following Tanzania's active participation in regional integration efforts, its T&A exports to the region have grown substantially, allowing for a comparison of outcomes across NVCs, RVCs, and GVCs. This chapter examines how NVCs and RVCs offer different opportunities for upgrading and competitiveness than GVCs, and how policies at the national, regional, and global levels promote value chain participation and upgrading. Our findings have implications for ongoing industrial policy development in Tanzania, suggesting a multi-scalar approach for improving industrial competitiveness with relevance for other LICs.[1]

Firm data draw from a 2019 survey of all eight operational large T&A firms, as well as firm-level trade data. The inclusion of exclusively large firms reflects their disproportionate contribution to value added, employment, exports, and productivity growth (Boys and Andreoni 2020). We present findings on functional, product, process, and end-market upgrading outcomes observed in NVCs, RVCs, and GVCs. We 'unbundle' the traditional packages of functions used in the literature and elicit information on the activities and services provided in each value chain type. Specifically, four functions are covered: cut, make, and trim (CMT); free on board or full package service (FOB); original design manufacturer (ODM); and own brand manufacturer (OBM). Given the limits to the upgrading framework identified in the literature review, we also use other performance metrics such as capacity utilization, employment, and local content (see Chapter 5 in this volume for discussion of technology use and local linkages in the Tanzanian textiles and apparel sector).

Policy analysis draws on semi-structured interviews with firms and policy makers; trade and tariff data; and official notifications, legislation, and regulations. We focus on concrete measures that allocate rents between actors where possible. For NVCs this includes analysing the valuation of imported products using international trade data, as well as public procurement policy and the granting of duty remission, drawing on official documents. For RVCs we use trade data to assess the rents provided by the SADC and EAC free trade areas (FTAs) and the impact of EAC policy towards used clothes. In GVCs we examine US African Growth and Opportunity Act (AGOA) rules and associated rents, along with the use of EPZs to create additional rents for GVC-oriented firms. Rents from duty-free trade arrangements are calculated simply as the product of trade values and most favoured nation (MFN) tariff rates, that is, approximately the tariff payments that would otherwise have been due.

[1] The authors are grateful for the support received in the preparation of this study, particularly from UNU-WIDER, SOAS University of London, and Gatsby Africa.

3.2 Literature review

The chapter speaks to two main streams of literature, the first on firm performance in different value chains and the second on industrial policy rents in the contemporary multi-scalar context. Trade directionality—that is, the destination of exports—is important for structural transformation in late industrializers, with greater 'learning effects' from South-South trade (Amsden 1986). Through the lens of value chains, the regionalization of trade represents a change of 'value chain directionality', i.e. a shift from GVCs to RVCs. Studies of apparel GVCs have found different end markets in the global North to offer distinct upgrading opportunities (Palpacuer et al. 2005), and this chapter contributes to the emerging literature on the implications for structural transformation of value chain regionalization in the South (Morris et al. 2016).

The interconnected capital-intensive textile and labour-intensive apparel sectors are favourites for GVC studies, giving rise to two organizing concepts: value chain governance and upgrading (Gereffi 1999). This literature posits a functional upgrading trajectory from basic apparel assembly operations (CMT), to providing a full package service (FOB) to high-value activities like design (ODM) and branding (OBM), with the possibility of vertical integration to textile manufacture (Staritz et al. 2017). Several major criticisms of this framework guide this research. First, studies tend to assume that firms operate in a single value chain serving a single end market, neglecting the potential for firms to engage *simultaneously* with multiple value chains and serve different end markets across regions (Navas-Alemán 2011). Second, the study of GVCs has resulted in an overriding preoccupation with exporting firms, yet there is evidence that firms carry out higher-value functions in NVCs serving domestic markets (Bazan and Navas-Alemán 2004). Third, the upgrading concept is criticized because upgrading need not be accompanied by greater surplus generation or capture, with strategic downgrading sometimes preferred (Tokatli 2013).

Recent research on T&A value chains in the global South has addressed some but not all elements of these critiques. Staritz and Whitfield (2018) go beyond upgrading to develop a matrix of sector-specific technological capabilities, yet they focus exclusively on GVC exporters despite the numerous Ethiopian firms serving the lucrative domestic market. Likewise, Phelps et al. (2009) focus on the FDI-driven, GVC-oriented segment of the Kenyan apparel industry, neglecting the domestically owned firms serving local markets. Morris et al. (2016) examine value chain upgrading by firms in sub-Saharan Africa (SSA) but with ownership characteristics as their central analytical focus. Tanzania has not featured in recent academic research on the T&A sector in SSA despite having potential to address the gaps identified.

This chapter also engages with the political economy of industrial policy rents in the context of overlapping value chains and trade regimes at the national, regional, and global levels.[2] Despite dissenting voices, mainstream development thinking continues to advise countries to conform to their (static) comparative advantage rather than defy it (Lin and Chang 2009; Cherif and Hasanov 2019) and prioritize entering GVCs and widening participation therein (Taglioni and Winkler 2016). In Tanzanian T&A, this means encouraging FDI in labour-intensive, low-skill apparel assembly for global markets using imported inputs, rather than backward integration to capital-intensive textiles manufacture or value addition of domestic inputs (Dinh and Monga 2013). Preferential trade agreements such as AGOA encourage the GVC approach by providing rents to global exporters, supported by relaxed rules of origin (ROO), which allow apparel made from imported fabrics to qualify for duty-free market access (Pickles et al. 2015).

GVC-based strategies contrast with the NVC approach of Hirschman (1977), who focused on multiple linkage dynamics within countries as drivers of the 'multidimensional conspiracy' for development. They also differ from strategies of east Asian newly industrialized countries, which emphasized building domestic productive capabilities through rents fostering strategic value chain integration, first through import substitution (building NVCs) and then by export promotion (insertion into RVCs and GVCs) (Chang 1994; Andreoni 2019; Chang and Andreoni 2020). Among industrial policy scholars, there remains a bias against NVCs, with the assumption that exposure to global competition through exporting is necessary to induce 'learning for productivity' (Whitfield et al. 2015), despite the high levels of import competition in the liberalized domestic markets of many countries in the global South.

With shifts in demand-growth dynamism from north to south, increasing concerns about value chains resilience, and renewed efforts towards regional integration by developing countries, RVCs have emerged as a basis for industrial policy (Barrientos et al. 2016). Regional trade agreements (RTAs) such as the East African Community (EAC) and Southern African Development Community (SADC) create rents aimed at promoting RVCs, with ROO critical to determining who benefits in the T&A sector (UNCTAD 2019). Yet the design and enforcement of domestic and regional policies in many ways still favour GVCs, such as the case of export processing zone (EPZ) regimes (Whitfield et al. 2015), indicating a strategic misalignment of market opportunities and rent allocation. Rents allocation within these EPZ tax incentive schemes are susceptible to corruption, as documented for the case of Tanzania (Andreoni et al. 2022).

The academic literature on industrial policy has not kept pace with changes in the global economy, with a lack of research into the complexities of policy making at the national, regional, and global levels simultaneously (Behuria 2019; Boys and

---

[2] A rent is an incremental change in income created by institutions and can be generated by industrial policies to encourage firm entry and learning in currently unprofitable but socially desirable areas like manufacturing (Khan 2017).

Andreoni 2023b). Further, questions of power and political economy are rarely given due attention in value chain studies (Andreoni et al. 2020). This chapter examines policies at different levels and how they interact, the effects on rent distribution among competing actors, and the extent to which multi-scalar industrial policy is successfully supporting strategic engagement in different value chains by Tanzanian T&A firms.

3.3 NVCs, RVCs, and GVCs: firm strategies, policy drivers, and outcomes

Table 3.1 presents the survey results, grouping firms by value chain directionality through their integration into NVCs, RVCs (African), or GVCs, and the activities carried out in each, from backward integration to final products. In the following sub-sections these results are analysed and discussed for different clusters of firms in the context of NVCs, RVCs, and GVCs.

3.3.1 National value chains

The three NVC firms surveyed source their main input, cotton lint, domestically and sell the overwhelming majority of outputs in Tanzania. They were all established as state-owned enterprises (SOEs) from the 1960s, often with the support of concessional loans or aid from bilateral donors, and benefited from rents in the protected domestic market. NVC firms have struggled to maintain competitiveness since privatization and liberalization, with nine other businesses closed at the time of the survey (TDU 2019).

Factories of current NVC firms were privatized during the 1990s, losing the rents associated with state ownership. Survey respondents indicated that the rapidly changing political and institutional context of privatization resulted in assets being acquired for less than market value. Textile plants were acquired by Tanzanian family-owned trading groups of south Asian origin with little experience running industrial enterprises. Ownership has changed little since privatization, and managers interviewed were mostly from the same families. As a result, NVC firms are part of diversified business groups, with intra-group financing often important in lean periods (see also Andreoni and Sial 2020). The wider groups often engage in unrelated activities, such as gold mining, or areas with apparently contradictory interests to their textile factories (e.g. used clothing imports).

Privatization coincided with trade liberalization such that the new owners lost trade protection rents and struggled to remain competitive in the domestic market. The applied weighted average tariff rates on manufactured T&A products fell sharply from 35.6 per cent in 1993 to 14.5 per cent in 1997, then increased after

Table 3.1 Summary of survey results

		NVC firms	RVC firms	GVC firms
Number of large firms		3	2	3
Ownership		Local	Local	Foreign
Privatized		Yes	No	No
EPZ status		No	No	Yes
Domestic inputs		Cotton	Cotton	Cotton, packaging
Regional inputs		Cotton	Cotton, yarn	-
Global inputs		Dyes, yarns, etc.	Yarns, trims, etc.	Fabrics, trims, etc.
Backward integration functions	Spin	3/3; N, R, G	1/2; N, R, G	1/3; G
	Weave/finish	3/3; N, R	1/2; N, R	-
	Knit/finish	1/3; N	2/2; N, R, G	-
Apparel and fabric value chain functions	Design	3/3; N, R	2/2; N, G	-
	Sample	3/3; N, R	2/2; N, R, G	1/3; G
	Input source	3/3; N, R	2/2; N, R, G	1/3; G
	Cut/sew/finish	1/3; N	2/2; N, R, G	2/3; G
	Print	3/3; N, R	2/2; N, R, G	-
	Embroidery	1/3; N, R	2/2; N, R, G	1/3; G
	Wash	3/3; N, R	1/2; N	1/3; G
	Brand	3/3; N, R	2/2; N, G	-
	Distribution	3/3; N	1/2; N	-
Employees—range		500–2,600	1,200–2,500	150–2,560
Employees—average		1,667	1,850	1,753
Capacity utilization range		35–70%	60–100%	50–91%

Capacity utilization average		49%	80%	75%
Product groups		Fp, Fi, A, Y	A, Fp, Fi, Y	A, Y
Sales by end market (average)	National	80%	38%	0%
	Regional	19%	60%	0%
	Global	1%	2%	100%
Upgrading outcomes	Function	1/3	-	-
	Product	-	-	1/3
	Process	2/3	1/2	2/3
	End market	1/3	1/2	-
Export UV, $/kg, all products		4.84	6.43	4.79
Export UV, $/kg, apparel only		-	9.76	8.70
Policy rents		Procurement contracts; national duty remission	SADC and EAC duty-free market access	AGOA duty-free market access, EPZ policy

Notes: Figures by value chain functions (3/3, 2/3 etc.) indicate how many of the firms in each group perform the function. **Bold** indicates all firms in the group perform the function and *italics* indicate some firms perform it. N/R/G indicates for which end markets (national, regional, or global) functions are performed. Product groups are in order of importance for each group of firms: A: apparel; Fp: processed fabric; Fi: intermediate fabric; Y: yarn. Export UVs (unit values) are weighted averages for 2017 and exclude cotton lint and waste, used clothes, bed nets and netting, sacks, and bags. For further description of value chain activities, see Boys and Andreoni (2020).
Source: Authors' survey data and national authorities.

the implementation of the EAC customs union to reach 24.1 per cent in 2018.[3] Although there is a duty remission scheme for inputs (discussed in Section 3.3.2), this is under-utilized in Tanzania, so tariffs on inputs reduce competitiveness without providing rents sufficient to stimulate investment.

Liberalization was followed by increased import competition because of tariff reductions and the competitiveness of Asian producers, particularly China. Tanzanian manufacturers interviewed complained of unfair competition, claiming importers under-report the value of goods to evade taxation and sell in the domestic market at lower prices. Andreoni and Tasciotti (2019) corroborate this, showing with mirror statistics that T&A products are among the most important for trade mis-invoicing of imports, with underreporting of US$563 million in 2017, resulting in foregone tax revenue of US$165 million.

Under-reported imports of K&K fabrics, a speciality of NVC firms and their main product line, are viewed as particularly harmful. Tanzania's import unit values are comparable to those in Kenya and Uganda but much lower than those in Rwanda, whose values are closest to those reported by China for its exports (Boys and Andreoni 2020: Figure 8). This suggests the rent from the 50 per cent EAC tariff on K&K does not fully benefit regional producers. Although import valuation data are suggestive of unfair competition for NVC firms, more important challenges are likely to be the export competitiveness of China already mentioned and declining national demand for K&K fabrics. Historically a fashion mainstay in East Africa, they are now losing ground as consumer tastes move towards Western-style clothing, especially with the availability of cheap used clothes.

Firm operations and strategy

The current business models of NVC firms largely date from their establishment as vertically integrated woven textile producers, but one firm recently added knitting and apparel capacity. NVC firms all carry out high-value functions, namely design, branding, and distribution. Being vertically integrated and having design capability is critical to the remaining competitiveness of NVC firms, enabling them to respond quickly to buyer demands for made-to-order products. Design capacity varies, with two only copying buyer samples using computer software and another employing more designers to respond to buyer specifications, producing its own samples based on original designs. Firms report that capacity for original design has been eroded over time, representing a partial downgrading (not shown in Table 3.1).

The principal products of NVC firms are processed fabrics such as K&K and bedsheets, with some sales of curtains, masai shuka (striped or chequered cloth),

---

[3] Data are from UNCTAD-TRAINS (2020). Tanzania applies tariffs of 10 per cent on yarns; 25 per cent on trims, fabrics, garments; 35 per cent on used clothing; and 50 per cent on khanga and kitenge (K&K) printed fabrics.

grey fabric for further processing, and yarn. Although their main market is Tanzania, exports (formal and informal) account for 19 per cent of total sales on average (ranging between 5 and 40 per cent), and are almost entirely to regional markets, though one firm exports small quantities of surplus yarn to Europe. Apparel production is for the domestic market only, consisting of uniforms for the public sector as well as T-shirts and polo shirts sold under the firm's own brand.

Facing intense import competition, declining domestic demand for traditional products and a lack of affordable credit, NVC firms want to diversify but struggle to accumulate or borrow capital to finance investment in new ventures. The entry to apparel manufacture by an NVC firm was enabled by two policy-based rents from national authorities, namely public procurement contracts and duty remission. A procurement contract for public-sector uniforms provided a secure enough revenue stream to allow the firm to invest in learning to manufacture apparel. Tanzanian procurement rules allow special preference (a margin of up to 15 per cent) for domestic suppliers (URT 2013). Such a rent can compensate for the risk and cost of learning associated with developing capabilities in a new activity, if accompanied by sufficiently strict disciplining measures such as quality requirements by buying institutions (Khan 2017). Other NVC firms expressed interest in upgrading to apparel manufacture if public procurement contracts could be secured.

Tanzanian authorities provided targeted rents to NVC firms through the EAC duty remission (DR) scheme, which exempts firms from duties on inputs. Although nominally a regional policy, national authorities can grant exemptions unilaterally on the condition that the resulting finished products cannot be sold duty free in other EAC countries, that is, are only for the national domestic market, termed 'national DRs'.[4] These have only been granted to NVC T&A firms since 2018, suggesting their under-utilization. Combining information from official DR notifications, EAC Gazettes (EAC 2020), with average unit prices from international trade data for the same inputs imported into Tanzania in the same years, we value the duty exemptions granted to NVC firms at around US$5 million in 2018 and 2019. The final products to be made from the inputs are designated in the notifications and include K&K but also apparel, suggesting the rent is conditional on being used productively by NVC firms to diversify away from traditional products.

Outcomes
Upgrading outcomes among NVC firms have been diverse. The clearest success is the case of functional upgrading to knitting and apparel manufacture, but this initiative is still in its early stages and for the domestic market only, despite aspirations

---

[4] This condition attached to a nationally granted DR aims to maintain a level playing field between EAC producers. 'Regional DRs' are agreed between EAC governments and allow duty-free sale across EAC countries but are less common.

to export to regional and then global markets. No cases of product upgrading were observed, with NVC firms making the least complex products of the three firm groups. Technical reports find fabric quality to be lower than international standards, with defects covered in the printing process for K&K (Salm et al. 2012). The apparel manufacturer currently focuses on the most basic products, namely uniforms and round-neck T-shirts but can also make more complex polo shirts.

There was one case of end-market upgrading in the group, an NVC firm that recently started exporting to regional markets. Otherwise there has been little change in end markets served in recent years according to export data, with no growth in exports overall (Boys and Andreoni 2020: Figure 6). Although exports account for a minority of sales, export UVs were slightly higher than those of GVC firms on average (see Table 3.1 and Figure 7 in Boys and Andreoni 2020), but this is mainly because one GVC firm exclusively exports low-value yarn.

NVC firms had the oldest production technologies of any group, but factories have seen some recent investments in process upgrading. Two firms had invested in machinery, one replacing nearly half the ring frames in its spinning section and another upgrading most of its weaving section with Chinese looms. This was motivated by the need to maintain competitiveness and difficulties getting spare parts for older equipment—in some cases, technologies were twenty to thirty years old or more at the time of the survey.

In non-upgrading outcomes NVC firms performed worst, except on local sourcing because of their use of domestic cotton lint. Capacity utilization was lowest among NVC firms, with one firm achieving only 35 per cent. In social outcomes NVC firms did slightly worse than others, having the fewest employees on average due to their focus on capital-intensive textile production. NVC firms are not obliged to prove compliance with international standards around labour, safety, and environmental issues so cannot be measured against those, but firms reported complying with national requirements.

3.3.2 Regional value chains

There were two large Tanzanian T&A firms oriented principally to regional markets and designated as RVC firms, although they retain a strong foothold in the Tanzanian market with own-branded products. RVC firms were established as private businesses in the mid-1960s by Tanzanian entrepreneurs of south Asian descent and have remained predominantly in the control of the same families ever since as part of diversified business groups. While not affected directly by privatization, RVC firms have been strongly affected by other issues affecting NVCs described earlier, especially liberalization in Tanzania and across regional markets.

Rents from RTAs are crucial to RVC firm competitiveness, particularly duty-free market access to South Africa under SADC and Kenya via the EAC. The SADC FTA allows for duty-free trade in goods originating in member states, with restrictive 'double transformation' ROO for apparel and fabrics. Being vertically integrated, Tanzanian RVC firms comply and can export duty free to South Africa, a highly prized market that makes up around 60 per cent of total SSA apparel imports. By contrast, GVC firms that import fabrics and produce apparel (e.g. on a CMT or FOB basis) are not eligible to export duty free to South Africa. The SADC FTA and accompanying ROO therefore have the effect of providing a targeted rent to vertically integrated, regionally oriented producers. The rent is disciplined by market relations because to benefit, firms must maintain good relationships with South African buyers and comply with requirements on cost, quality, and delivery timelines.

The EAC FTA and customs union allows for duty-free trade between members and is complemented by a 25 per cent tariff on most finished T&A products, which gives regional producers extra rent to help them compete with imports. EAC ROO are more relaxed than in SADC, with the same double transformation requirements for knitted fabrics (HS 60) but only single transformation rules for apparel (i.e. manufacture from imported fabric is allowed). Only one of the RVC firms carries out its own spinning so is eligible to export knitted fabrics duty free, but both firms can export apparel duty free. GVC firms operating on a CMT or FOB basis would also be able to export apparel duty free to the EAC, but they do not because of different market conditions.

Another important aspect of the market context for RVC firms is imports of used clothing (*mitumba*) across the region, which are in direct competition with their own apparel products.[5] Since trade liberalization, EAC imports of used clothing have exploded from almost nothing to nearly US$350 million in 2018, and this was consistently highlighted by industry stakeholders as a major factor in the decline of the domestic industry. In 2015 EAC leaders announced their intention to phase out used clothes, confirming in March 2016 that this would take place over three years and subsequently raised tariffs on used clothes (Wolff 2020). When one of the main US-based exporters of used clothes to the EAC complained, the Trump administration threatened to remove AGOA eligibility if the tariff increase was not reversed. This created a choice for Tanzanian authorities between maintaining several thousand jobs in GVC firms in the short term and longer-term NVC and RVC development. After lengthy negotiations, Tanzania complied with US demands, unlike Rwanda, which lost AGOA access.

---

[5] Imports of used clothes affect both NVC and RVC firms, but the latter are far more focused on apparel, and because EAC policy towards used clothes has a strongly regional element, it is addressed here.

One aspect of the used clothing issue is firmly within the purview of EAC governments, namely their valuation by customs authorities. Firms surveyed complained of import undervaluation for the purposes of tax evasion, making it even more difficult to compete with used clothes in the domestic market. Evidence suggests that Tanzania has consistently valued used clothes lower than other EAC countries, but a 50 per cent increase in unit value from 2017 to 2018 indicated a change of approach (Boys and Andreoni 2020: Figure 9).

Firm operations and strategy

RVC firms are vertically integrated but to different degrees, one doing spinning, knitting, weaving, finishing, and apparel while the other buys yarn and does only knitting and apparel production. Both firms provide a full package service for buyers in the markets they serve, sourcing the inputs they do not produce themselves. Both companies carry out higher-value design and branding functions in the domestic market and one also does so in global markets, albeit for small share of sales. One firm also engages directly in distribution through its own depot.

The more vertically integrated firm produces a diverse range of products, selling the least complex products—processed fabrics (K&K, suiting and shirting fabrics, tablecloths, masai shuka) and uniforms—in the domestic market; assorted products—cotton yarn, grey knitted and woven fabrics (for processing by others), knitted cotton shirts, and T-shirts—in regional markets; and knitted cotton T-shirts in global markets. The other firm mainly sells T-shirts, polo shirts, and underwear in Tanzania; T-shirts, polo shirts, leggings, and fleece tracksuits in regional markets; and T-shirts in global markets. There is a roughly equal split of cotton and non-cotton products overall. RVC firms earn 60 per cent of their revenues in regional markets on average, with the EAC taking more than SADC in 2016 and 2017 overall (see Table 3.1, and Figure 10 in Boys and Andreoni 2020). The overwhelming majority of apparel exports have gone to South Africa in recent years.

Capitalizing on the targeted rents available through SADC for exports to South Africa is a core element of RVC firms' strategy. We estimate the magnitude of these rents using publicly available trade and tariff data, cross-checked against transaction-based data at firm level from national authorities for available years. Virtually all of Tanzania's T&A exports to South Africa are knitted apparel articles (HS 61), almost all of which are manufactured by the two RVC firms in our sample, and all are eligible for duty-free market access as opposed to South Africa's MFN tariff of 45 per cent. The total rent generated by the SADC FTA is approximated by the tariff payments that would otherwise have been due to be around US$18.9 million over the five years to 2018 (Boys and Andreoni 2020: Table 5). We take this as principally benefiting Tanzanian RVC firms because South African buyers are able to import duty free from Lesotho and Swaziland, so if tariffs were due on imports from Tanzania, buyers would be able to shift the burden to supplying firms through lower prices. However, in the absence of duty-free market access it is unlikely that the same level of exports would have been seen, given that even GVC firms are not competitively exporting to South Africa with tariff barriers. This is supported by the fact that apparel exports from Tanzania to South Africa were at much lower levels before the implementation of the SADC FTA in 2008, after which the rate of growth increased substantially.

By exporting to Kenya under the EAC, RVC firms can access another important source of rents, albeit less targeted than SADC because GVC firms also comply with EAC ROO. Using the same approach as above, we value these rents at around US$6.4 million in the five years to 2018 (Boys and Andreoni 2020: Table 6). Because the RVC firms in our sample make up almost the entirety of Tanzania's exports of these products to Kenya, and because Kenyan buyers would be able to source from domestic suppliers in the presence of tariffs on imports from Tanzania, we suggest this rent accrues principally to Tanzanian RVC firms, following the same logic as for SADC rents and with the same caveats.[6] The EAC could provide additional rents through its DR scheme, but RVC firms have had less success accessing these than NVC firms. One of the RVC firms in the sample sought a regional DR, that is, one that would not affect its ability to sell within the EAC, but it was instead granted a national DR, which ruled out duty-free sale to Kenya so it chose to withdraw from the scheme altogether.

Outcomes

Instances of upgrading among RVC firms were scarce with no cases of functional or product upgrading reported in recent years or planned. Export UVs for RVC firms have not shown a clear trend that would indicate product up- or downgrading generally, except for mild downgrading for cotton shirts (Boys and Andreoni 2020: Figure 7 and Table 2). Table 3.1 shows that RVC firms had higher export UVs for apparel than GVC firms in 2017, but these are absolute values that reflect product type above all, with the heavier cotton jeans/trousers for the US market in particular dragging down US$/kg UVs. Table 2 in Boys and Andreoni (2020) suggests that relative UVs of RVC firms' main exports are below the global benchmark, while those of GVC firms are above, but this could reflect either product specificities (e.g. complexity, quality) or production cost, so no strong conclusions can be drawn.

End-market upgrading outcomes were positive overall. RVC firm exports to Europe declined, but this was mostly accounted for by lower value yarn, while over the same period exports of higher-value apparel to South Africa have risen considerably (Boys and Andreoni 2020: Figure 10). In 2019, one RVC firm started

---

[6] RVC firms also export woven fabrics and yarn to Kenya but the trade values are relatively low, so the rents generated are smaller, and NVC firms also export these products so rents are less targeted. For simplicity, they are excluded from the analysis.

exporting to the United States under AGOA for the first time starting with polo shirts for children, representing a case of end-market upgrading. It follows previous end-market upgrading by the same firm. In 2012 apparel production was for Tanzania, Uganda, and Kenya only; in 2013 exports to South Africa started and increased substantially in the following years; and finally some exports to Canada and Japan have been achieved. The firm's management reported that quality standards for the US market were higher than for South Africa, which was more demanding than Kenya and Tanzania in turn. This suggests support for an emerging finding in the literature that NVCs and RVCs can serve as stepping stones to GVCs (Beverelli et al. 2019).

Unlike NVC firms, RVC firms have engaged in a fairly continuous process of technological upgrading since their establishment, although one had not seen significant investment for a few years. One firm had machinery between five and fifteen years old at the time of the survey with variation by section, while the other used more recent technologies, all being less than five years old. The firm starting sales to the United States is also upgrading in terms of compliance, factory organization, and production-system management in response to and with the active support of new US buyers.

In other economic outcomes, RVC firms were the biggest group of exporters in our sample until 2015 when they were overtaken by GVC firms, and overall, there was little growth in RVC firm exports to 2017 (Boys and Andreoni 2020: Figure 6). One RVC firm reported full capacity utilization in 2018, the only such case in the whole survey, while the other RVC firm achieved only 60 per cent capacity utilization, resulting in a higher average than for other firm groups. One firm reported having recently doubled their knitting capacity, an important outcome that does not fit neatly in the upgrading framework.

On local content, the firm doing spinning buys cotton lint mainly within Tanzania, having stopped sourcing from Uganda (despite superior lint quality there) because of delays receiving refunds for value added tax (VAT) paid on imported cotton. The other firm sources cotton yarn regionally, and both companies import inputs not available locally (e.g. synthetic yarn, accessories, dyes) from Asia. Although firm-level data on values of imported and locally sourced inputs are not available, RVC firms likely fall between NVC and GVC firms in terms of share of local content.

RVC firms perform well on social outcomes, employing 2,500 and 1,200 employees each, more than any other group of firms on average. RVC firms comply with a range of international and national labour, safety, and environmental standards,[7] but neither are currently certified by WRAP (Worldwide Responsible

---

[7] Certifications held include OEKO-TEX (for the safety and sustainability of fabrics), ISO 9001:2015 (for quality management system), SA8000 (for social welfare compliance), and the Global Organic Textile Standard.

Accredited Production), one of the most well-known social compliance schemes. The RVC firm selling to the United States is instead audited according to the buyer's own code of conduct, viewed by the Tanzanian firm as more stringent than WRAP, which they had previously participated in.

3.3.3 Global value chains

The three GVC firms operating in Tanzania have all been established with EPZ status by foreign investors since 2009 and are owned by (separate) companies with headquarters in China. The main driver of Tanzanian integration into GVCs is preferential market access, especially the unilateral trade preferences of the United States. Other factors include relatively low unit labour costs, the cultivation of cotton in Tanzania, and the incentives provided by EPZs.

AGOA is currently the most important preferential scheme for Tanzania, providing duty-free market access across 97.5 per cent of tariff lines. Key to the uptake of AGOA for T&A products is its relaxed single transformation ROO, particularly the third-country fabric (TCF) provision which permits apparel to be made from fabric originating anywhere. This creates significant rents for apparel assemblers, incentivizing them to create labour-intensive jobs in industrial districts of eligible countries. As a result, AGOA underpins a large number of urban jobs and is a powerful foreign policy tool for the United States, as shown by most EAC countries reversing used clothes tariff increases on the threat of AGOA's withdrawal (see Section 3.3.2).

AGOA's expiry is scheduled for 2025, and the United States would prefer bilateral trade deals involving reciprocal tariff reductions over either AGOA renewal or the African Union proposal for an FTA between the African Continental Free Trade Area (AfCFTA) and the United States. The US approach is prevailing with Kenya opening negotiations on a bilateral deal to safeguard its US market access. It appears likely that Tanzania's duty-free US market access would continue in some form, but uncertainty over its future is reducing incentives for new GVC investment in the apparel sector, with interviewees preferring at least a ten-year time horizon of policy stability for new investment, and existing firms anticipate having to find alternative markets or reducing their production.

AGOA has broader impacts on T&A value chain development at the national and regional levels. The TCF provision increases the value of rents to manufacturers in eligible countries but also reduces incentives for investment in local textile production (Pickles et al. 2015). Furthermore, the incentives created by AGOA are different across value chain types because US MFN tariff rates are higher (at 25–32 per cent) for synthetic than cotton apparel products (13–17 per cent) (Staritz 2011). By reducing tariffs on all T&A products to zero, AGOA provides greater duty advantages for manufacturers using synthetic over cotton fabrics such that Tanzania's second-largest apparel export is non-cotton T-shirts to the United States (Boys and Andreoni 2020: Table 2), despite the presence of an established cotton sector in Tanzania. Thus, although AGOA promotes integration into T&A GVCs, its current design ensures that the local demand generated for fabric will be met through imports rather than backward integration, and linkages with NVCs and RVCs are likely to remain weak.

The Tanzanian and EAC-level policy framework towards EPZs is one of the most prominent national/regional industrial policy instruments in the T&A sector and actively favours integration into GVCs. EPZs give favourable fiscal incentives and other arrangements to investors, on the condition that no more than 20 per cent of output may be sold in the 'domestic' market, that is, the EAC single customs territory in this case. The priority on export is justified by the potential to earn foreign exchange and the discipline imposed on exporters by global markets, requiring firms to meet the highest standards, although the export requirement is sometimes weakly enforced (Whitfield et al. 2015). Discussions are ongoing around changing EPZ rules (e.g. by weakening export requirements) so as to extend rents to RVC and NVC firms to finance upgrading or allow a partial re-orientation of GVC firms to EAC markets.

Firm operations and strategy

One GVC firm is a spinning mill only, while the others are apparel manufacturers carrying out assembly operations in Tanzania on a CMT basis, although one also does embroidery and washing. The apparel firms are part of triangular manufacturing networks with production in Tanzania to access AGOA rents, with all strategic decisions on sourcing and production made at headquarters overseas. Even routine management and decision-making are driven by parent companies through involvement in daily production planning, with daily and even real-time progress reports. Buyers influence the decision-making of parent companies but also engage with factory management directly (e.g. through the provision of training, technical advice, and product quality inspections), in one case with buyer representatives being present on a full-time basis. None of the GVC firms do any higher-value functions such as design, branding, or distribution in Tanzania, reserving these for headquarters with no plans to change the functions carried out in Tanzania.

The spinning mill produces only cotton yarn for export to China. One apparel manufacturer produces cotton jeans and woven trousers while the other makes sportswear from knitted polyester fabric, mostly T-shirts, long-sleeved polo shirts, and shorts. Both apparel manufacturers are overwhelmingly oriented to the US market, selling to major brands and retailers, although one firm is looking to open new markets in anticipation of the expiry of AGOA. They reported interest in the South African market, but SADC's double transformation ROO means GVC firms would have to pay tariffs, which are seen as prohibitively high.

AGOA rents are central to GVC apparel firm strategy, being the principal reason for their location in Tanzania. As before, it is possible to use bilateral tariff and trade data to estimate the size of AGOA rents, at US$9.4 million in the five years to 2018 (Boys and Andreoni 2020: Table 7). Tanzania's apparel exports to the United States are composed almost entirely of the output of the GVC firms in our survey, and because US buyers can easily source duty free from other countries, the rent is considered to principally benefit the Tanzanian GVC firms and their foreign owners.

The EPZ regime provides rents to GVC firms, mainly through a ten-year corporation tax holiday. Although firm-level profit data are not available, official data from ASIP (2018) allow the calculation of a close proxy for profit—gross operating surplus—for apparel firms employing 500 or more employees, which captures the two GVC apparel firms in our sample only.[8] After converting to US dollars with average annual exchange rates and assuming the standard corporate tax rate of 30 per cent in the absence of EPZs, the revenue foregone by national authorities and therefore the rent to GVC firms was US$0.255 million, US$0.659 million, and US$1.244 million in 2013, 2015, and 2016, respectively (US$2.158 million in total). Other advantages for EPZ firms are exemptions from withholding taxes on dividends and other payments to owners overseas (usually at 10 per cent) as well as from customs duty, VAT, and other taxes on imports. EPZ firms also often have access to serviced land in publicly maintained industrial parks at subsidized rates and benefit from facilitated customs administration. There are doubts about the effectiveness of these incentives at promoting investment, with a 2011 survey of investor motivations finding that 91 per cent would have invested in Tanzania without incentives (James 2013). Evidence presented here suggests that the EPZ rents are significant in magnitude, with the corporate tax holiday alone worth two-thirds of AGOA rents in 2016, but may have accrued to the Chinese owners rather than the Tanzanian firms.

Outcomes

Few cases of upgrading were found among GVC firms and no functional upgrading, reflecting the 'non-embedded' characteristics of their owners (Morris et al. 2016). The survey results provide further evidence that greater incentives for product and process upgrading are present with the more 'hierarchical' governance arrangements found in GVCs (Bazan and Navas-Alemán 2004).

---

[8] Gross operating surplus is gross output less intermediate consumption, less employee compensation, which amounted to TZS1.360 billion, TZS4.374 billion, and TZS9.024 billion in 2013, 2015, and 2016, respectively, for GVC apparel firms. This differs from profit because it does not consider, for example, depreciation, taxes, interest, or office costs, but it does provide a rough approximation, especially for a labour-intensive industry with comprehensive tax exemptions and negligible local financing.

One GVC apparel firm interviewed has recently started producing a new product for a new end market—Canada—as it explores options to remain competitive after AGOA. The product is more complex, and this represents a case of product upgrading (the only one in our survey), but because Canada is on par with the United States in terms of buyer requirements, we do not call it end-market upgrading. This case echoes Pipkin and Fuentes's (2017) finding that upgrading often occurs in response to 'vulnerability shocks', which threaten the viability of firm strategies, but in this case merely the threat of losing duty-free market access to the United States was enough. Export data suggests successful product upgrading, with rising exports alongside rising export UVs for GVC firms generally, and one successful and one failed product upgrading case for the US market (Boys and Andreoni 2020: Figures 6 and 7, and Table 2). Table 3.1 shows that GVC firms had the lowest export UVs of all groups on average, mainly because of the substantial exports of yarn by the spinning mill. When this is removed and export UVs of apparel are viewed in isolation, RVC firms show higher figures, but as discussed earlier, this is because of product type rather than quality or production efficiency.

GVC firms report being engaged in continuous process upgrading by replacing machinery to improve productivity, refining production processes, and providing ongoing skills training for workers. The technology used was less than ten years old at the time of the survey, with not all machinery being new upon installation in Tanzania. Live order tracking is a requirement of US buyers, so both apparel factories have invested in computerized systems to track their production. Quality requirements are high and rising, so products are inspected as they leave production lines and reject/rework rates are closely monitored, with one firm reporting dramatic improvements around the time of the survey.

In other outcomes, GVC firms have rapidly grown their exports and by 2017 contributed more to export earnings than the other two groups put together (see Figure 6 in Boys and Andreoni 2020). Capacity utilization among GVC firms was slightly below that of RVC firms, with the main constraints to full utilization being absenteeism in apparel factories and lack of availability of cotton lint for the spinning mill. GVC apparel manufacturers have been the main contributors to employment growth in Tanzanian T&A in recent years, but average employment in GVC firms was slightly below that of RVC firms because of the presence of the capital-intensive spinning mill. Local content was very high for the spinning firm that sources cotton locally and negligible for the apparel manufacturers who import all production inputs from Asia. On labour, safety, and environmental standards, as was seen with RVC firms, no GVC firm currently holds WRAP certification; instead, buyers carry out regular audits to ensure their own standards are met.

3.4 Conclusion and industrial policy implications: managing rents for upgrading

This section takes stock of the findings of this study by outlining the heterogenous upgrading outcomes observed in NVCs, RVCs, and GVCs; the role of rents at the national, regional, and global levels; and how industrial policies at different levels could evolve to maximize the contribution of each value chain type for structural transformation and resilient growth in the wake of the COVID-19 pandemic. We find that value chain directionality affects upgrading outcomes and can be shaped by multi-scalar industrial policy regimes.

Firm-level survey data reveal a spectrum of engagement with NVCs, RVCs, and GVCs, with significant variations in firm set-up and outcomes according to value chain directionality. GVC firms focus on a narrow range of lower-value functions (mostly apparel assembly) because of being foreign owned and the structure of AGOA trade rents, while RVC and NVC firms perform a wider range of functions including vertical integration to textile manufacture and higher-value activities (e.g. design and branding). Only one recent case of functional upgrading was found, an NVC firm that used highly targeted, firm-specific rents from public procurement contracts and DR to start manufacturing apparel for the local market, a model that could be replicated in other cases, potentially with added incentives or compulsions to start exporting to the region within a specified timeframe.

Results in the area of end-market upgrading confirmed the hypothesis that NVCs and RVCs can serve as 'learning grounds' or 'stepping stones' to more demanding but lucrative global markets, as demonstrated by the RVC firm able to start meeting the higher requirements of US buyers, building on its OBM status in domestic markets and experience exporting to the region. This case demonstrates that adequate rents are present in both regional and global export markets, from trade agreements and unilateral preferences, to support end-market upgrading trajectories from NVCs to RVCs and eventually GVCs, which could in principle be replicated. Product and process upgrading outcomes were best among GVC firms because of the nature of rents and governance arrangements, with GVC firms closest to the technological frontier followed by RVC and NVC firms, but process upgrading was observed in all groups.

In other economic and social outcomes, GVCs have made the greatest contribution to recent employment generation and export growth. Interestingly, there was little difference between RVC and GVC firms in terms of compliance with accredited international labour and safety standards, with no company being WRAP accredited, but global buyers have similarly demanding codes of conduct enforced by regular audits. Compliance with accredited social compliance schemes is not necessary for integration into GVCs, which is surprising, but whether this is a peculiarity of the buyers present in Tanzania or represents a broader change in the apparel industry remains to be seen. NVC firms performed best on local content with all firms relying on Tanzanian cotton, while some RVC and GVC firms also procure local cotton depending on firm set-up but otherwise depend on imported inputs.

Regional and international duty-free market access arrangements, especially SADC, EAC, and AGOA, were critical sources of rents for RVC and GVC firms. The design of ROO in these arrangements determines which firms benefit and what kind of investment takes place. Importantly for the design of RTAs in Africa, the double transformation ROO in SADC and Tanzania's resulting privileged access to the South African market have not resulted in significant new investment. One vertically integrated RVC firm is even moving away from serving the South African market, preferring to sell to US buyers under AGOA's single transformation ROO. This suggests policy makers negotiating the design of ROO in the Tripartite Free Trade Area and AfCFTA should be sceptical of the idea that double transformation ROO for T&A products will create sufficient incentives for new manufacturing investment in the regional cotton-to-clothing value chain. Instead, more relaxed ROO favouring export-oriented apparel producers might eventually result in a backward linkage effect (i.e. new investment in textile manufacture) by creating a critical mass of demand for fabrics, as seen in the case of Ethiopia.

The US unilaterally granted AGOA trade preferences have driven recent investment in Tanzanian apparel manufacturing and are an important source of rents for GVC firms, but ROO mitigate against backward integration by encouraging the import of raw materials and negligible local content. It appears likely that Tanzania's duty-free market access to the United States will continue in some form after the scheduled expiry of AGOA in 2025, but the potential 'vulnerability shock' of its loss is already reducing incentives for investment and, in line with other studies (e.g. Pipkin and Fuentes 2017), causing GVC firms to explore alternative products and end markets, with upgrading already happening as a result. As mentioned, GVC firms' current business models do not comply with SADC ROO so the South African market is not an option. The design of ROO in AfCFTA will be critical to determine the extent to which other regional markets could replace the United States. Changes to EPZ rules in Tanzania and the EAC may also play a role, such as the idea to relax export requirements to enable GVC firms to re-orient themselves to NVCs and RVCs (potentially coupled with commitments to increase local content).

Although a number of successful upgrading cases were observed, supported by various kinds of rents, the policy stance is unfavourable in several ways. At the national level, Tanzania's toleration of import undervaluation by customs authorities, particularly for K&K and used clothes, makes it difficult for NVC and RVC firms to accumulate capital for investment in upgrading, with little new capacity for textile manufacture added since liberalization. This undermines progress towards the stated policy goal of an integrated Tanzanian 'cotton-to-clothing' value chain (URT 2016), the best hope for which may paradoxically be through orienting rents primarily towards apparel production for RVCs and GVCs and only later targeting the development of backward linkages, as was also argued at the regional level.

The EAC CET, which has nominally governed tariff rates in Tanzania since 2005, is currently under review, offering the potential to address a number of failings for the T&A sector. First, tariffs on finished goods are seen as too low at 25 per cent, so the proposal to increase them to 30–35 per cent will be welcomed by producers but is unlikely to stimulate new investment. Second, T&A manufacturers complain that intermediate goods such as thread and fabric often attract the top rate of 25 per cent, which may be addressed by the proposed reallocation of intermediates across bands. Third, intermediate products made from synthetic and cotton fibres often receive the same tariff treatment despite the production of the latter in the EAC but not the former, which could be changed under a proposal to impose higher tariffs on intermediates available in the EAC. The criteria for availability will be critical to the impact of this measure because some cotton-based intermediates are or could be produced in the EAC but not always at internationally competitive prices, so incentivizing local sourcing by raising tariffs on imports will harm the competitiveness of manufacturers. The EAC scheme for duty remission on imported inputs could address this issue but has been under-utilized by NVC firms. Furthermore, the use of unilaterally granted national DRs, which rule out the sale of finished goods in other EAC countries, denies a potentially important source of rents to RVC firms.

The COVID-19 pandemic caused untold disruption to supply chains worldwide (UNIDO 2022), with the T&A sector hit particularly hard by lockdowns reducing demand for new clothes in major end markets. Scepticism about the reliability of GVCs for supporting resilient growth was reinforced as global buyers cancelled orders and provided little support to suppliers, with female workers in the global South suffering disproportionately (Castañeda-Navarrete et al. 2021). On the other hand, evidence that South African buyers were more reliable in honouring contractual agreements and supporting suppliers (Pasquali and Godfrey 2022) builds hope that RVCs may offer a viable pathway to sustained, resilient industrialization.

References

Amighini, A., and M. Sanfilippo (2014). 'Impact of South–South FDI and Trade on the Export Upgrading of African Economies'. *World Development*, 64: 1–17.

Amsden, A. H. (1986). 'The Direction of Trade—Past and Present—and the "Learning Effects" of Exports to Different Directions'. *Journal of Development Economics*, 23(2): 249–74.

Andreoni, A. (2019). 'A Generalised Linkage Approach to Local Production Systems Development in the Era of Global Value Chains, with Special Reference to Africa'.

In R. Kanbur, A. Noman, and J. Stiglitz (eds), *The Quality of Growth in Africa* (pp. 264–94). New York: Columbia University Press.

Andreoni, A., J. Boys, and O. Therkildsen (2022) 'The Political Economy of "Specialism" in Tanzania: How to Make Export Processing Zones Work via Conditional Special Licensing'. Working Paper, Anti-Corruption Evidence Consortium, SOAS. London: ACE.

Andreoni, A., P. Mondliwa, S. Roberts, and F. Tregenna (2020) *Structural Transformation in South Africa: The Challenges of Inclusive Industrial Development in a Middle-Income Country.* Oxford: Oxford University Press.

Andreoni, A., and F. Sial (2020). 'Not Business as Usual: The Development of Tanzanian Conglomerates under Different Regimes of Capitalist Accumulation'. Working Paper 22. Anti-Corruption Evidence Consortium, SOAS. London: ACE.

Andreoni, A., and L. Tasciotti (2019). 'Lost in Trade: Towards a Red-Flag System to Target Trade Misinvoicing and Tax Evasion in Tanzania'. Working Paper 19. Anti-Corruption Evidence Consortium, SOAS. London: ACE.

ASIP (2018). 'Annual Survey of Industrial Production 2016'. Dodoma: National Bureau of Statistics of Tanzania.

Barrientos, S., P. Knorringa, B. Evers, M. Visser, and M. Opondo (2016). 'Shifting Regional Dynamics of Global Value Chains: Implications for Economic and Social Upgrading in African Horticulture'. *Environment and Planning A*, 48(7): 1266–83.

Bazan, L., and L. Navas-Alemán (2004). 'The Underground Revolution in the Sinos Valley: A Comparison of Upgrading in Global and National Value Chains'. In H. Schmitz (ed.), *Local Enterprises in the Global Economy: Issues of Governance and Upgrading* (pp. 110–39). Cheltenham: Edward Elgar.

Behuria, P. (2019). 'Twenty-First-Century Industrial Policy in a Small Developing Country: The Challenges of Reviving Manufacturing in Rwanda'. *Development and Change*, 50: 1033–62.

Beverelli, C., V. Stolzenburg, R. B. Koopman, and S. Neumueller (2019). 'Domestic Value Chains as Stepping Stones to Global Value Chain Integration'. *The World Economy*, 42(5): 1467–94.

Boys, J., and A. Andreoni (2020). 'Value Chain Directionality, Upgrading, and Industrial Policy in the Tanzanian Textile and Apparel Sectors', WIDER Working Paper 93/2020. Helsinki: UNU-WIDER.

Boys, J., and A. Andreoni (2023a). 'Upgrading through Global, Regional or National Value Chains? Firm-Level Evidence from the East African Textiles & Apparel Sector'. *Geoforum*, 144: 103809. https://doi.org/10.1016/j.geoforum.2023.103809.

Boys, J., and A. Andreoni (2023b). 'Does Regionalism Increase Industrial Policy Space? An Analytical Framework Applied to the East African Textiles and Apparel Sector'. *Third World Quarterly*, 44(8): 1680–98.

Castañeda-Navarrete, J., J. Hauge, and C. López-Gómez (2021). 'COVID-19's Impacts on Global Value Chains, as Seen in the Apparel Industry'. *Development Policy Review*, 39: 953–70.

Chang, H.-J. (1994). *The Political Economy of Industrial Policy.* New York: Macmillan.

Chang, H.-J., and A. Andreoni (2020). 'Industrial Policy in the 21st Century'. *Development and Change*, 51(2): 324–51.

Cherif, R., and F. Hasanov (2019). 'The Return of the Policy That Shall Not Be Named: Principles of Industrial Policy'. Working Paper No. 19/74. Washington, DC: IMF.

Dinh, H.T., and C. Monga (2013). *Light Manufacturing in Tanzania: A Reform Agenda for Job Creation and Prosperity.* Washington, DC: World Bank.

EAC (2020). 'EAC Gazettes'. Arusha, Tanzania: East Africa Community.

Gereffi, G. (1999). 'International Trade and Industrial Upgrading in the Apparel Commodity Chain'. *Journal of International Economics*, 48(1): 37–70.

Hirschman, A. O. (1977). 'A Generalized Linkage Approach to Economic Development with Special Reference to Staples'. *Economic Development and Cultural Change*, 25: 67–98.

James, S. (2013). 'Tax and Non-Tax Incentives and Investments: Evidence and Policy Implications'. Investment Climate Advisory Services, Washington, DC: World Bank Group.

Kabissa, J. (2014). *Cotton in Tanzania: Breaking the Jinx*. Bukoba and Oxford: Tanzania Educational Publishers and Africa Book Collective.

Khan, M. (2017). Introduction: Political Settlements and the Analysis of Institutions. *African Affairs Virtual Issue*, 117 (469): 670–94.

Lin, J., and H.-J. Chang (2009). 'Should Industrial Policy in Developing Countries Conform to Comparative Advantage or Defy It? A Debate between Justin Lin and Ha-Joon Chang'. *Development Policy Review*, 27(5): 483–502.

Morris, M., L. Plank, and C. Staritz (2016). 'Regionalism, End Markets and Ownership Matter: Shifting Dynamics in the Apparel Export Industry in Sub-Saharan Africa'. *Environment and Planning A: Economy and Space*, 48(7): 1244–65.

Msami, J., and S. Wangwe (2016). 'Industrial Development in Tanzania'. In C. Newman, J. Page, J. Rand, A. Shimeles, M. Söderbom, and F. Tarp (eds), *Manufacturing Transformation: Comparative Studies of Industrial Development in Africa and Emerging Asia* (pp. 155–73). Oxford: Oxford University Press.

Navas-Alemán, L. (2011). 'The Impact of Operating in Multiple Value Chains for Upgrading: The Case of the Brazilian Furniture and Footwear Industries'. *World Development*, 39(8): 1386–97.

Palpacuer, F., P. Gibbon, and L. Thomsen (2005). 'New Challenges for Developing Country Suppliers in Global Clothing Chains: A Comparative European Perspective'. *World Development*, 33(3): 409–30.

Pasquali, G., and Godfrey, S. (2022). 'Governance of Eswatini Apparel Regional Value Chains and the Implications of COVID-19'. *The European Journal of Development Research*, 34: 473–502.

Phelps, N. A., J. Stillwell, and R. Wanjiru (2009). 'Broken Chain? AGOA and Foreign Direct Investment in the Kenyan Clothing Industry'. *World Development*, 37(2): 314–25.

Pickles, J., L. Plank, C. Staritz, and A. Glasmeier (2015). 'Trade Policy and Regionalisms in Global Clothing Production Networks'. *Cambridge Journal of Regions, Economy, and Society*, 8(3): 381–402.

Pipkin, S., and A. Fuentes (2017). 'Spurred to Upgrade: A Review of Triggers and Consequences of Industrial Upgrading in the Global Value Chain Literature'. *World Development*, 98: 536–54.

Reinert, E. S. (2007). *How Rich Countries Got Rich . . . and Why Poor Countries Stay Poor*. London: Constable and Robinson.

Salm, A., P. Dinsdale, D. MacDonald, C. Martelli, K. Hill, and J. Kabissa (2012). *Tanzania Textiles and Garment Situational Analysis and Development Strategy*. Dar es Salaam: Ministry of Industry and Trade.

Staritz, C. (2011). 'Making the Cut? Low-Income Countries and the Global Clothing Value Chain in a Post-Quota and Post-Crisis World'. Washington, DC: World Bank.

Staritz, C., and L. Whitfield (2018). 'Local Firms in the Ethiopian Apparel Export Sector: Building Technological Capabilities to Enter Global Value Chains'. CAE Working Paper 2018: 2. Roskilde: Roskilde University.

Staritz, C., L. Whitfield, A. T. Melese, and F. M. Mulangu (2017). 'What Is Required for African-Owned Firms to Enter New Export Sectors? Conceptualizing Technological Capabilities within Global Value Chains'. CAE Working Paper 2017: 1. Roskilde: Roskilde University.

Taglioni, D., and D. Winkler (2016). *Making Global Value Chains Work for Development*. Washington, DC: World Bank.

TDU (2019). *Survey of Textile and Apparel Factories in Tanzania, 2018*. Dar es Salaam: Ministry of Trade and Industry, Textile Development Unit of Tanzania.

Tokatli, N. (2013). 'Toward a Better Understanding of the Apparel Industry: A Critique of the Upgrading Literature'. *Journal of Economic Geography*, 13(6): 993–1011.

UNCTAD (2019). 'Economic Development in Africa Report 2019. Made in Africa—Rules of Origin for Enhanced Intra-African Trade'. Geneva: United Nations Conference on Trade and Development.

UNCTAD-TRAINS (2020). UNCTAD TRAINS database. New York: United Nations.

UNIDO (2022). 'Industrial Development Report 2022. The Future of Industrialization in a Post-Pandemic World'. Vienna: United Nations Industrial Development Organization.

URT (2016). *Cotton-to-Clothing Strategy 2016_2020*. Geneva: International Trade Centre.

URT (United Republic of Tanzania) (2013). 'The Public Procurement Act Regulations'. Dar es Salaam: Government Printer.

Whitfield, L., O. Therkildsen, L. Buur, and A. Kjaer (2015). 'Tanzania: Intense Contestation within a Weak Dominant Party'. In *The Politics of African Industrial Policy* (pp. 208–32). Cambridge: Cambridge University Press.

Wolff, E. A. (2020). 'The Global Politics of African Industrial Policy: The Case of the Used Clothing Ban in Kenya, Uganda and Rwanda'. *Review of International Political Economy*, 28(5): 1308–31.

4

Trade, technology, and local linkages in the Tanzanian textiles and garments sector

Amrita Saha, André Castro, Marco Carreras, and Daniele Guariso

4.1 Introduction

Low-income countries (LICs) have attracted the most labour-intensive segments of the textiles and garments global value chain—cutting, making (sewing), and trimming. In these segments, upgrading takes place in terms of process, applying new technology or changes in existing production; or in terms of product, shifting into higher value-added product lines (Gereffi 1999). Therefore, participation in these parts of the value chain has been important for the pursuit of industrial development and export competitiveness in LICs—key for firms to build resilience in sustaining their growth and development. However, severe gaps between the available technologies and what are known as best practices continue to present challenges for the adoption of more efficient production processes (Saha et al. 2019) or for a move up the chain into higher value-added functions, that is, functional upgrades or organizational changes in distribution and production. Gaps are apparent in the Tanzanian textiles and garments sector, which lies at the lower end of the global technology frontier, and whose productivity differential continues to increase with respect to other economies at similar stages of development. In fact, the sustainability of moving to higher value-added, and its impact on wider processes of social and economic transformation has received wide attention for LICs (Ponte 2019).[1]

The main way forward for LIC firms in the buyer-driven textiles and apparel value chain (Gereffi 1999) is to adopt new technology or adopt frontier ones and master the ability to produce patterns that can help to establish direct relationships with first-tier buyers. This is frequently the route to higher value addition

[1] Support from UNU-WIDER is gratefully acknowledged. We also thank the International Growth Centre (IGC) for funding previous research on the topic in a project entitled 'Identifying Pathways to Economic Development through India's South-South Knowledge Transfers and Exchange: Evidence from Cotton Apparel in Tanzania', which enabled us to collect the primary data. We are grateful to Ben Shepherd for his advice and contributions to the IGC project; to Ideas in Action, Tanzania; and to all the respondents for working with us—notably Frank Maimu and Frank Dafa. We are grateful to Margaret McMillan and Mia Ellis for sharing the merged Census of Industrial Production and Annual Survey of Industrial Production data sets.

Amrita Saha et al., *Trade, technology, and local linkages in the Tanzanian textiles and garments sector.*
In: *Sustaining Tanzania's Economic Development.* Edited by: Oliver Morrissey, Joseph Semboja, and Maureen Were, Oxford University Press. © UNU-WIDER (2024). DOI: 10.1093/oso/9780192885746.003.0004

(Whitfield and Staritz 2017). But such upgrading requires access to technology which often comes from abroad. The successful deployment of these technologies is dependent on different factors—the sum of which might even result in negative effects on functional upgrading (Fukunishi et al. 2013; Giuliani et al. 2005). These factors include gaps in firm capabilities, weak local linkages, inadequate access to finance, and low government support, which can impede firms' ambitions to adopt the technologies in a sustained manner and use them for future learning. For firm capabilities in particular, the shortage of skilled labour is a major constraint in LICs, and linkages between firms and local networks can be a means of facilitating integration of technology and building resilience.

This chapter investigates technology use in the textiles and apparel sector in Tanzania (Chapter 3 addresses the integration of Tanzanian firms in value chains), a growing East African hub of textiles and apparel production, as a representative case of an LIC struggling to move up the value chain due to inadequate technologies, lack of skilled labour, and insufficient resources. These constraints are expected to be further exacerbated by the COVID-19 crisis (see Chapter 10). In particular, we examine the relationship between firms' productivity and imported technology. Our focus is threefold. First, we consider the role of a firm's absorptive capacity—the capacity of a recipient to assimilate value and use the knowledge transferred (Cohen and Levinthal 1990)—in mediating the effect of imported technology on firm's productivity. Second, we consider differential effects across geographical clusters, in terms of both local linkage types and absorptive capacities within the clusters. Third, we consider current technology, gaps in firms' capabilities, and challenges in the sector, in order to identify specific policy implications. In addition to these three main objectives, the chapter also briefly reviews the role of technology from the global South and its potential to bring LIC firms closer to the technological frontier.

The analysis combines quantitative data with qualitative semi-structured interviews. First, we use panel data constructed from the Census of Industrial Production (CIP) for 2013 and the Annual Survey of Industrial Production (ASIP) for 2015 and 2016. Second, we use primary data from a structured survey with a sample of twenty firms that are representative of the Tanzanian textiles and apparel sector (Saha et al. 2019). Third, we use qualitative data from semi-structured interviews with the firms and a group of key policy stakeholders. Additionally, we reached out to key stakeholders to collect their reflections on how firms and the government are responding to the consequences of the COVID-19 crisis.

The remainder of the chapter is organized as follows. Section 4.2 presents a brief overview of Tanzania's textiles and apparel sector. Section 4.3 outlines the data sets we utilize and discusses the methods used in the analysis. Section 4.4 presents the results, highlighting their relevance for the literature and the Tanzanian context. Finally, Section 4.5 summarizes findings and draws targeted policy implications.

4.2 Overview of the Tanzanian textiles and apparel sector

Strategically located in the East African Community (EAC), the Tanzanian textiles and apparel sector still lags behind in competitiveness, despite its growth in recent years. The sector contributes about 4 per cent of value added in total manufacturing (Trading Economics 2020); and accounts for about 27 per cent of total employment in agro-processing activities (Mazungunye 2019). Firms in this sector are at a lower tier in the global textiles and apparel value chain—primarily assembling pieces and selling them to foreign intermediaries, which then sell them on to global retailers and manufactures. This characterizes most LIC firms in the textiles and apparel sector, which is a typical buyer-driven value chain (Gereffi 1999).

Tanzania has harvested cotton since the colonial era, albeit with relatively low agricultural yields, inadequate quality as a raw material, and insufficient amounts to meet the demands of the domestic industry. Over 75 per cent of the output being shipped overseas and cotton exports are mostly in raw form, valued at US$29.5 million equivalent to 0.53 per cent of total Tanzanian exports (Observatory of Economic Complexity 2020). Although there is evidence that among Tanzanian firms, the textile sector invests more than the national average in research and development (R&D), connectivity, and formal training (Goedhuys 2007), only 25 per cent of the cotton output is processed locally (according to ASIP and CIP data). Looking at the share of local sales and exports for the textiles and apparel sector (Table 4.1), on average, only about 15 per cent of the sector's output was exported between 2013 and 2016; and a large majority of production was sold to the domestic market, with a decline in export shares.

Greater integration with external markets, which could in turn benefit local firms, is impeded by several challenges. Investments in the sector are only made when a threshold demand consistent with a minimum efficient scale is reached, whether local or international. The threshold is difficult to reach because export markets demand stringent standard requirements for suppliers, in terms of not only quality control but also production lead times and delivery deadlines, design specifications, etc. (Calignano and Vaaland 2017). Furthermore, firms face

Table 4.1 Share of local sales and exports, by sector

	Manufacture of textiles, %				Manufacture of wearing apparel, %			
	2013	2015	2016	All years	2013	2015	2016	All years
Share of local sales	75.2	85.2	83.0	82.1	91.2	92.3	94.4	92.8
Share of exports	24.8	14.8	17.0	17.9	8.8	7.7	5.6	7.2

Note: Table 4.1 reports the share of local sales and exports for the textiles and apparel sector.
Source: Authors' calculations based on data from ASIP and CIP.

extensive minimum criteria for accessing global value chains—structured and diversified financing, integrated logistics, and labour and environmental standards (Staritz et al. 2017)—often either unaffordable or unknown to the majority of local firms in Tanzania.

The local network of Tanzanian firms is relatively homogeneous (Dantas et al. 2007). There is limited foreign direct investment (Calignano and Vaaland 2017), which mostly comes from the EAC-integrated consumer market. Limited linkages, both domestic and foreign, reduce the extent to which the Tanzanian textiles and apparel sector can learn via interactions, resulting in a less dynamic environment for firm innovation (Goedhuys 2007).

4.3 Data and methodology

4.3.1 Data

The main analysis is based on secondary data for a representative sample of Tanzanian firms operating in the manufacture of textiles (International Standard Industrial Classification—ISIC, Division 13) and wearing apparel (ISIC Division 14). We extracted this data from a panel data set also used in Diao and McMillan (2018); further details in Saha et al. (2020a). This is supplemented with primary quantitative data collected in mainland Tanzania between June and August 2019, using a carefully structured survey with a target sample of thirty firms for 2018 to 2019 (Saha et al. 2019; 2020a).[2] Ultimately, the survey yielded a sample of twenty firms (a 67 per cent response rate) that responded to a structured set of questions. This structured primary data[3] is used to identify two geographical clusters and map the linkages among firms within those clusters. The local linkages among firms are mapped for each cluster.

Qualitative data collected between June and August 2019 using a semi-structured questionnaire with the same firms from which we had collected quantitative data, and with relevant policy stakeholders, is used to facilitate drawing policy implications.[4] First, we asked firms open-ended questions about performance, value addition, government policy, and linkages with other firms. Second, we asked government stakeholders about the current status and potential of the textiles and apparel industry in Tanzania. Third, we asked about the levels of engagement and linkages with countries in the global South. Finally, in

---

[2] Due to the limited size of the textiles and apparel industry in Tanzania, this number is quite close to the universe of firms.

[3] The panel data is from 2013–14 to 2016–17, and the primary data is from interviews conducted in 2018–19. The network information is especially comparable for 2016–17, as there is only a very small lag. Further, the additional questions in our primary survey support the validity of this comparison.

[4] For a full list of policy stakeholders, see Saha et al. (2020a).

April 2020 we conducted another round of interviews with key informants to gather implications of COVID-19. Overall, the qualitative analysis helped us to contextualize the findings and identify directions for future research.

4.3.2 Research hypotheses

Differences in adoption lags and intensity of use regarding new technologies explain a large part of the income divergence among countries over the past two centuries (Comin and Mestieri 2018). We focus on two key hypotheses in relation to these differences:

> H1: The relationship between the adoption of new technologies and productivity is mediated by absorptive capacity—a firm's ability to learn from such technology from abroad.

First, in an environment of rapid technological change, firms demand technology in order to be able to innovate and stay connected to the global value chain. A firm's intellectual capital is an important source of competitive advantage that determines its ability to learn (Yeoh 2009). Firms can import new technology to improve productivity (Dearden et al. 2006); to promote skills transfer; for the imitation and/or improvement of engineering and managerial processes that lower costs, that is, learning by doing (Gereffi et al. 2005); or to work towards functional upgrades that entail the movement of the firm's production process towards more complex functions in a certain value chain. These can result in a firm's upwards movement along the value chain and a strengthening of backward linkages (Gereffi et al. 2005). However, a low absorptive capacity, measured by the firm's lack of human capital (Eaton and Kortum 1996) or of its own R&D, can reduce or even impede such learning from technology transfers.

> H2: Being in a geographical cluster with greater linkages among local firms is an important factor in explaining a firm's productivity.

Second, the existence of locally owned firms is an important differential in the retention of technologies in the recipient country, enabling further investments and ultimately embedding these local firms into global value chains. Local ownership of firms is evidenced as an important factor that drives profits and capabilities in several countries, including Ethiopia and Lesotho (Morris and Staritz 2017; Whitfield and Staritz 2017). Furthermore, local linkages among firms can bring easier access to sources of finance or capacity-building programmes and can aid matchmaking with global buyers. We attempt to capture whether the differential effects between imported technology and productivity, mediated by absorptive capacity, are correlated with a firm's clustering through different forms of linkage, such as the sharing of information and awareness, or other complementarities in decision-making. To capture the role of such networks, we control for two different geographical clusters in mainland Tanzania, which are characterized by differences in local network linkages among firms and their absorptive capacities.

4.3.3 Empirical model

Our empirical model is based on Boothby et al. (2010), which examined the combined effects of the adoption of new technologies and training on productivity. We apply this model to investigate the role of imported technology and absorptive capacity (the latter captured as training or technology upgrade planning) in firm productivity in Tanzania, accounting especially for the geographical location of clusters. Table 4.2 summarizes the variables used for the quantitative analysis.

Table 4.2 Summary of variables of interest for empirical analysis

Variable	Variable description
Productivity (PP)	
Value added	(Log) Value added: gross output minus intermediate consumption
Imported technology (Imported Tech.)	
Imported technology	Use of imported technology—dummy variable with value 1 if the firm imports any technology from abroad in a given year
Absorptive capacity (Abs.Cap)	
Training employees	Training for employees—dummy variable with value 1 for firms that provide training for employees in a given year, and 0 for firms that do not provide any training in that year
Control variables	
Firm size	(Log) Total persons engaged in the firm—number of employees on the permanent payroll, together with any temporary or seasonal workers
Age	Years since operations first started
Foreign	Foreign ownership—dummy variable with value 1 for firms with any foreign ownership, and 0 otherwise
Exporter	Exporting to foreign markets—dummy variable with value 1 where the firm is an exporter, and 0 otherwise
South	Being in the South cluster—dummy variable that identifies firms in the South cluster (1) relative to those in the North (0)

Note: Table 4.2 reports the main variables used for the empirical analysis.
Source: Authors' compilation based on data from ASIP and CIP, and primary data collected by the authors.

To explore the two hypotheses outlined above, we estimate the following specification:

$$PP_{it} = \beta_0 + \beta_1 \, Imported \; Tech._{it} + \beta_2 \, Abs. \; Cap_{it} + \beta_3 \, Imported_{it} {}^* Abs.Cap_{it}$$
$$+ \rho x + \nu_t + \varepsilon_{it} \qquad\qquad (1)$$

where PP is a productivity measure for firm i at time t; *Imported Tech.* measures a firm's reliance on technology from abroad; *Abs.Cap* reflects a firm's absorptive capacity, using a proxy measure; *Imported*Abs.Cap* is the interaction term; x is a vector of control variables that may affect productivity; ν_t is the year fixed effect; ε is an error term. $\beta_1, \beta_2, \beta_3$, and ρ are coefficients and vectors of coefficients to be estimated.

Productivity is measured using value added of the firm (in logs), following the definition provided in the 2013 CIP as gross output (value of goods produced, receipts from services rendered, and non-industrial services) minus intermediate consumption (electricity, water and fuels, raw materials and supplies, industrial and non-industrial services).

The key explanatory variables include *imported technology*. This comprises manual, semi-automated, and fully automated technology that is not locally manufactured. This classification is based on the current status of the plant technology being used by the firms. We use a dummy variable that identifies the use of imported technology. The measurement of absorptive capacity for Tanzania's manufacturing sector is challenging given data limitations. The panel data are used to construct a proxy measure, *training employees*, a dummy variable that captures whether firms provided training in a given year. An interaction term between imported technology and absorptive capacity is included to investigate whether the effect of imported technology is mediated by the absorptive capacity of the firm (Giuliani and Bell 2005).

The set of control variables comprise, first, *firm size* (the total number of employees, in logs) to account for size-related characteristics that affect productivity. Second, the *age* of the firm is measured from the year the firm started operations until the year in which the information was collected, to account for the role of firms' experience. Third, *foreign* is a dummy variable that identifies foreign owners, examining whether foreign-owned firms are more productive than purely domestic firms. Fourth, similar to Boothby et al. (2010), the *exporter* dummy identifies whether a firm exports any output, an important incentive to innovate due to exposure to international competition (Baldwin and Gu 2004). Finally, we include a dummy variable for *South* that takes the value of 1 for firms located in southern Tanzania, and 0 for firms in northern Tanzania; the grouping is also based on linkages among firms in each cluster.

We recognize that there may be two main limitations, given the scope of our econometric analysis. First, on account of the small number of observations, we cannot account for possible endogeneity. Second, there may be an omitted variable bias, as the possibility to control for variables is driven to a certain extent by data availability. However, the sectoral focus of the analysis in combination with an in-depth qualitative enquiry allows us to better contextualize the findings in the Tanzanian economy.

4.4 Results

The majority of sample firms report having used either manual or semi-automated technology consistently over the years, only a limited number of firms report the use of fully automated technology. The majority of these technologies are sourced from the local market—as second-hand machinery, due to the absence of a domestic machinery industry.[5] A breakdown of technology use types by disaggregated sectors—textiles and apparel—indicates (Saha et al. 2020a): first, in textiles, firms appear to increase their share of imported manual machinery over the years; however, there is a decline in imported semi-automated and fully automated machinery. Second, in apparel, most machinery is procured from local sources over the three years.

Figure 4.1 presents the network linkages[6] for the Tanzanian textiles and apparel sector, split according to the two geographical clusters in this study. Panel A is the *North cluster*—Mwanza, Shinyanga, Arusha, and Kagera; panel B is the *South cluster*—Dar es Salaam, Morogoro, Tanga, and Pwani. On the left of each panel, the nodes are also identified by absorptive capacity measured (using the primary data) as employee training; on the right, the nodes reflect technology upgrade/innovation plans. The numbers represent specific firms in the primary data sample. In terms of activities, firms in both clusters conduct some or all of the following: weaving and spinning textiles, sewing, knitting, and production of apparel. Among our sample firms, ginning is concentrated in the North (57 per cent), where most cotton is grown, while most knitting/weaving, dyeing/printing, and sewing is done in the South (54 per cent).

The network in the North is characterized by relationships based on common membership of associations (67 per cent), and the interactions are quite infrequent (78 per cent occur less than once a month). The network in the South shows a

[5] However, from our primary data, we find that by 2018–19 many firms were purchasing new machinery (55 per cent) or equipment (80 per cent), which was largely imported (91 per cent and 63 per cent respectively).

[6] Prepared using NEATO visualization software. The geometric distance in the layout between any two nodes approximates their path distance in the network.

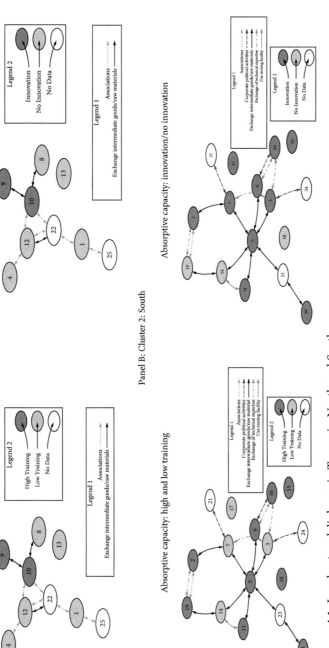

Figure 4.1 Local network linkages in Tanzania, North and South

Note: The numbers represent anonymized firms from the primary survey of thirty target firms in Tanzania's textiles and apparel sector. Legend 1 lists the nature of the interactions. Legend 2 lists absorptive capacity.

Source: Authors' illustration.

more diversified pattern of relationships, predominantly exchanges of intermediate goods and raw materials (50 per cent), followed by exchanges of technical
expertise (22 per cent), with the former not occurring very often (89 per cent
occur less than once a month). Firms in the South appear to be more connected
on average: the average degree (i.e. the average number of links for each node) is
2.25, against two in the North (+12.5 per cent). This is also true when weighted
by the frequencies of the interactions: the average weighted degree is 0.78 in the
South and 0.67 in the North (+16 per cent).

We find that in the North cluster, on average, 80 per cent of firms report the use
of manual technology; only 40 per cent and 20 per cent report the use of semi-
automated or fully automated technology respectively. In the South cluster, we
observe that only 50 per cent of firms report the use of manual technology, while
more than 60 per cent report the use of semi-automated technology; the share of
firms reporting fully automated technology is similar to the share in the North
cluster. If we look at the source of the technologies, while the manual technology
in the North cluster is almost equally split between local and imported technology, in the South cluster the share of local technology is greater than the imported
share, albeit with a decreasing trend over the years. If we look at semi-automated
and fully automated technology, a greater share in both clusters comes from the
local market, with a relatively higher share of imported technology in the North
cluster.

Table 4.3 reports firms' characteristics for all, by cluster, and by imported technology status (Saha et al. 2020a reports firms' main characteristics by years and by
foreign ownership status). On average, firm value added is TZS7,822,000. In terms
of imported technology, only about 30 per cent of firms make use of any type of
imported technology. For absorptive capacity measured as training, we find that
only a fifth of the firms in our sample have provided any form of training for their
employees.

Firms in the South cluster report higher average value added compared with
the North, with a sharp increase registered in 2015. Further, while 50 per cent
of the firms in the North report the use of imported technology, the majority (80 per cent) of firms in the South rely on local technology. While we note
some differences at cluster level in terms of the utilization of imported technology, the number of employees, and the share of firms providing training for
employees, the significant differences are in terms of financial resources for training activity: the quality and extent of employee training is greater in the South
cluster. Finally, firms in the North are on average younger than their southern
counterparts and report a higher value of exports and lower total production
and sales.

In terms of absorptive capacity, using our primary data, we observe that the
South cluster is characterized not only by more diversified and frequent interactions, but also by a larger proportion of firms with greater absorptive capacity

Table 4.3 Firms' main characteristics, by cluster and by imported technology status

	(1) All	(2) Cluster: North	(3) Cluster: South	(4) Without imported technology	(5) With imported technology
Dependent variables					
(Log) Value added	12.8	12	13	13	12
	(2.8)	(3)	(3)	(3)	(3)
Explanatory variables				0%	100%
Imported technology	29.9	46	20	(0)	(0)
(dummy), %	(45.9)	(50)	(40)		93
Training employees	22.7	22	23	31	24
(dummy), %	(42.0)	(42)	(42)	(46)	(43)
Control variables					
Firm size	248.1	238	254	13	11
	(533.3)	(594)	(495)	13	11
Age	12.2	9.1	14.1	318	85
	(12.2)	(10.1)	(13.0)	(618)	(142)
Foreign, %	26.0	29	24	29	20
	(44.0)	(46)	(43)	(45)	(40)
Exporter, %	22.7	22	23	29	9
	(42.0)	(42)	(42)	(45)	(29)
Exported value	11,966.4	19,574	7471	13,215	2289
(000 TZS) if >0	(12,642.2)	(15,106)	(8448)	(12,886)	(3148)
Number of firms	**154**	**59**	**95**	**108**	**46**

Note: Table 4.3 reports the main firms' characteristics for all firms (All), by cluster (North and South), and by imported technology status (with and without). Standard deviations in parentheses.
Source: Authors' calculations based on data from ASIP and CIP.

(proxied by employee training)[7]—69 per cent, compared with 28 per cent in the North. Hence, the two geographical clusters are characterized by different proportions of firms with high absorptive capacity.

Only 30 per cent of firms have used any imported technology. Interestingly, firms that have not used any imported technology across the three years report on average higher value added, higher shares of expenditure on training for employees, higher shares and total values of exports, and higher levels of production and sales. During our semi-structured interviews, firms stated a preference for local, older machinery. Three reasons were given for this. First, spare parts are easily and cheaply available. Second, frequent power cuts mean that the seasonal availability of cotton results in inconsistency in production plans—plant closures occur during part of the year, and costs from depreciation of non-operational machinery

---

[7] We do not consider firms for which we are able to infer linkages from the survey but that we did not interview, as we do not have data on their average level of training.

are high. Third, access to long-term finance is still limited and expensive. Hence, it appears that a mismatch between other available inputs and lack of access to higher-quality capital may be affecting firms' decisions regarding the sourcing of technology, which will also likely affect productivity.

We investigate the relationship between technology and firm productivity, focusing on the role played by absorptive capacity; estimating a model of the type proposed by Boothby et al. (2010), and applying it to imported technology for the Tanzanian textiles and apparel sector. To examine the productivity effects between the two groups of firms differentiated by their reliance on imported technology, Table 4.4 presents the results of ordinary least squares (OLS) regressions using value added as the dependent variable and the absorptive capacity measure—training employees dummy (further results including robustness

Table 4.4 Imported technology, absorptive capacity, and firm productivity

	Dependent variable: value added			
	(1)	(2)	(3)	(4)
Imported technology	−0.710**		−0.638*	−0.898**
	(0.339)		(0.340)	(0.365)
Abs.Cap.		0.660*	0.575	0.259
		(0.353)	(0.353)	(0.390)
Interaction				1.634*
				(0.892)
Control Variables				
Firm size (ln)	0.649***	0.681***	0.666***	0.690***
	(0.133)	(0.133)	(0.133)	(0.132)
Age	0.039***	0.036***	0.037***	0.037***
	(0.013)	(0.013)	(0.013)	(0.013)
Foreign	1.820***	1.752***	1.762***	1.792***
	(0.430)	(0.433)	(0.429)	(0.426)
Exporter	0.611	0.661	0.542	0.425
	(0.419)	(0.418)	(0.419)	(0.420)
South	0.904***	1.075***	0.913***	0.919***
	(0.322)	(0.311)	(0.320)	(0.318)
Year dummies	Yes	Yes	Yes	Yes
Observations	154	154	154	154
R-squared	0.619	0.616	0.626	0.634

Note: Table 4.4 presents the results of ordinary least squares (OLS) regressions using value added as the dependent variable. In column (1), we introduce the imported technology dummy variable. Column (2) reports results for the training employees dummy as absorptive capacity measure. Column (3) includes both imported technology and the absorptive capacity measure. Finally, we introduce the interaction term between the two in column (4), where we find a positive and statistically significant coefficient that affirms the mediating role played by absorptive capacity. Standard errors in parentheses. *** $p<0.01$, ** $p<0.05$, * $p<0.1$.
Source: Authors' calculations based on data from ASIP and CIP.

checks are reported in Saha et al. 2020a). In columns (1) and (3), it is interesting to note that imported technology has a consistently negative and statistically significant coefficient. Absorptive capacity measured by employee training alone is positive and statistically significant in column (2). With both of the aforementioned variables together in column (3), the coefficient for absorptive capacity turns insignificant. However, when we introduce the interaction term in column (4), we find a positive and statistically significant coefficient that affirms the mediating role played by absorptive capacity in the productivity–imported technology relationship.[8] These results are robust to the use of different measures for imported technology (Saha et al. 2020a). Using the alternative proxy for absorptive capacity, we also find similar results to those above, which suggests that our findings are also robust to this alternative measurement.

The finding that imported technology alone may have a negative impact on firm-level productivity aligns with the literature, which identifies that the successful adoption and integration of new technologies requires the acquisition of new skills or the upgrade of the existing workforce's skill levels. Okafor et al. (2017) and Yasar (2013) found similar results for the cases of Ghana and China respectively: absorptive capacity mediates the effect of imported technology on productivity. The meta-analysis employed by Zou et al. (2018) also found similar results: absorptive capacity mediates the effect of innovation and knowledge transfer on financial performance, which is largely positively correlated with firm productivity.

In the semi-structured interviews, while the majority of firms that imported new technology stated that increasing production capacity and improving production quality were their main motivations, a binding constraint on higher productivity levels appears to have been associated with the lack of skilled labour, corroborating the crucial role of absorptive capacity in mediating the effect of imported technology on productivity. Indeed, foreign technical experts are also hired to train local staff on the correct usage of machinery.

Girma (2005) found an analogous result for the United Kingdom regarding the mediating role of absorptive capacity on productivity. When developing countries are considered, the expected positive correlation between imported technology and firm-level productivity is actually much more nuanced (Habiyaremye 2013), and even negative for some industries and sectors (López 2008). However, even in the case of developed countries, a negative correlation holds in some cases (Fagerberg and Verspagen 2000). Our results contrast with some other findings in the literature, mostly for either developed countries (Mendi 2007; Vuori 1997) or countries with a well-established industrial park (Hasan 2002; Jacob and Meister

---

[8] The interaction effect is significant at 10 per cent, so while our results provide support for the association between the main variables of interest, given the low significance levels, we conduct a set of robustness checks.

2005; Kim 1980; Parameswaran 2009; Zhao 1995). Furthermore, the results are also different from general evidence regarding Tanzania's manufacturing sector, such as Nyantakyi and Munemo (2017).

Notwithstanding caveats regarding the interpretation of the trade indices in the *Doing Business Reports* (DBRs) (Sharafeyeva and Shepherd 2020; World Bank 2020), Tanzania is ranked 141 out of 190 countries, the lowest among its East African peers (World Bank 2020). However, our qualitative interviews differed slightly. In contrast with its fair score in the DBRs, all the firms we interviewed stated that electricity was the main barrier, not only because of its high cost in general (and the high costs of acquiring back-up generators), but also because of the frequent power cuts, which bring plants grinding to a halt. Several respondents also indicated an oligopolistic local market for textile raw materials, dominated by a couple of large firms able to charge higher prices, rendering smaller companies less competitive—an issue not covered by the DBRs. While we do not model them directly, we also find that a number of firms cannot increase production levels due to a lack of access to finance and the high costs of borrowing for the purchase of machinery and raw materials, once again in contrast with the DBRs, which give credit the highest score of all topics for Tanzania (although it is still low compared with more developed countries). Further research on factors such as electricity and sources of finance would therefore add value to the modelling of productivity effects for Tanzanian firms.

Among the control variables, the only non-significant coefficient is related to the status of firms as exporters. This suggests that firms export products with limited processing so being an exporter does not have a significant impact on value addition. The coefficients for number of employees, age, and foreign ownership are positive and statistically significant, as expected. The positive and statistically significant relationship between productivity and foreign ownership aligns with responses during the semi-structured interviews. While sample firms reported that they could compete on quality, they were unable to compete on price with international firms, mostly those from South and South-East Asia. The exception were firms with some foreign ownership, which reported being competitive with overseas products. However, most firms expressed the need for interim protection from textile and garments imports. This is not surprising, as these firms simultaneously reported linkages with a number of other firms, including foreign ones—importing inputs from the global South, especially China and India.

Being located in the South cluster with diversified linkages is correlated with higher productivity, corroborating the summary statistics presented earlier. However, generally the scope of local networks in the Tanzanian textile and garments industry is still limited. Only a few domestic firms report working with other domestic firms—mostly smaller firms collaborate to increase their production capacity and meet orders during demand spikes. Moreover, only a few smaller firms purchase inputs, mostly fabrics, from larger firms (three in total). Two firms stated that they purchased second-hand foreign machinery and parts from other domestic firms, whereas such purchases from abroad are common. Even in these two firms, the domestic transfer of technology took place because of the closure of companies and the subsequent sale of machinery and equipment.

Despite the limited extent of the local network of firms more generally, the domestic market is very important for many Tanzanian firms. Using an average from the ASIP and CIP data, we find that approximately 85 per cent of the sectoral output is sold locally, with the rest being exported. Most of these firms turn to the local market due to a lack of capacity or awareness to supply first-tier international buyers, even though firms recognize that growth based on the domestic market is structurally limited by chronically low purchasing power. In contrast, some Ethiopian firms use the local market as a springboard from which they tap into global value chains; in these cases, the local market cross-subsidizes operations with international markets, such as testing branded product lines and controlling production to meet stringent requirements (Whitfield and Staritz 2017), evidence of which our survey did not find in Tanzania.

Overall, our results reveal that to benefit from imported technology, firms need to invest in building their absorptive capacities. Imported technology can have a detrimental impact on a firm's productivity if it is not combined with training or technology upgrade plans. Access to foreign technologies does not necessarily translate into higher productivity, due to firms' limited ability to identify and develop such technologies. The crucial role of absorptive capacity in determining the effect of imported technology on firms' productivity highlights the need for a combination of foreign technology and investment in capacity for local firms.

Furthermore, low labour productivity has been an issue. While we do not model this, our semi-structured interviews found evidence of high rates of labour turnover and absenteeism in the industry. Firms reported that besides being unpunctual and inconsistent in going to the factory floor, workers often tended not to stay at the same firm for long periods of time, and to change firms quite often. Firms may therefore not only be disincentivized to offer training, but also have to adopt costly measures to manage the high labour turnover. Additionally, there is limited availability of workers for managerial and supervisory positions, which are then filled by expatriates, mostly from South Asia. However, labour regulations regarding the hiring of foreign workers remain fairly stringent. In this respect, easing immigration policy for skilled workers in relevant predetermined sectors and activities would address a key constraint for firms. This would also be in line with the role that absorptive capacity plays in mediating the effect of imported technology on firms' productivity.

Where firms in LICs may lack the means to build these capabilities, development practitioners and initiative can provide support—especially facilitating the exchange of knowledge from other partners in the global South. One route to fix this gap could be to facilitate the inflow and exchange of knowledge and technology from partners in the global South, especially by means of South-South cooperation, which can bring in cost-effective and adaptable technologies with other South partners (Mohanty et al. 2019; Saha et al. 2020b).

Finally, in the context of the consequences of COVID-19, three broad groupings of firms are visible in the market. First, large firms that are engaged in cut, make, and trim, with offices in Mauritius and Hong Kong, are facing hits to capacity utilization, with lower foreign demand and changes in purchasing behaviour. Second, firms that export primarily to regional markets have had order cancellations, and as a response shifted to the production of face masks using different fabrics, in an initiative spearheaded by TEGAMAT and coordinated with the Ministry of Industry and Trade. However, these firms faced difficulties in accessing inputs imported from abroad. Third, smaller firms that produce a local fabric called *kanga kitenge* for mainly local markets (mostly farmers) expect to face depressed demand. As a result of the COVID-19 crisis, at the end of 2020, several firms expected to cut hours, grant extended leave, and furlough half of their workforce, raising questions about firm resilience and sustainability (see further discussion in Chapter 10).

4.5 Conclusions and policy implications

This chapter explored the case of Tanzanian textiles and apparel firms, focusing on the role of imported technology for improving productivity and absorptive capacity, with implications for building resilience in sustaining their growth and development. The main finding is that absorptive capacity plays a mediating role in the effect of imported technology on productivity in the Tanzanian textile and apparel industry. Where firms introduced new products or processes between 2013 and 2016, those products and processes were new to the firm only, not to the domestic market; this highlights the inadequate access to technology and the low levels of upgrading. The majority of firms that purchased either new machinery or equipment largely imported them from India or China. In this regard, although machinery is largely exempt from import duty under the EAC Common External Tariff, bureaucracy around imports is still problematic. Firms in our sample reported that customs procedures, and value-added tax (VAT) refunds for the import of capital inputs such as machinery, are cumbersome, and significant human resources have to be allocated specifically for this long process.

We also find that firms faced issues regarding the availability of raw materials, which, coupled with import restrictions on raw cotton, prevented smaller firms from increasing their production capacity. In addition to facing high cotton prices, many firms have to import certain processed inputs that are subject to import duties, such as yarn, due to the low quality of locally available inputs. In this context, firms demand a more candid dialogue among all parties—farmers, industry, and government—to discuss the scope for the government, via the TCB, to purchase raw materials from farmers at higher subsidized prices in order to meet industry needs at lower subsidized prices.

The second main finding captures geographical differences: the southern region of Tanzania is characterized by diversified linkages among local textile firms, which is correlated with higher firm productivity. However, northern Tanzania lags behind, where firms expressed the need for government support to effectively build local capacity to link into global value chains, facilitating easier access to sources of finance and capacity-building programmes, or to aid matchmaking with global buyers. Although all firms are members of sectoral and industry associations, which are good networks for coordinating interests with the government, it appears that few firms know how to actually accrue effective and tangible benefits.

In light of overcoming the challenges brought about by COVID-19, continuing policy action and support will be needed for technology adoption and skills development, especially in LICs (Castañeda-Navarrete et al. 2021; Pasquali and Godfrey 2022). At the end of 2020, the Tanzanian government had taken some measures already (i.e. redirecting industrial capacity towards the production of face masks and other personal protective equipment). However, textiles and apparel firms sought more concrete steps in order to alleviate the impact of the exogenous price and demand shocks and remain resilient. In particular, firms voiced support for: clearance of outstanding debts, the waiving of interest charges on overdrafts and short-term loans, the reduction of payroll taxes, VAT, and corporate tax rates, and a restriction on imports of second-hand clothing.

References

Baldwin, J., and W. Gu (2004). 'Trade Liberalization: Export-Market Participation, Productivity Growth, and Innovation'. *Oxford Review of Economic Policy*, 20: 372–92.

Boothby, D., A. Dufour, and J. Tang (2010). 'Technology Adoption, Training and Productivity Performance'. *Research Policy*, 39(5): 650–61. https://doi.org/10.1016/j.respol.2010.02.011

Calignano, G., and T. I. Vaaland (2017). 'Supplier Development in Tanzania: Experiences, Expectations and Motivation'. *Extractive Industries and Society*, 4: 385–97. https://doi.org/10.1016/j.exis.2017.01.012

Castañeda-Navarrete, J., J. Hauge, and C. López-Gómez (2021). 'Covid-19's Impacts on Global Value Chains, as Seen in the Apparel Industry'. *Development Policy Review*, 39(6): 953–70. https://doi.org/10.1111/dpr.12539

Cohen, W. M., and D. A. Levinthal (1990). 'Absorptive Capacity: A New Perspective on Learning and Innovation'. *Administrative Science Quarterly*, 35: 128–52. https://doi.org/10.2307/2393553

Comin, D., and M. Mestieri (2018). 'If Technology Has Arrived Everywhere, Why Has Income Diverged?' *American Economic Journal: Macroeconomics*, 10: 137–78. https://doi.org/10.1257/mac.20150175

Dantas, E., E. Giuliani, and A. Marin (2007). 'The Persistence of "Capabilities" as a Central Issue in Industrialization Strategies: How They Relate to MNC Spillovers, Industrial Clusters and Knowledge Networks'. *Asian Journal of Technology Innovation*, 15: 19–43. https://doi.org/10.1080/19761597.2007.9668636

Dearden, L., H. Reed, and J. Van Reenen (2006). 'The Impact of Training on Productivity and Wages: Evidence from British Panel Data'. *Oxford Bulletin of Economics and Statistics*, 68(4): 397–421. https://doi.org/10.1111/j.1468-0084.2006.00170.x

Diao, X., and M. McMillan (2018). 'Toward an Understanding of Economic Growth in Africa: A Reinterpretation of the Lewis Model'. *World Development*, 109: 511–22. https://doi.org/10.1016/j.worlddev.2016.12.008

Eaton, J., and S. Kortum (1996). 'Trade in Ideas Patenting and Productivity in the OECD'. *Journal of International Economics*, 40(3–4): 251–78. https://doi.org/10.1016/0022-1996(95)01407-1

Fagerberg, J., and B. Verspagen (2000). 'Productivity, R&D Spillovers and Trade'. In: B. van Ark, S. K. Kuipers, and G. H. Kuper (eds), *Productivity, Technology and Economic Growth* (pp. 345–60). Boston, MA: Springer. https://doi.org/10.1007/978-1-4757-3161-3_12

Fukunishi, T., K. Goto, and T. Yamagata (2013). 'Aid for Trade and Value Chains in Textiles and Apparel'. Geneva: WTO, OECD, and IDE/JETRO.

Gereffi, G. (1999). 'International Trade and Industrial Upgrading in the Apparel Commodity Chain'. *Journal of International Economics*, 48: 37–70. https://doi.org/10.1016/S0022-1996(98)00075-0

Gereffi, G., J. Humphrey, and T. Sturgeon (2005). 'The Governance of Global Value Chains'. *Review of International Political Economy*, 12: 78–104. https://doi.org/10.1080/09692290500049805

Girma, S. (2005). 'Absorptive Capacity and Productivity Spillovers from FDI: A Threshold Regression Analysis'. *Oxford Bulletin of Economics and Statistics*, 67: 281–306. https://doi.org/10.1111/j.1468-0084.2005.00120.x

Giuliani, E., and M. Bell (2005). 'The Micro-determinants of Meso-level Learning and Innovation: Evidence from a Chilean Wine Cluster'. *Research Policy*, 34(1): 47–68. https://doi.org/10.1016/j.respol.2004.10.008

Giuliani, E., C. Pietrobelli, and R. Rabellotti (2005). 'Upgrading in Global Value Chains: Lessons from Latin American Clusters'. *World Development*, 33: 549–73. https://doi.org/10.1016/j.worlddev.2005.01.002

Goedhuys, M. (2007). 'Learning, Product Innovation, and Firm Heterogeneity in Developing Countries: Evidence from Tanzania'. *Industrial and Corporate Change*, 16: 269–92. https://doi.org/10.1093/icc/dtm003

Habiyaremye, A. (2013). 'Imported Capital Goods and Manufacturing Productivity: Evidence from Botswana's Manufacturing Sector'. *South African Journal of Economics*, 81: 581–604. https://doi.org/10.1111/saje.12015

Hasan, R. (2002). 'The Impact of Imported and Domestic Technologies on the Productivity of Firms: Panel Data Evidence from Indian Manufacturing Firms'. *Journal of Development Economics*, 69: 23–49. https://doi.org/10.1016/S0304-3878(02)00051-2

Jacob, J., and C. Meister (2005). 'Productivity Gains, Technology Spillovers and Trade: Indonesian Manufacturing, 1980-96'. *Bulletin of Indonesian Economic Studies*, 41: 37–56. https://doi.org/10.1080/00074910500072674

Kim, L. (1980). 'Stages of Development of Industrial Technology in a Developing Country: A Model'. *Research Policy*, 9: 254–77. https://doi.org/10.1016/0048-7333(80)90003-7

López, R. A. (2008). 'Foreign Technology Licensing, Productivity, and Spillovers'. *World Development*, 36: 560–74. https://doi.org/10.1016/j.worlddev.2007.04.016

Mazungunye, P. P. (2019). 'Industrialization for Economic Transformation: Economy-wide Impacts of Agro-processing Development in Tanzania'. SA-TIED Working Paper 42. Helsinki: UNU-WIDER.

Mendi, P. (2007). 'Trade in Disembodied Technology and Total Factor Productivity in OECD Countries'. *Research Policy*, 36: 121–33. https://doi.org/10.1016/j.respol.2006.09.028

Mohanty, S. K., L. Franssen, and S. Saha (2019). 'The Power of International Value Chains in the Global South'. Geneva: ITC. https://www.intracen.org/uploadedFiles/intracenorg/Content/Publications/Global%20South%20value%20chains_final_Low-res.pdf

Morris, M., and C. Staritz (2017). 'Industrial Upgrading and Development in Lesotho's Apparel Industry: Global Value Chains, Foreign Direct Investment, and Market Diversification'. *Oxford Development Studies*, 45: 303–20. https://doi.org/10.1080/13600818.2016.1237624

Nyantakyi, E. B., and J. Munemo (2017). 'Technology Gap, Imported Capital Goods and Productivity of Manufacturing Plants in Sub-Saharan Africa'. *Journal of International Trade & Economic Development*, 26(2): 209–27.

Observatory of Economic Complexity (2020). 'Which Countries Export Raw Cotton?' Available at: https://oec.world/en/visualize/tree_map/hs92/export/show/all/5201/2016/ (accessed 28 April 2020).

Okafor, L. E., M. Bhattacharya, and H. Bloch (2017). 'Imported Intermediates, Absorptive Capacity and Productivity: Evidence from Ghanaian Manufacturing Firms'. *World Economy*, 40: 369–92. https://doi.org/10.1111/twec.12467

Parameswaran, M. (2009). 'International Trade, R&D Spillovers and Productivity: Evidence from Indian Manufacturing Industry'. *Journal of Development Studies*, 45: 1249–66. https://doi.org/10.1080/00220380902862911

Pasquali, G., and S. Godfrey (2022). Governance of Eswatini Apparel Regional Value Chains and the Implications of Covid 19. *European Journal of Development Research*, 34: 473–502. https://doi.org/10.1057/s41287-021-00383-3

Ponte, S. (2019). *Business, Power and Sustainability in a World of Global Value Chains*. London: Bloomsbury Publishing.

Saha, A., D. Guariso, A. Castro, and B. Shepherd (2019). 'Technology Demand and the Role of South-South Trade in Tanzania's Textiles and Apparel: Examining Linkages with India'. Working Paper. London: IGC.

Saha, A., A. Castro, M. Careras, and D. Guariso (2020a). 'Trade, Technology, and Absorptive Capacity: Firm-level Evidence across Geographical Clusters in the Tanzanian Textiles and Apparel Sector'. Working Paper 2020/96. Helsinki: WIDER.

Saha, A., J. Thorpe, P. O. F. Flynn, and H. Bucher (2020b). *Designing for Impact: South-South Trade and Investment*. Geneva: ITC.

Sharafeyeva, A., and B. Shepherd (2020). 'What Does "Doing Business" Really Measure? Evidence from Trade Times'. *Economics Letters*, 192: 109215. https://doi.org/10.1016/j.econlet.2020.109215

Staritz, C., L. Whitfield, A. T. Melese, and F. M. Mulangu (2017). 'What Is Required for African-Owned Firms to Enter New Export Sectors? Conceptualizing Technological Capabilities within Global Value Chains'. CAE Working Paper 2017/1. Roskilde: Roskilde Universitet, Centre of African Economies.

Trading Economics (2020). 'Tanzania: Textiles and Clothing (% of Value Added in Manufacturing)'. Available at: tradingeconomics.com/tanzania/textiles-and-clothing-percent-of-value-added-in-manufacturing-wb-data.html (accessed 7 July 2020).

Vuori, S. (1997). 'Interindustry Technology Flows and Productivity in Finnish Manufacturing'. *Economic Systems Research*, 9: 67–80. https://doi.org/10.1080/09535319700000005

Whitfield, L., and C. Staritz (2017). 'Mapping the Technological Capabilities of Ethiopian-Owned Firms in the Apparel Global Value Chain'. CAE Working Paper 2017/4. Roskilde: Roskilde Universitet, Centre of African Economies.

World Bank (2020). *Doing Business 2020: Comparing Business Regulation in 190 Economies*. Washington, DC: World Bank. https://doi.org/10.1596/978-1-4648-1440-2.

Yasar, M. (2013). 'Imported Capital Input, Absorptive Capacity, and Firm Performance: Evidence from Firm-Level Data'. *Economic Inquiry*, 51: 88–100. https://doi.org/10.1111/j.1465-7295.2010.00352.x.

Yeoh, P.-L. (2009). 'Realized and Potential Absorptive Capacity: Understanding their Antecedents and Performance in the Sourcing Context'. *Journal of Marketing Theory and Practice*, 17: 21–36. https://doi.org/10.2753/MTP1069-6679170102.

Zhao, H. (1995). 'Technology Imports and their Impacts on the Enhancement of China's Indigenous Technological Capability'. *Journal of Development Studies*, 31: 585–602. https://doi.org/10.1080/00220389508422379.

Zou, T., G. Ertug, and G. George (2018). 'The Capacity to Innovate: A Meta-Analysis of Absorptive Capacity'. *Innovation*, 20: 87–121. https://doi.org/10.1080/14479338.2018.1428105.

5

Drivers of manufacturing export performance and competitiveness in Tanzania

Roseline Misati and Kethi Ngoka

5.1 Introduction

Growth in international trade over the past decades has been much faster than that of world output, driven by supportive policies, innovation, and changing business models that have brought down the cost of cross-border trade. Tanzania has benefited from export growth and diversification away from primary commodity dependence to an increasing share of manufactured exports (albeit primarily resource-based), and this supported economic growth. Since the late 2000s, however, this growth has slowed down due to structural and cyclical factors, coupled with the long-lived impacts of the global recession that followed the 2007–08 global financial crisis. Trade elasticities (the change in the value of global trade relative to the change in world output) declined to 0.9 per cent from 1.8 per cent in the pre-crisis period, affecting all product groups—albeit by different magnitudes (UNCTAD 2015: 5). While the volume of world merchandise trade increased by 1.5 per cent in 2016 and 4.6 per cent in 2017, growth was only 0.2 per cent in 2019 (WTO 2017, 2018, 2022). World merchandise trade contracted by 5 per cent in 2020 due to lockdowns and disruption in global supply chains occasioned by the COVID-19 pandemic, although growth recovered to 9.8 per cent in 2021, following easing of lockdowns and restoration of global supply chains (WTO 2022). However, shortages of manufacturing inputs due to weak supply chains limit prospects of sustaining this recovery, and new pressures emerged with the outbreak of the war in Ukraine in April 2022, especially reductions in food and fertilizer supply generating high global food price inflation (WTO 2022). An emerging theme from these episodes of volatility and uncertainty for growth and trade prospects, especially for emerging and developing economies, is the need to rebuild resilience against shocks through diversifying exports of goods and enhancing competitiveness,

Roseline Misati and Kethi Ngoka, *Drivers of manufacturing export performance and competitiveness in Tanzania*.
In: *Sustaining Tanzania's Economic Development*. Edited by: Oliver Morrissey, Joseph Semboja, and Maureen Were,
Oxford University Press. © UNU-WIDER (2024). DOI: 10.1093/oso/9780192885746.003.0005

especially of manufactures, which generate strong positive externalities to the economy.[1]

Tanzania's Development Vision 2025 seeks to achieve a diversified and semi-industrialized economy with a substantial industrial sector comparable to typical middle-income countries. In this regard, some of the interventions entail shifting Tanzania's production structure to high-value manufactured goods as well as integrating and deepening regional and global value chains (GVCs) to achieve annual real gross domestic product (GDP) growth rates of 8–10 per cent to deliver improved incomes and higher standards of living. The specific measures that have been deployed to date to drive the growth and competitiveness of manufactured exports encompass aspects of infrastructure, innovation, and technology (Misati and Ngoka 2021). Despite the strategic investments made in Tanzania, the share of manufacturing exports to total merchandise exports continues to remain relatively low at 15.1 per cent in 2019, dropping to 11.4 per cent in 2020 due to the effect of COVID-19 and recovering slightly to 13.8 per cent in 2021 (World Bank 2022). In addition, manufactured exports continued to be of low skill and technology intensity, limiting benefits to the economy. Medium- and high-technology exports constituted only a small share of manufactured exports, averaging 15.1 per cent between 1997 and 2015, whilst integration into global and regional value chains that currently constitute a large share of international trade remains limited. As a result, Tanzania's long-term growth aspirations, which are predicated on the performance and competitiveness of manufactured exports, may not be achieved.

Previous analysis highlights a number of constraints to manufacturing exports without providing quantitative evidence of the key determinants of manufacturing export competitiveness in Tanzania. Classifying Tanzania's manufacturing exports in terms of skill and technology intensity shows that growth since 2000 has been mainly in low-technology and low to medium skill-level products. Against this background, this chapter seeks to establish determinants of competitiveness and export performance in the manufacturing sector in Tanzania over the period 1997–2018. We focus not only on growth, but also on different performance dimensions, such as revealed comparative advantage (RCA) and participation in GVCs, with a view to identifying policies that can unlock the potential of these sectors (measures aimed at deepening the technology intensity of manufactured

[1] We are very grateful to UNU-WIDER and UONGOZI Institute for providing us with the opportunity and support to undertake this study. We would also like to express our gratitude to all the participants during the conference held in February 2020 for providing us with very insightful comments. In a special way, we sincerely thank Oliver Morrisey, Joseph Semboja, Josephat Kweka, and Maureen Were, who provided very useful input and exceptional support that greatly shaped the final version of this study. Any inadvertent errors and omissions are entirely our own responsibility.

exports are beneficial for tapping into international markets). The focus is on the following objectives:

1. Examination of the performance of Tanzania's manufacturing exports, focusing not only on growth but also on different performance dimensions, such as RCA and participation in GVCs.
2. Analysis of the performance for product types using the harmonized system of goods classification, allowing for processing stage and skill and technology intensity.
3. Identification of the main factors that have influenced the growth and competitiveness of Tanzania's manufactured exports.

In addressing these objectives, the study uses trend and descriptive analysis as well as quantitative methods based on panel data methods to assess the performance of manufacturing exports by different trade and industry classifications to give a holistic view. We utilize data compiled using the standard international trade classification (SITC) focusing on codes 5 and 6, chemicals and manufactured products at the two-digit level respectively, which are broadly consistent with the industry classification of manufactures (for detail see Misati and Ngoka 2021). In addition, the SITC data permit analysis of skill, technology, and capital intensities, and scale characteristics of manufactured exports (see Section 5.3). Given the relative importance of GVCs in international trade, we also consider specific GVC sectors that are a subset of the manufacturing industry.

Governments around the world including Tanzania are in the process of developing strategies to build resilience to shocks given the experience of the COVID-19 pandemic. Among some of the strategies towards building competitiveness, resilience to shocks and production capacities in Tanzania include the development, promotion, and diversification of exports. Three main approaches towards this end are identified in the UNCTAD (2022) report for Tanzania:

(i) Use of fiscal incentives to facilitate linkages between local and foreign firms through supporting activities that integrate SMEs into global supply chains.
(ii) Provision of assistance to local firms to penetrate export markets through provision of key information on overseas markets.
(iii) Efforts to enhance export diversification by lowering trade costs, reducing the cost of investing in new economic activities, ensuring that local producers have reliable access to inputs at competitive prices, using industrial policy to support reallocation of resources to manufacturing, and providing support for requirements to meet international quality standards.

5.2 Literature review

The theory of international trade has evolved over time, where the earlier schools of thought, such as comparative advantage theory and the Heckscher–Ohlin theory, assumed perfect competition and constant returns to scale while modern theories, such as the new trade theory (NTT), incorporate possibilities of market imperfections (Misati and Ngoka 2021). The NTT is founded on imperfect competition and increasing returns to scale, whereby product differentiation in open economies is the most important source of trade between countries with similar economies. Product differentiation reflects past investment in physical, human, and knowledge capital or technical improvements. Trade patterns are outcomes of profitable specialization in a cost structure independent of the country's attributes such as technology and endowments that are assumed as given in the old trade theory (Athanasoglou and Bardaka 2010; Neary 2009).

A relatively newer paradigm of international trade is GVCs. Although a comprehensive theoretical framework is yet to be fully developed, GVCs now constitute a large share of international trade. GVCs are characterized by fragmentation of production across countries, specialization by countries with regard to tasks and functions, and networks between suppliers and buyers (De Backer and Miroudot 2013). Due to the specialization and the organized production processes, similarities have been observed between GVCs and the traditional determinants of comparative advantage theories. Technology transfer and productivity improvements tend to be more intense within a GVC framework (Amador and Cabral 2016; Taglioni and Winkler 2016). This is attributed to the fact that goods produced are typically intended for international markets and entail close networks between buyers and suppliers since they embody requirements for customization. Improvements in export efficiencies coupled with enhanced GVCs promote a country's export competitiveness.

Studies on competitiveness focusing on Africa include Agbor and Taiwo (2014), who provide an assessment of export competitiveness from an exchange rate perspective: large current account deficits are associated with exchange rate appreciation, which in turn hampers the development of tradables, including manufactured exports. However, critiques of this theory contend that it is not applicable to African countries for two reasons. First, African countries mainly export primary products whose demand is not sensitive to the producer's exchange rate or to the domestic cost of production, but to world market prices. Second, changes in the real exchange rate (RER) in small open economies are not an accurate reflection of the country's competitiveness due to their vulnerability to external shocks. Nevertheless, based on panel data to analyse disaggregated manufacturing exports, Bogale (2017) concluded that depreciation of the real effective exchange rate improves all types of manufacturing exports in the East Africa region. Similarly, Wondemu and Potts (2016) analysed the impact of RER changes on export performance in Tanzania and Ethiopia, finding that while overvaluation is harmful to exports, undervaluation boosts export supply as well as export diversification.

Most existing literature on Tanzania adopts a broader approach to determinants of export competitiveness. Wangwe et al. (2014) conducted a survey on the evolution of the manufacturing sector in Tanzania and categorized the main constraints to industrial growth into five types: technical, financial, administrative, market, and policy challenges. All of these factors are relevant to competitiveness. Page (2016) reviews the performance, prospects for and public policy towards industrial development in Tanzania, mainly focusing on special economic zones, micro-, small-, and medium-sized firms, and trade logistics. The analysis revealed a need to strengthen Tanzania's infrastructure and institutional frameworks to levels that can attract investors to its special economic zones; adopt a more selective approach in strengthening the small and medium enterprises (SME) sector; and enhance efforts in improving the efficiency of the port of Dar es Salaam. Epaphra (2016) examined the determinants of export performance in Tanzania during the period 1966–2015: real GDP, trade liberalization, and a favourable exchange rate were found to positively affect export performance, while official development assistance and inflation negatively affect export performance in Tanzania. The study, however, omitted important factors such as institutional variables and infrastructure that have been identified as constraints to export performance in Tanzania and other sub-Saharan African countries.

5.3 Characteristics of Tanzania's manufacturing sector exports

Analysis of Tanzania's manufactured exports with regard to composition, technology, and skill intensity, and GVC participation shows that, prior to 2018, the composition of manufactured exports was dominated by basic metal industries. The share of fabricated metal products increased from 2002 to reach 36 per cent by 2018; the share of non-metallic minerals, food and beverages, and chemicals also increased from 2.7, 11.3, and 3.5 per cent in 2009 to 5.2, 12.9, and 14.5 per cent, respectively, in 2018 (Misati and Ngoka 2021). These trends are indicative of transition in the manufactured export structure towards high-value goods.

The transition to high-value goods has been accompanied by some slight technological deepening although technology-intensive manufactures remain at a very low level. Until the 2000s, primary products (traditional exports) accounted for most of Tanzania's exports, averaging almost 80 per cent between 1995 and 1997 but declining to 33 per cent by the period 2010–20 (Table 5.1). Table 5.1 shows the significant growth in non-agricultural resource-based (and unclassified) exports and that, despite growth, most manufactured exports are low technology. Using the UNCTAD classification of technological intensity (see Table 5.A1), the shares

Table 5.1 Technology intensity of merchandise exports in Tanzania (average shares)

Manufactured exports	1995–99	2000–09	2010–20
Primary products	78.5	45.9	33.0
Resource-based manufactures: agro-based	6.2	5.8	6.6
Resource-based manufactures: other	6.3	14.1	14.0
Low-technology manufactures: textile, garment, and footwear	3.0	2.8	2.8
Low-technology manufactures: other products	1.0	2.0	4.1
Medium-technology manufactures: automotive	0.8	0.4	0.4
Medium-technology manufactures: process	0.4	1.8	2.5
Medium-technology manufactures: engineering	0.8	1.3	2.1
High-technology manufactures: electronic and electrical	1.0	0.6	0.9
High-technology manufactures: other	0.2	0.4	0.6
Unclassified products	1.7	25.0	33.0

Note: UNCTAD classification of exports; technology intensity based on direct research and development intensity (see Table 5.A1).
Source: Authors' construction based on UNCTADstat data.

of low-technology manufactures (other) and medium-technology manufactures (process) in total merchandise exports rose from less than 1 per cent in the 1990s to average 4.1 per cent and 2.5 per cent, respectively, between 2010 and 2020. The recent dynamics show scope for making inroads into technology-intensive manufactures, especially in the medium-technology category.

Integration into global value chains has fuelled trade in manufactures, especially for textiles and garments (see Chapters 3 and 4). Global market shares between 2002 and 2018 for neighbouring countries show marginal growth, with Ugandan shares remaining low. Tanzania's share in the global market for final and intermediate apparel and footwear has improved significantly and outperforms Kenya (Table 5.2). However, in 2021 there was a reduction in global market shares across all the products which can be attributed to supply chains disruptions in the context of COVID-19. Rising global market shares are not always indicative of an increase in export competitiveness as shares also depend on global developments.

The growth in intermediate apparel and footwear and final textiles between 2002 and 2018 reflects various new products. In particular, Tanzania's global market share of 'other woven fabrics of polyester staple fibres' in the GVC chains increased to 1.57 per cent in 2018 (Misati and Ngoka 2021). Tanzania's market shares for final textiles also increased, reflected in textiles of cotton, manmade fibres, and other textiles. The main product markets include China and the United

Table 5.2 Market shares for selected comparator countries and years

Country	Years	Final Apparel & Footwear	Final Electronics	Final Textiles	Final Vehicles	Intermediate Apparel & Footwear	Intermediate Electronics	Intermediate Vehicles
Kenya	2002	0.066	0.001	0.004	-	0.004	0.001	0.006
	2018	0.081	0.002	0.018	0.005	0.002	0.002	0.002
	2021	0.101	0.001	0.005	0.002	0.001	-	0.002
Tanzania	2002	0.001	-	-	-	0.005	-	-
	2018	0.011	-	0.031	0.001	0.023	-	0.001
	2021	0.008	-	0.016	-	0.016	-	-
Uganda	2002	0.001	-	-	-	-	-	-
	2018	0.001	-	0.002	-	0.001	-	-
	2021	0.001	-	0.001	-	-	-	-

Note: Figures are the share of each country in global exports for the sector.
Source: Authors' construction based on World Integrated Trade Solution, World Bank.

States. The African Growth and Opportunities Act (AGOA) of the United States that provides duty-free access has contributed to the growth in textiles. Peferential tariffs for Tanzania's manufactured exports have reduced over time, especially for the textiles and wearing apparel GVC sectors mainly due to AGOA provisions (Misati and Ngoka 2021). Aside from tariff reductions, GVCs can also be enhanced through deep Preferential Trade Agreements (PTAs)—those that contain more provisions. Hofmann et al. (2017) categorize fifty-two policy areas that reoccur in agreements into fourteen World Trade Organization-plus (WTO+) provisions and thirty-eight WTO-extra (WTO-X) provisions. The WTO+ provisions are within the mandate of the WTO and include customs regulations, export taxes, and technical barriers to trade. The WTO-X provisions are not within the mandate of the WTO and embody broader policy areas, including market access, investment, competition policy, and harmonization of product regulations.

The number of PTAs covering WTO-X provisions are particularly relevant for the governance of GVCs and affect the decisions of firms to offshore or outsource certain tasks to a developing country. Tanzania's PTAs are mainly with regional partners and focus on competition policy. In addition, the improvements observed in the number of agreements between 2005 and 2015 are on account of new members assenting to join the existing blocs and not necessarily a reflection of Tanzania's efforts to negotiate new trade agreements. In addition, agreements negotiated between developed nations (North-North) and between developed and developing nations (North-South) have been observed to have more provisions. On the other hand, South-South trade agreements (those between developing nations) have been identified as being shallow in content, with a focus on the traditional policy issues that may not be supportive of new dynamics in international trade. PTAs are an important device for ensuring commitment to creating a reliable business environment, especially in the context of manufacturing exports and GVCs. However, deep trade agreements also tend to restrict policy autonomy; hence, authorities need to find a balance during negotiations.

5.4 Theoretical framework, variable definition, and data sources

In this section, we describe the standard export competitiveness model and provide the theoretical framework underpinning the variables that affect export competitiveness, consistent with Tanzania's characteristics and previous studies. We also describe the data sources as well as the justification of the estimation method. No consensus exists in the literature on the definition of competitiveness (Agbor and Taiwo 2014) or the role of demand factors, supply factors, and policy factors in export competitiveness.[2] Fagerberg (1988) defines competitiveness

---

[2] The exchange rate and foreign income are the main demand factors, while examples of supply factors include domestic demand, labour productivity, and infrastructure.

as the ability of a country to realize economic policy goals, especially growth in income and employment, without running into balance-of-payments difficulties. Fagerberg (1988) further developed a model of international competitiveness relating market share growth to the ability to compete in terms of price, technology, and capacity. Other authors have provided a consolidated view in the literature on competitiveness based on firm level, industry level, and country level, while emphasizing the strong interlinkages. Modern trade theories allow for market imperfections and increasing returns to scale (Athanasoglou and Bardaka 2010).

In this study, we adopt the definition of competitiveness at a country level; in line with previous studies, we use export performance and the revealed comparative advantage (RCA) of manufacturing exports as dependent variables.[3] Export performance is computed for manufactured exports and chemical exports classified using the SITC Rev.3 nomenclature at the two-digit level and total manufactured exports based on ISIC.[4] Since the RCA is available for products at the three-digit level, we use 2018 export weights to aggregate to the two-digit level. The RCA index is defined as the share of Tanzania's manufactured exports as a share of its total manufactured exports relative to the world manufactured exports as a share of global manufactured exports. This approach is used to compute the RCA index for total manufactured exports classified using the ISIC nomenclature. Trends of the RCA index and export performance show improvements in fabricated metal products, essential oils, textiles, and non-metallic mineral manufactures.[5]

The specification of competitiveness equation is based on a hybrid model that combines both demand and supply factors and other factors identified as relevant for developing countries in the literature (e.g. Atif et al. 2019; Biggs 2007). We thus include RER, foreign demand/income, foreign direct investment (FDI), imported intermediate inputs, tariffs, domestic demand, institutional quality, labour productivity, inflation, and mobile cellular phone subscriptions per 100 people as a proxy for infrastructure. Foreign income, measured by the weighted average of the GDP of a sample of Tanzania's foreign markets, is included to capture external

[3] We also considered the measuring export competitiveness index (MECI) and global competitiveness index (GCI) in the regression but the data are only available from 2007 and do not fit our sample covering the period 1997–2018, placing a constraint on the degrees of freedom. Similarly, data constraints also prevented us from using unit labour costs as a measure of competitiveness. As pointed out by Kweka et al. (2019), unit labour costs measure cost competitiveness but the data available from the Annual Survey of Industrial Production and Census of Industrial Production conducted in Tanzania is for 2008–16 and 2013, respectively. Correlation tests between GCI and RCA indices as well as export performance measures are reported in Misati and Ngoka (2021).

[4] Total manufactured exports include manufacture of metals, chemicals, wood, food, paper, basic metal industries, fabricated metal products, textiles, wearing apparel, leather and non-metallic minerals, and other manufactured exports, while key manufactured exports exclude food and beverages. Chemical exports comprise chemical products, dying, tanning, and colouring products, medicinal and pharmaceuticals manufactures, essential oils and perfumes, plastic in primary forms, and fertilizers.

[5] See details of the computation of RCA, RCA indices, and the ISIC classification of manufactured exports in Misati and Ngoka (2021).

demand for Tanzania's manufactured exports. A high level of foreign demand fosters international competitiveness in the manufacturing sector. This is countered if there are barriers in export markets; high tariffs imposed by importing partners reduce exports by increasing costs (Araujo and Flaig 2017; Hassan 2017). The exchange rate is defined as domestic currency per unit of foreign currency. The RER is defined as the nominal exchange rate multiplied by domestic price as a ratio of foreign price. A depreciated RER attracts foreign demand and increases a country's market share, which in turn leads to improvement in external positions (Esteves and Rua 2013). This implies a negative relationship, but the relationship can be positive if the import content in manufactured exported goods is high and if the exchange rate is highly volatile.

Domestic demand measured by GDP growth is included to capture the impact of supply-side factors on export competitiveness. This is plausible under the assumption that foreign sales and domestic sales are substitutes, in which case domestic conditions can influence a firm's willingness or ability to supply exports, implying a negative relationship between domestic demand and export competitiveness. In periods of slackened domestic demand, firms may try to compensate for the decline in domestic sales through increased effort to export and vice versa, although export entrepreneurs will always try to maintain exports if they had made substantial prior investment in entering foreign markets (Esteves and Rua 2013). Similarly, increased inflation tends to hamper the expansion of exports and to retard their diversification (Lovasy 1962).

Institutions form an important element of the general environment and influence competitiveness by shaping the incentives of economic actors. Weak institutions generally create uncertainty and distort longer-term investment decisions (Doan 2019; Stiglitz and Charlton 2006). This study uses an indicator that captures constraints on the executive. Constraints ensure that the country's policy environment is investment-friendly and that there are no incentives to introduce changes that are risky to the business environment. They also reduce the probability that future changes to policy have adverse effects on the institutional environment.

FDI augments domestic capital and facilitates transfer technology and access to new and large foreign markets. At the same time, FDI may lower or replace domestic savings and investment for indigenous exporting firms to the detriment of the host country's export sector and inhibit the expansion of indigenous firms with exporting potential (Goh et al. 2013; Zhang 2015). The a priori sign is thus ambiguous.

We also include imported intermediate inputs and GVC index as the two indicators measuring value addition. Imported intermediate inputs are included to capture the foreign value-added in exports. The literature identifies three channels through which imports or value addition may affect export activity. First, firm internalization is characterized by the existence of sunk costs, and some of them could be common between import and export activities. Second, importing new and more advanced goods relaxes some constraints on the production process, leading to improved firm productivity. Third, trade liberalization may promote the competitiveness of domestic firms through the reduction of input tariffs, leading to lower costs of imported inputs across all firms (Das and Gupta 2019; Turco and Maggioni 2012). The GVC participation index constitutes indirect value-added, domestic value-added, and foreign value-added. Similar to imported intermediate inputs, value addition is embedded in the concept of vertical trade chains. These entail a country specializing in particular stages of the production process, with two or more countries adding value in the production sequence; a priori, a positive sign is expected between intermediate inputs/GVC index and export competitiveness.

Various indicators have been used to measure infrastructure in previous work, including telephone subscriptions/lines, air transport, mobile phone subscriptions, railway network, road length, energy/electricity production or access, and access to water resources (Prince 2019; Vickers and Pena-Mendez 2015). In this study, we use mobile phone subscriptions per 100 people, access to electricity, air transport, and an index comprising electricity, telephone networks, air transport, internet use, and communication. Consistent data for road and railway transport were not available.

Improved labour productivity is manifested in higher output per unit of labour input or gross value-added per worker. The linkage may be explained through the technology effect and competitive pricing channels. The technology effect manifests itself as an increase in new products or new markets, while the competitive pricing channel is reflected in low unit labour costs for domestic producers. It is assumed that firms that are more productive self-select themselves into foreign markets. A positive sign is expected a priori (Atkinson 2013; Greenaway and Kneller 2004).

5.4.1 Empirical model and estimation method

We use panel data covering the period 1997–2018 on Tanzania's exports of chemicals and manufactured goods at the two-digit SITC level (see Appendix Table 5.A1; exports, RCAs, and tariffs are measured at the product level, other variables are at a country level). The data on total manufactured exports are obtained from the World Bank's World Integrated Trade Solution (WITS) and consist of export products from the manufacturing industry. Data on intermediate imports and average (preferential) tariffs are also obtained from WITS. Additional data for the same period are retrieved from the World Development Indicators (WDI), specifically for GDP growth, FDI to GDP, mobile phone subscriptions per 100 people, and consumer price index (CPI). GVC-related indicators are obtained from the UNCTAD-EORA Global Value Chain Database. Institutional quality is measured by a variable on constraints on the executive, obtained from the Polity IV data set, capturing the extent to which constraints on decision-making are institutionalized and how these limitations are imposed by a framework of accountability. The RCA index for respective chemical and manufactured export products is obtained from the UNCTAD database. Our analysis also includes a variable on productivity, measured by output per employed person, and growth in output per employed person obtained from the 2019 Total Economy Database. For the RER, we derive an index (2005 = 100) on the basis of Tanzania's annual nominal exchange rate obtained from the IMF's International Financial Statistics and CPI relative to the US CPI.

The empirical model specified in equation (1) follows the discussion above, where export performance at the manufacturing product level and the RCA index are used separately as dependent variables. Equation (1) represents the standard export competitiveness equation in the literature, where i and t denote manufacturing product and period, respectively, X represents export performance and export competitiveness, Y represents foreign income, RER signifies the RER, and *Control* represents a vector other product-specific and macro variables that affect export performance and competitiveness. The term ε_t corresponds to the error term:

$$X_{it} = \delta_1 Y_t + \delta_2 RER_t + \delta_3 Control_{it} + \varepsilon_{it} \qquad (1)$$

Consistent with other studies, our analysis includes the following set of variables referred to as *Control* in (1): institutional quality, foreign demand, GVC index/imported intermediate inputs, domestic demand, inflation, RER, tariff, labour productivity, FDI, and mobile cellular phone subscriptions per 100 people as a proxy for the telecommunications aspect of infrastructure (Hassan 2017). The variables that are common for all products include domestic demand, institutional quality, imported intermediate inputs, GVC, inflation, and infrastructure variables. Export performance, RCA index, and tariffs are measured at the product level. This specification is consistent with similar previous studies that have both firm-/product-specific and macro variables in the same framework (Agur 2016). The study uses panel data with a product fixed effects estimator (supported by a Hausman test to choose between fixed and random effects).[6]

5.5 Empirical results

The estimation results of the determinants of the performance and competitiveness of manufactured exports are presented in Tables 5.3 and 5.4. Eight models

---

[6] Due to missing data for some years for some of the variables, the study uses unbalanced panel data.

are estimated: four for export performance (Table 5.3) and four for the RCA competitiveness measure (Table 5.4), where the dependent variables for alternative export sectors—key manufactures (includes chemicals), chemicals only, total manufactures, and total manufactures incorporating a GVC index as an explanatory variable instead of imported inputs. As a robustness check, we estimated the same models but replaced FDI, mobile phone subscriptions, and tariffs with investment (gross fixed capital formation), electricity access, and a proxy for tariff preferences, respectively (results are similar; see Misati and Ngoka 2021). The role of government in promoting export competitiveness is also included in each of the models with alternative measures.

The results show that both supply-side factors and demand-side factors explain export competitiveness. The coefficient of FDI is negative and significant in all the models in Tables 5.3 and 5.4 except for chemical exports, suggesting that FDI substitutes rather than complements export performance. This is consistent with other studies (Chakraborty et al. 2017; Chiara 2013); FDI can have a negative effect on competitiveness if it is concentrated in the enclave natural resources sector, as is the case in most African countries, including Tanzania. Most of the FDI inflows to Tanzania are to the mining sector rather than manufacturing. The significant negative effect is consistent with Dutch Disease, although the generally insignificant effect of RER implies these effects of resource sectors are weak (perhaps because specific extractive resources do not dominate Tanzanian exports). The positive and significant effect of total investment in five of the reported models, however, is consistent with the argument that investment in capital and infrastructure has positive implications for export performance, for example, by reducing transport costs (Limao and Venables 2001).

The coefficients of mobile subscription are positive and significant, underpinning the importance of quality telecommunications infrastructure in reducing connection costs and boosting international trade (Shinyekwa and Ntale 2017). Labour productivity is positive and generally significant, at least for key manufactures, signifying the importance of investment in human capital and research and development and specialized skills in enhancing manufacturing competitiveness. The coefficient of institutional quality is statistically significant, even if weakly so, for all RCA models and for total manufactured exports; strengthening institutions provides incentives for innovation, reduces costs of doing business, and encourages entrepreneurship (Alvarez et al. 2018).

High tariffs in the importing partner, at least for key and total manufactures, and inflation in most cases reduce export competitiveness (significant negative coefficients), consistent with acting as a disincentive to the manufacture of high-productivity non-traditional exports. High inflation implies increased production costs and an adverse economic environment that deters exports. High import tariffs (for Tanzania) reduce competitiveness of firms that rely on imported goods (Atif et al. 2019; Hassan 2017)—the results also show that, where significant, the

Table 5.3 Empirical results with export performance

Dependent variable	Model 1 Export performance of key manufactured goods	Model 2 Export performance of chemical exports	Model 3 Export performance of total manufactured exports	Model 4 Export performance of total manufactured exports with GVC
FDI	−0.147 (−5.09)***	−0.073 (−0.87)	−0.207 (−2.29)**	−0.36 (−1.89)**
Domestic demand	0.003 (0.01)	−0.196 (−3.32)***	−0.743 (−3.03)***	−0.059 (−0.22)
Mobile	0.253(1.78)*	0.519 (3.45)***	0.315 (3.06)***	0.025 (1.74)*
RER	−0.018 (−1.88)*	0.008 (0.51)	0.002 (0.49)	−0.005 (−0.67)
Tariff	−0.082 (−1.77)*	0.245 (1.52)	−0.106 (−3.70)***	
Imported inputs	7.25E−05 (0.23)	0.0003 (1.87)*	0.0003 (2.73)***	3.15E−06 (0.54)
GVC				0.002 (4.41)***
Foreign income	−0.111 (−0.87)	0.325 (1.90)**	0.418 (1.51)	3.081 (2.00)**
Institutional	−0.845 (−0.79)	0.167 (0.87)	0.884 (2.57)***	−0.165 (−0.53)
CPI	−0.053 (−2.79)***	−0.017 (−1.86)*	−0.008 (−2.93)***	−0.039 (−3.13)***
Labour	0.002 (3.28)***	0.081 (2.13)**	−0.009 (−0.42)	0.001 (2.17)**
R^2	0.85	0.72	0.83	0.82
Number of observations	126	144	162	162

Note: for all the coefficients, the *t*-statistics are in parentheses; * , ** , *** denote 10 per cent, 5 per cent, and 1 per cent significance levels, respectively.
Source: Authors' calculations.

Table 5.4 Empirical results with RCA as the measure of competitiveness

Dependent variable	Model 5 RCA for key manufactured exports	Model 6 RCA for chemical exports	Model 7 RCA for total manufactured exports	Model 8 RCA for total manufactured exports, with GVC
FDI	−0.157 (−1.82)*	−0.112 (−2.34)**	−0.341 (−2.86)***	−0.197 (−1.95)**
Domestic demand	−0.095 (−1.27)	−0.928 (−3.00)***	−0.330 (−0.97)	−0.504 (−1.67)*
Mobile	0.021 (2.50)**	0.535 (4.05)***	−0.135 (−1.09)	0.042 (2.65)***
RER	−0.0001 (−0.18)	0.001 (0.21)	−0.015 (−2.66)***	0.008 (1.01)
Tariff	−0.059 (−2.47)***	0.080 (0.99)	−0.078 (−2.53)***	6.71E−06 (1.47)
Imported inputs	0.0003 (3.39)***	−0.806 (−1.00)	−0.0001 (−2.29)**	
GVC				0.925 (3.40)***
Foreign income	0.053 (0.86)	0.387 (2.44)***	0.612 (2.32)**	2.478 (1.90)**
Institutional	0.148 (2.02)**	0.149 (1.77)*	0.866 (2.85)***	0.894 (1.92)**
CPI	−0.037 (−4.19)***	−0.018 (−5.94)***	−0.001 (−0.58)	−0.040 (−2.49)***
Labour	0.001 (2.71)***	0.070 (2.54)***	−0.013 (−0.72)	−0.015 (−0.83)
Number of observations	170	144	162	171
R^2	0.76	0.77	0.78	0.75

Note: for all the coefficients, the t-statistics are in parentheses; * , ** , *** denote 10 per cent, 5 per cent, and 1 per cent significance levels, respectively.
Source: Authors' calculations.

coefficient on imported inputs is generally positive (except for RCA of total manufactures). However, tariffs are not typically highest on manufactures; Karingi et al. (2016) show that Tanzania exports the highest number of sensitive products (mostly agriculture-based) and has the highest share of sensitive products in the value of exports (12 per cent, compared to Rwanda and Burundi at 6 per cent and Kenya at 2 per cent).[7]

The foreign income coefficient (weighted using trade shares) bears the expected positive sign in five of the reported models in Tables 5.3 and 5.4. This implies that growth dynamics in Tanzania's key five main trading partners (Zambia, Democratic Republic of Congo, Kenya, Rwanda, and the United States), constituting over 66 per cent of total trade, are critical for its export competitiveness. The skewed nature of Tanzania's export market makes it highly vulnerable to the business cycles of these five economies and signifies the need to diversify export destinations and expand manufactured exports so as to boost its competitiveness. The coefficient of the RER is negative and significant in five of the reported models, consistent with the theory that exchange rate depreciation increases export competitiveness.

The coefficients of intermediate inputs and GVC are positive and significant in most of the reported models, irrespective of Tanzania's relatively low share of intermediate inputs from the neighbouring countries, at 21 per cent compared to Kenya at 44 per cent and Uganda at 22 per cent (Karingi et al. 2016). In the last column of Tables 5.3 and 5.4, we consider the same variables but replace imported intermediate inputs with a broader measure of value-added—the GVC index. The coefficient of GVC is positive and significant, signalling the possibility of backward and forward linkages in manufactured products in Tanzania. This result would be a pointer towards the need to encourage measures to facilitate import content in Tanzania as a way to enhance competitiveness.

5.6 Conclusions and policy implications

The manufacturing sector in Tanzania has been growing in the recent past, but with a less diversified export structure, concentrated in food products, textiles, wearing apparel and leather, chemicals, and basic metal industries and fabricated metal products. The growth is, however, far below the targets set for the sector in the Tanzanian Integrated Industrial Development Strategy 2025. Moreover, attainment of long-term development goals was further derailed by the impact of COVID-19 in key sectors of the economy, especially manufacturing, and recovery prospects from the pandemic are also being slowed down by the conflict in

---

[7] Most of the sensitive items are food products that are highly protected, with very high tariffs on grounds of food security, poverty reduction, and protection of vulnerable domestic production.

Ukraine. Recent analysis of the impact of COVID-19 on the economy in Tanzania shows a variety of shocks to the manufacturing sector that also negatively affect other sectors including agriculture due to associated linkages.

To understand the drivers of Tanzania's export competitiveness, the chapter used fixed effects models on panel data covering the period 1997–2018. Different models for export performance and competitiveness based on RCA indicators of selected manufactured exports, chemical exports, and total manufactured exports were estimated. The results show that although both demand and supply factors determine export competitiveness in Tanzania, supply factors are more dominant. Specifically, the findings indicated that FDI, tariffs in export markets, and inflation have a negative effect on export competitiveness while total investment, labour productivity, infrastructure, and institutions are associated with manufacturing exports and competitiveness. The negative effect of FDI may be because most is in resource sectors, especially mining, rather than manufacturing (suggesting a Dutch Disease effect). There is thus a need to understand the drivers of FDI inflows to Tanzania and attract foreign investment in manufacturing. Trade policies and deeper regional integration should reduce tariffs faced by exporters. The positive effect of total investment is consistent with the positive coefficients on infrastructural indicators; competitiveness benefits from targeted investment in infrastructure, including roads, communications, and regular electricity. The results also seem to suggest the need to continue enhancing human capacity, given the positive significance of labour productivity in this study, as well as continued strengthening of the institutional framework.

There is evidence that GVC engagement supports export performance and competitiveness, signalling the need to encourage use of intermediate and value-enhancing imports through policies that facilitate integration into GVCs while safeguarding the domestic value-added component. However, Tanzania's GVC participation remains limited, with notable increases only in textiles, apparel, and footwear. Achieving (regional) integration to benefit exports requires negotiation of deeper PTAs with diverse regions, attracting investment in potential growth sectors such as electronics and vehicles, while deepening existing GVCs in textiles and apparel. The content of the PTAs should be geared towards scaling up technology intensity of manufactures while leveraging the available low- and medium-skill labour.

Attainment of the long-term development goals were slowed down by the impact of COVID-19 in key sectors of the economy and especially manufacturing in Tanzania. Lessons from the COVID-19 pandemic imply a need to accelerate current strategies to enhance competitiveness as well as design and adopt new strategies to ensure resilience to shocks and sustained manufacturing competitiveness. Studies that analysed the impact of COVID-19 on various sectors in Tanzania showed that shocks in the manufacturing sector had more effects in absolute terms and in the number of other sectors affected due to linkages. Moreover, the impact was also amplified due to the sector's sensitivity to internal and external factors that affect the value chain of the production processes from sourcing raw materials to storage and selling the final products. The manufacturing sector was affected by different sub-sectors' including factories, warehouses, and transporters, as well as farms, some of which were forced to stop production (Pantaleo and Ngasamiaku 2021).

The studies further showed that SMEs were more affected than larger firms. Notably, findings from a survey conducted in 2021 showed that firms in Tanzania reported an average decline in sales of 36 per cent, which jeopardized the solvency of more than three-quarters of SMEs. Most affected firms never benefited from any type of government support, and respondents suggested that tax deferrals for firms in the most severely affected sectors, including tourism and related services would be appropriate (Stanslaus 2021). The Government of Tanzania like many other countries focused interventions and measures on firms in the health and related sectors to mitigate the effects of COVID-19. For instance, exemptions from value-added tax (VAT) and customs duties were granted for imports of medical equipment and supplies (UNCTAD 2022). To promote production and strengthen competitiveness of domestically manufactured items, the government granted a duty remission for one year on raw materials sourced by domestic manufacturers of items used in the diagnosis, prevention, treatment, and management of the COVID-19 pandemic, including masks, sanitizers, ventilators, and personal protective equipment (Bishagazi 2021).

Mitigation measures against COVID-19 were, however, temporary and mainly focused on health and related firms yet part of the lessons learnt from COVID-19 pandemic signalled that a shock to the manufacturing sector has more individual impacts than the rest of the sectors and this sector also negatively affects the highest number of other sectors including agriculture due to associated linkages. This points to a need to accelerate current strategies to enhance manufacturing sector competitiveness as well as design and adopt new strategies to ensure resilience to shocks and sustainability of the sector particularly manufacturing exports' competitiveness.

References

Agbor, J., and O. Taiwo (2014). 'The Fundamental Determinants of Competitiveness in African Countries'. Working Paper 463. Cape Town: Economic Research Southern Africa.

Agur, I. (2016). 'Products and Provinces: A Disaggregated Panel Analysis of Canada's Manufacturing Exports'. Working Paper 16/193. Washington, DC: IMF https://doi.org/10.5089/9781475541335.001

Alvarez, I. C., J. Barbero, A. Rodríguez-Pose, and José L. Zofío (2018). 'Does Institutional Quality Matter for Trade? Institutional Conditions in a Sectoral Trade

Framework'. *World Development*, 103: 72–87. https://doi.org/10.1016/j.worlddev. 2017.10.010

Amador, J., and S. Cabral (2016). 'Global Value Chains: A Survey of Drivers and Measures'. *Journal of Economic Surveys*, 30(2): 278–301. https://doi.org/10.1111/joes. 12097

Araujo, S., and D. Flaig (2017). 'Trade Restrictions in Brazil: Who Pays the Price'. *Journal of Economic Integration*, 32(2): 283–323. https://doi.org/10.11130/jei.2017.32. 2.283

Athanasoglou, P., and I. Bardaka (2010). 'New Trade Theory, Non-Price Competitiveness and Export Performance'. *Economic Modelling*, 27(1): 217–28. https://doi.org/ 10.1016/j.econmod.2009.09.002

Atif, R., H. Mahmood, L. Haiyun, and H. Maoet (2019). 'Determinants and Efficiency of Pakistan's Chemical Products' Exports: An Application of Stochastic Frontier Gravity Model'. *PLoS One*. https://doi.org/10.1371/journal.pone.0217210

Atkinson, D. (2013). 'Competitiveness, Innovation and Productivity: Clearing Up the Confusion'. Available at: http://www2.itif.org/2013-competitiveness-innovation-productivity-clearing-up-confusion.pdf (accessed 8 February 2021).

De Backer, K., and S. Miroudot (2013). 'Mapping Global Value Chains'. Trade Policy Paper 159. Paris: OECD.

Biggs, T. (2007). 'Assessing Export Supply Constraints: Methodology, Data, Measurement'. Available at: http://aercafrica.org/wp-content/uploads/2018/07/2BiggsT_Assessing.pdf.

Bishangazi, P. (2021). 'The Socio-Economic Impact of the COVID-19 Pandemic on Women and Girls in Tanzania'. Available at: https://www.researchgate.net/publication/356993752 (accessed July 2022)

Bogale, F. (2017). 'Real Exchange Rate and Manufacturing Export Competitiveness in Eastern Africa'. *Journal of Economic Integration*, 32(4): 891–912. https://doi.org/10. 11130/jei.2017.32.4.891

Chakraborty, D., J. Mukherjee, and J. Lee (2017). 'FDI Inflows Influence Merchandise Exports? Causality Analysis for India over 1991–2016'. *Global Economy Journal*, 17(3): 1–10. https://doi.org/10.1515/gej-2017-0020

Chiara, F. (2013). 'Exports and FDI Motivations: Empirical Evidence from U.S. Foreign Subsidiaries'. *International Business Review*, 22(1): 47–62. https://doi.org/10. 1016/j.ibusrev.2012.02.002

Das, D., and N. Gupta (2019). 'Climbing Up India's Manufacturing Export Ladder: How Competitive Are Intermediate Goods'. Working Paper 371. New Delhi: Indian Council for Research on International Economic Relations.

Doan, H. (2019). 'Trade, Institutional Quality and Income: Empirical Evidence for Sub-Saharan Africa'. *Economies*, 7(48): 1–23. https://doi.org/10.3390/economies7020048

Epaphra, M. (2016). 'Determinants of Export Performance in Tanzania'. *Journal of Economics Library*, 3(3): 470–87.

Esteves, P., and A. Rua (2013). 'Is There a Role for Domestic Demand on Export Performance'. Working Paper 1594. Frankfurt: European Central Bank.

Fagerberg, J. (1988). 'International Competitiveness'. *The Economic Journal*, 98(2): 355–74. https://doi.org/10.2307/2233372

Goh, S. K., K. N. Wong, and S. Y. Tham (2013). 'Trade Linkages of Inward and Outward FDI: Evidence from Malaysia'. *Economic Modelling*, 35: 224–30. https://doi.org/10. 1016/j.econmod.2013.06.035

Greenaway, D., and R. Kneller (2004). 'Exporting and Productivity in the United Kingdom'. *Oxford Review of Economic Policy*, 20(3): 358–71. https://doi.org/10.1093/oxrep/grh021

Hassan, T. (2017). 'An Analysis of Prime Determinants and Constraints of Bangladesh's Export Market: Stochastic Frontier Gravity Model Approach. *World Customs Journal*, 11(2): 77–92.

Hofmann, C., A. Osnago, and Michele Ruta (2017). 'Horizontal Depth: A New Database on the Content of Preferential Trade Agreements'. Policy Research Working Paper 7981. Washington, DC: World Bank. https://doi.org/10.1596/1813-9450-7981

Karingi, S., O. Pesce, and L. Sommer (2016). 'Regional Opportunities in East Africa'. WIDER Working Paper 2016/160. Helsinki: UNU-WIDER. https://doi.org/10.35188/UNU-WIDER/2016/204-5

Kweka, J., M. McMillan, N. Gooroochurn, and F. Sooi (2019). 'A Diagnostic Manufacturing Competitiveness Study: Challenges, Prospects and Policy Options for Tanzania'. Dar es Salaam: REPOA.

Limao, N., and T. Venables (2001). 'Infrastructure, Geographical Disadvantage, Transport Costs, and Trade'. *World Bank Economic Review*, 15(3): 451–79. https://doi.org/10.1093/wber/15.3.451

Lovasy, G. (1962). 'Inflation and Exports in Primary Producing Countries'. *IMF Staff Papers*, 9(1): 37–69. https://doi.org/10.2307/3866081

Misati, R., and K. Ngoka (2021). 'Constraints on the Performance and Competitiveness of Tanzania's Manufacturing Exports'. WIDER Working Paper 2021/35. Helsinki: UNU-WIDER. https://doi.org/10.35188/UNU-WIDER

Neary, J. (2009). 'Putting the "New" into the New Trade Theory: Paul Krugman's Nobel Memorial Prize in Economics'. *Scandinavian Journal of Economics*, 111(2): 217–50. https://doi.org/10.1111/j.1467-9442.2009.01562.x

Page, J. (2016). 'Industry in Tanzania: Performance, Prospects and Public Policy'. WIDER Working Paper 2016/5. Helsinki: UNU-WIDER. https://doi.org/10.35188/UNU-WIDER/2016/048-5

Pantaleo, I., and Ngasamiaku, W. (2021). 'Are Sectors Hit Equally by Covid-19 Pandemic? Some Insights from Assessing the Economic Impacts of the Pandemic on Selected Sectors in Tanzania'. *African Journal of Economic Review*, IX(III): 51–69.

Prince, F. (2019). 'The Determinants of Economic Growth: The Role of Infrastructure'. Working Paper 93101. Munich: MPRA.

Shinyekwa, I., and A. Ntale (2017). 'The Role of Economic Infrastructure in Promoting Exports of Manufactured Products: Trade Facilitation and Industrialization in the EAC'. Research Paper 265773. Kampala: Economic Policy Research Centre.

Stanslaus, V. (2021). 'Assessment of the Social Economic Effects of Covid-19 and the Policy Response in Tanzania'. *International Journal of Academic Research in Business and Social Sciences*, 11(10): 385–96.

Stiglitz, J., and A. Charlton (2006). 'Aid for Trade'. *International Journal of Development Issues*, 5(2): 1–41. https://doi.org/10.1108/eb045861

Taglioni, D., and D. Winkler (2016). *Making Global Value Chains Work for Development: Trade and Development*. Washington, DC: World Bank Group. https://doi.org/10.1596/978-1-4648-0157-0

Turco, A., and D. Maggioni (2012). 'On the Role of Imports in Enhancing Manufacturing Exports'. *The World Economy*, 36(1): 93–120. https://doi.org/10.1111/twec.12020

UNCTAD (2015). 'Key Statistics and Trends in International Trade 2015'. Available at: https://unctad.org/en/PublicationsLibrary/ditctab2015d1_en.pdf.

UNCTAD, (2022). 'Enhancing Productive Capacities in the United Republic of Tanzania: A Coherent and Operational Strategy'. Available at: https://unctad.org/system/files/official-document/aldc2022d3_en.pdf.

Vickers, B., and B. Pena-Mendez (2015). 'Mobile Technology and Trade in Sub-Saharan Africa'. *The Commonwealth*, 123: 1–6.

Wangwe, S., D. Mmari, J. Aikaeli, N. Rutatina, T. Mboghoina, and A. Kinyondo (2014). 'The Performance of the Manufacturing Sector in Tanzania: Challenges and the Way Forward'. WIDER Working Paper 2014/085. Helsinki: UNU-WIDER. https://doi.org/10.35188/UNU-WIDER/2014/806-3

Wondemu, K., and D. Potts (2016). 'The Impact of Real Exchange Rate Changes on Export Performance in Tanzania and Ethiopia'. Working Paper 240. Abidjan: African Development Bank.

World Bank (2022). World Development Indicators. Available at: https://databank.worldbank.org/source/world-development-indicators (accessed July 2022).

WTO (2017). 'World Trade and GDP Growth in 2016 and Early 2017', *World Trade Statistical Review 2017*, Chapter III. Available at https://www.wto.org/english/res_e/statis_e/wts2017_e/wts2017_e.pdf.

WTO (2018). 'Highlights of World Trade in 2017', *World Trade Statistical Review 2018*, Chapter II. Available at: https://www.wto.org/english/res_e/statis_e/wts2018_e/wts2018chapter02_e.pdf.

WTO (2022). 'Russia–Ukraine Conflict Puts Fragile Global Trade Recovery at Risk', Press/902. Available at https://reliefweb.int/report/world/ukrainerussia-war-continues-africa-food-crisis-looms.

Zhang, K. (2015). 'What Drives Export Competitiveness? The Role of FDI in Chinese Manufacturing'. *Contemporary Economic Policy*, 33(3): 499–512. https://doi.org/10.1111/coep.12084

Table 5.A1 Data sources and definitions

Data	Data source	Definition
Resource-based, low-, medium-, and high-technology manufactured exports	UNCTAD	Defined as direct research and development intensity using the Lall classification.
Chemical exports	UNCTAD	Third revision of the SITC nomenclature at the two-digit level.[a] Eight products are covered.
Manufactured exports	UNCTAD	Same as above. Nine products are covered.
Total manufactured exports	WITS	ISIC nomenclature. It captures chemicals, food, leather, non-metallic and metals, wood, paper, and other. Nine manufacturing-industry-specific products are covered.
RCA index for chemical exports	UNCTAD and authors' calculations	RCA is available at the three-digit product level. The study used 2018 trade weights (Tanzania's exports for each of the three-digit level products as a share of each of the respective two-digit product level) to aggregate RCAs at the three-digit to the two-digit product level.
RCA index for manufactured exports	UNCTAD	Same as above.
RCA index for total manufactured exports	Authors' calculations	Computed using the formula in Misati and Ngoka (2021) Appendix B.
Intermediate imports	WITS	Values.
Preferential tariffs	WITS	Weighted average of the applied tariff (PTA rate where applicable) in importing country for Tanzanian exports by product group.
Tanzania's GDP	WDI	Real GDP.
Foreign GDP	WDI	Weighted using chemical and manufactured exports to Tanzania's major destinations. The weights are applied to real GDPs of the respective countries to get a composite foreign GDP.
FDI	WDI	Ratio to GDP.

Data	Data source	Definition
Mobile	WDI	Subscriptions to a public mobile telephone service using cellular technology per 100 people.
GVC index	UNCTAD-EORA Global Value Chain Database	The GVC participation index indicates the extent to which a country is involved in a vertically fragmented production process.
GVC by product of interest	WITS	Constructed using data on gross exports and imports to compute participation in GVCs across seven product categories grouped in three industries.
Institutional quality	Polity IV Database	Constraints on the executive and encompasses decision rules.
RER	IMF's International Financial Statistics	Computed as an index (2005 = 100) on the basis of Tanzania's annual nominal exchange rate, obtained from the CPI relative to the US CPI.
Labour productivity	Total Economy Database	Measured by output per employed person and growth in output per employed person, obtained from the 2019 release of the Total Economy Database.

Note: Data on chemical and manufactured exports are measured at the product level. [a] The SITC is a statistical classification of the commodities entering external trade. The current international standard is SITC, Rev.3.
Source: Authors' construction.

6

Addressing gender and innovation gaps

Laura Barasa

6.1 Introduction

The gender performance gap is a key area of female entrepreneurship that has received significant attention in the past decade. Persistence in factors causing gender differences in firm performance undermine the growth potential of female-owned enterprises and ultimately economic growth (Sabarwal et al. 2009). Gender gaps imply that human capital is underutilized or misallocated, and if female entrepreneurs are disadvantaged it is likely physical capital is also underutilized (for example if they face more difficulties accessing credit). The existence of gender gaps undermines the sustainable growth of female-owned enterprises. This chapter addresses gender innovation gaps in Tanzanian enterprises.

Enhancing participation of women in private sector development is vital for achieving the global development agenda contained in the Sustainable Development Goals (SDGs).[1] In particular, women's participation in private-sector development promotes the achievement of gender equality and women's empowerment (SDG 5). In addition, the global development agenda recognizes the need for supporting and achieving economic growth through innovation and socio-economic inclusion for all (SDG 8, SDG 9, and SDG 10). At the continental level, Africa's Agenda 2063 encapsulates the importance of achieving gender equality by eliminating obstacles impeding female entrepreneurship and innovation. Furthermore, Agenda 2063 underscores that science, technology, and innovation (ST&I) underpins inclusive and sustainable growth. In line with this, the Science, Technology, and Innovation Strategy for Africa 2024 (STISA-2024) was developed in tandem with Agenda 2063 because Africa's success is hinged on research and development (R&D) investment and innovation (African Union 2014).

---

[1] The SDGs refer to the global goals adopted by all the United Nations member states in 2015. They are a universal call to action aimed at ending poverty, protecting the planet, and ensuring that 'all people enjoy peace and prosperity by 2030' (United Nations 2015).

Laura Barasa, *Addressing gender and innovation gaps*. In: *Sustaining Tanzania's Economic Development*.
Edited by: Oliver Morrissey, Joseph Semboja, and Maureen Were, Oxford University Press.
© UNU-WIDER (2024). DOI: 10.1093/oso/9780192885746.003.0006

Policies aimed at guiding R&D in Tanzania have evolved over several decades. The 1960s era focused on science policies, evolving into science and technology policies in the early 1970s. The 1980s saw the introduction of ST&I policies, which integrated R&D into the national development strategy. Tanzania's Development Vision 2025 underpins the importance of achieving industrial growth through gender equality and innovation as outlined in the Five-Year Development Plan 2016/17–2020/21 (FYDP II). Tanzania's Development Plans and ST&I policies identify gender inequality and limited technological advancement as fundamental challenges. Wide disparities exist in accessing R&D resources and opportunities. The National Economic Empowerment Council and the Tanzania Commission for Science and Technology have embarked on affirmative action initiatives ensure that R&D activities do not discriminate against disadvantaged groups. Notwithstanding, innovation is still constrained by limited public-sector and private-sector R&D investment. This is further exacerbated by an inadequately skilled labour force. Taking gender into consideration, women are generally under-represented in business ownership (Ritter-Hayashi et al. 2019). Furthermore, female-owned enterprises—defined as businesses that are wholly or majority female owned—may face gender-based challenges that undermine investment in productive assets and human capital capabilities that are critical for improving innovation performance. These factors undermine firm productivity and resilience, putting Tanzania's development agenda of sustained growth at risk.

Existing studies examine the gender gap in firm performance indicators comprising sales growth and employment growth (Conroy and Weiler 2016). Little is known regarding the gender gap in innovation relating to gender inequality in the introduction of new or significantly improved products and manufacturing methods: product innovation and process innovation. The innovation gap thus reflects the difference in innovation performance between female-owned and male-owned enterprises (Dohse et al. 2019; Marvel et al. 2015). There is sparse empirical evidence on factors contributing to innovation performance differences between female-owned and male-owned enterprises in sub-Saharan Africa (Amoroso and Link 2018; Idris 2009; Strohmeyer et al. 2017). The research questions this chapter addresses aim to fill this gap. Do gender differences in innovation exist in the private sector in Tanzania and what factors contribute to innovation gaps between female-owned and male-owned enterprises?

The chapter makes several contributions. First, it adds to the growing body of literature concerning the gender innovation gap. Second, it sheds light on specific factors constraining innovation in female-owned enterprises. Lastly, it promotes the debate on mainstreaming gender perspectives in the formulation and implementation of ST&I policies.

6.2 Theoretical background

Two strands of literature dominate the subject of female entrepreneurship. These include the constraint-driven gaps theory and the preference-driven gaps theory. The constraint-driven gaps framework theorizes that female entrepreneurship is constrained by gender-based barriers that undermine firm performance. Some of the barriers that may hamper innovation include difficulties that female entrepreneurs face in accessing financial resources and information (Idris 2009). Social norms also undermine female participation by limiting mobility and time spent on running an enterprise. In addition, social and cultural norms have been found to constrain female ownership of productive assets, further widening gender asset and wealth gaps (Doss et al. 2014; Ravazzini and Chesters 2018). These challenges pose serious obstacles to innovation and overall firm growth for female-owned enterprises (Sabarwal et al. 2009).

The preference-driven gaps theory acknowledges that there are inherent differences in male and female entrepreneurship. Preference gaps linked to innovation include the choice of industry and risk taking. Female entrepreneurs are more likely to cluster in industries with low innovation potential, as the choice of industry may be linked to inequality of opportunity, while female entrepreneurs engaging in innovation activities are likely to encounter industry-specific skills gaps and skills shortages (Marvel et al. 2015; Sabarwal et al. 2009). Furthermore, technological innovation typically occurs in high-technology industries that are generally male dominated. Considering that entrepreneurial innovation involves significant risk and uncertainty, the gender innovation gap may exist since women are more risk averse than men (Hillesland 2019; Klapper and Parker 2011; Sabarwal et al. 2009).

This chapter adopts both theories to examine the gender innovation gap. These theories provide valuable insight into how gender differentials may affect innovation. In addition, both frameworks set out the factors that may cause gender differentials in innovation performance in the context of Tanzania. In particular, Rutashobya (2001) suggests that the female-entrepreneurship landscape in Tanzania faces severe constraints arising from social and cultural norms. For instance, women are disadvantaged in the acquisition of high-return productive assets. Furthermore, gender roles encourage women to adopt household-centred strategies rather than business-centred strategies. Consequently, female entrepreneurs are likely to cluster in low-technology industrial sectors.

6.2.1 Firm investment and the gender innovation gap

Private firm investment is instrumental in driving economic growth in developing countries in Africa. Firm investment refers to the acquisition of fixed assets aimed at boosting future returns. Acquisition of fixed assets is generally associated with increased productivity and innovation (Islam et al. 2018). It is also an innovation activity when firms purchase assets that have substantially different characteristics than the existing equipment used in production processes. Substantial capital outlays are generally required to purchase fixed assets, so financial constraints associated with acquisition of assets by female entrepreneurs hamper firm performance. Moreover, female entrepreneurs are more likely to operate small or micro businesses, with low investment and concomitantly low innovation prospects.

Investment in fixed assets also involves significant risk and uncertainty. However, women tend to be more risk averse and are more likely to make small-scale investments. Thus, the main sources of capital for female entrepreneurs in Tanzania include informal social networks, family networks, personal savings, and the community credit system (Nziku and Struthers 2018). These sources are also more likely to offer smaller amounts of capital for the purchase of fixed assets when compared to formal sources of financing. Various authors suggest that breaking into the 'old boys' network might play a critical role in facilitating female entrepreneurs' access to economic networks and financial resources in a male-dominated society (McAdam et al. 2019), although this does not diminish the hurdles women presently face in the acquisition, ownership, and management of productive assets (Doss et al. 2019; Rutashobya 2001). This chapter considers the proposition that:

> H1. Firm investment is positively associated with the gender gap in innovation.

6.2.2 Type of industry and the gender innovation gap

Various studies demonstrate that female entrepreneurs invest in small-scale and low-value industries such as the retail and service industry (Weiler and Bernasek 2001). Female entrepreneurs are also less likely to conduct business in high-technology industries and the construction industry. These industries remain highly male dominated (Sabarwal et al. 2009) but have high growth potential and are generally more innovative (Osabutey and Jin 2016; Sospeter et al. 2014). However, the industries have characteristics that result in increased transaction costs which might discourage female entrepreneurs disproportionately (Rutashobya 2001). For instance, the Tanzanian construction industry is characterized by delays in project completion, time and cost over-runs, that increase operating costs in addition to capital investment requirements (Sambasivan et al. 2017). Choice of industry is also driven by technical and financial barriers and related to balancing business and domestic demands (Kuada 2009). Innovation typically involves substantial risks and uncertainty while more-risk-averse (female) entrepreneurs prefer industries associated with risk minimization. This implies that industry choice by female entrepreneurs is likely to be associated with poor innovation outcomes.

Consequently, risk minimization strategies by female entrepreneurs encourage engaging in low innovation business, generating an innovation gender gap. Furthermore, the choice of industry might be linked to inequality of opportunities that result in less-educated and less-skilled female entrepreneurs (Sospeter et al. 2014). This results in female entrepreneurs operating business in small-scale, low-risk businesses that ultimately yield low innovation returns, suggesting a second hypothesis:

> H2. The manufacturing industry and the construction industry are positively associated with the gender gap in innovation in comparison to the service industry.

6.2.3 Skills gaps and the gender innovation gap

While formal qualifications matter for innovation, van Uden et al. (2017) suggest that a wide range of skills and competencies play a pivotal role in fostering innovation. Some of the workforce characteristics and competencies that foster innovation include creativity, cognitive abilities, adaptability to change, social skills, communication skills, technical skills, and problem-solving skills (OECD/Eurostat 2018). Innovation requires these specific types of skills, fostered by (if not requiring) relatively high levels of education, yet most countries in Africa have an abundance of semi-skilled and unskilled labour. This suggests the presence of skills gaps: the difference between the skills that firms need and the skills that employees possess; Freel (1999) and van Uden et al. (2017) find that skills gaps hamper innovation activities by firms in East Africa. Skills gaps therefore pose a major challenge for innovation in both male-owned and female-owned enterprises.

Female-owned enterprises are likely to be disproportionately affected by the skills gaps for a number of reasons. First, female-owned enterprises are likely to be small and informal, so they are less attractive to skilled workers; more-educated females are likely to seek wage employment, especially in the public sector. Second, female-owned enterprises are less likely to invest in recruiting, training, and retaining highly qualified manpower due to financial constraints. Lastly, female entrepreneurs in male-dominated industries must compete for skilled labour with their male counterparts. Female entrepreneurs are thus required to overcome gender biases to succeed (Rutashobya 2001). Consequently, female entrepreneurs face more protracted obstacles relative to their male counterparts. This suggests a third hypothesis:

> H3. Skills gaps are positively associated with the gender gap in innovation.

6.2.4   Female managers and gender innovation gap

Managerial capabilities influence the manner in which firms exploit resources for innovation. However, female-owned enterprises might generally face impediments in acquiring managers that embody dynamic managerial capabilities, possibly due to resource constraints, limited economic and social networks (McAdam et al. 2019), or gender biases that result in subordination by current and potential workers (Ritter-Hayashi et al. 2019; Rutashobya 2001).

Female ownership might also result in gender diversity in the top management, which is likely to benefit knowledge-sharing, performance of managerial tasks, and decision-making, which enhance innovation (Dohse et al. 2019; Ritter-Hayashi et al. 2019). However, increasing female participation does not guarantee desirable innovation outcomes in an unfavourable organizational climate (Cropley and Cropley 2017). In addition, findings from various studies suggest that female entrepreneurs are likely to be more biased towards hiring female managers (Beugnot and Peterlé 2020). However, female managers might lack peer support and business networks in comparison to their male counterparts (McAdam et al. 2019; Rutashobya et al. 2009). Such networks are critical in fostering the exchange of ideas that foster innovation. Female managers are also likely to handle a bigger proportion of family responsibilities.

Women typically face barriers in accessing education, training, and employment (Carrasco 2014), with adverse effects on the skills and experience females gain in the labour market. Consequently, women are generally under-represented in science, technology, engineering, and mathematics (STEM) and in managerial positions (Dohse et al. 2019; Ritter-Hayashi et al. 2019). As such, hiring female managers might compound the obstacles faced by female-owned enterprises in accessing resources and acquiring skilled labour (Rutashobya 2001). In addition, considering that women are likely to be more risk averse, female managers might also experience bottlenecks associated with risky business ventures such as innovation. This suggests a final hypothesis:

> H4. Female managers are positively associated with the gender gap in innovation.

6.3   Data and methods

The analysis is based on data from the 2015 Tanzania Firm-Level Skills Survey (TFLSS) conducted from April 2015 to August 2015 by the World Bank. A comprehensive skills module was developed alongside a firm-level survey that collected information on innovation and innovation activities, managerial, firm, and industry characteristics. The collection of data on innovation and innovation activities was governed by the Oslo Manual guidelines (OECD 2005). The stratified random sampling technique was used to select the survey sample. Firms were stratified according to industry, firm size, and region. Two sampling frames were used. The first was the 2011/12 Central Registry of Establishment (CRE) obtained from the National Bureau of Statistics. This sampling frame was used to select firms in mainland Tanzania. The second sampling frame comprised the 2012 CRE of the Office of Chief Government Statistician that was used to select firms located in Zanzibar (World Bank 2016).

Data from the 2015 TFLSS is suitable for investigating the gender gap in innovation for several reasons. First, the survey collects detailed information that measures the main determinants of innovation. This data includes managerial characteristics such as gender, age, experience, and education. It also includes firm-level characteristics: age, size, and industry. Second, the survey includes information on innovation activities such as R&D expenditure and innovation outcomes. Third, this is a recent survey that captures skills gaps which are likely to contribute to the gender innovation gap.

The survey instrument asked whether firms introduced new or significantly improved products or processes over the last three years. In total, 424 firms were interviewed although we only use data from 403 firms with complete information on the variables of interest (twenty-one firms were dropped because they were 'not in business' over the period covered in the survey instrument—the previous three fiscal years).

Innovation was measured as the introduction of new products and processes. The survey asked firms whether new or significantly improved products and services or methods of manufacturing products or offering services were introduced 'over the last three years'. This definition and measurement of product innovation and process innovation is consistent with the guidelines found in the Oslo Manual (OECD/Eurostat 2018). Innovation was thus measured as a dummy variable taking 1 if the firm introduced new or significantly improved products or processes, and 0 if otherwise. Other variables captured in the survey are listed below.

Female ownership
A female-owned enterprise is defined as a business that is wholly or majority female owned (i.e. at least 51 per cent ownership by women). Female ownership was measured as a dummy variable taking 1 where firms reported female entrepreneur share capital holdings of not less than 51 per cent, and 0 if otherwise.

Firm investment
This variable relates to the purchase of fixed assets. It encompasses the acquisition of new or used machinery, equipment, land or buildings, and vehicles. It was measured as a dummy variable taking 1 if the firm reported purchasing fixed assets in 2014, and 0 if otherwise.

Industry

Three industrial sectors were included in the sample: manufacturing, construction, and services. Industry was measured using a dummy variable taking 1 if the industrial sector was manufacturing or construction, and 0 if otherwise. The service sector was therefore the reference category.

Skills gap

Skills gap was constructed from eight items used to rate the level of skills that the establishment 'needs against the skills of current permanent employees' at the firm level. The items included interpersonal and communication skills, writing skills, problem-solving skills, critical-thinking skills, work ethic, English skills, computer skills/general information technology skills, and technical skills other than computers/vocational job-specific skills. This measure was coded as 0 when a firm reported that the skills met the firm's requirements and 1 if the skills fell below the firm's requirements. The scores of the separate skills items were added for each firm. The resulting value was then divided by the total number of skills items and finally multiplied by 100 to make it a percentage. This measure reflected the degree of the skills gap in a firm. A high score on this measure was equated to a high degree of skills gap.

Female manager

This variable captured the gender of the firm's manager. It was measured as a binary variable taking a value of 1 if the firm's top manager was female and 0 if male.

Managerial experience

This measures the number of years of experience the top manager has in the sector. The natural log of the years of experience in the respective sector was used in the analysis.

Firm age

The age of the firm was calculated as the difference between the year of the survey and the year that the firm began its operations. Firms were then categorized as young (≤5 years), mature (6–15 years), and old (>15 years). A dummy variable reflecting these categories was then used to measure firm age. The dummy variable took the value 1 when the firm was categorized as mature or old, and 0 if otherwise. The reference category was therefore young firms.

Firm size

Firms were categorized as a small enterprise (5–19 employees), medium-sized enterprise (20–99 employees), and a large enterprise (100 employees and more).

A dummy variable was generated to reflect the firm size measures. It took the value 1 when a firm was classified as a small enterprise or medium-sized enterprise and 0 if otherwise. Large enterprises were therefore the reference category.

Formal R&D

The survey instrument asked whether the firm incurred formal R&D expenditure on activities that were either in-house or contracted. This variable was measured as a dummy taking 1 where the firm reported incurring R&D expenditure and 0 if otherwise.

Regional dummies

The 2015 TFLSS comprised five regions: Arusha, Dar es Salaam, Mbeya, Mwanza, and Zanzibar. Region was measured as a dummy variable taking 1 when a firm was situated in Arusha, Dar es Salaam, Mbeya, or Mwanza, and 0 if otherwise. Zanzibar was therefore the reference category.

6.3.1 Estimation method

The Blinder–Oaxaca approach was used for decomposing mean differences in innovation based on regression models in a counterfactual manner (Blinder 1973; Oaxaca 1973). This approach is generally applied in labour market outcomes to examine the gender wage gap based on group differences such as race and gender. This study applied a non-linear decomposition technique because innovation was measured as a binary variable (Yun 2004).

The Blinder–Oaxaca decomposition was used to divide the innovation differential between female-owned enterprises and male-owned enterprises into two components: the endowments effect and the coefficients effect. The endowments effect represents the 'explained' part, the gender innovation gap arising from differences in endowments between female-owned and male-owned firms. The endowments effect measures the extent to which differences in observed managerial, firm, and industry characteristics account for differences in innovation. The coefficients effect represents the 'unexplained' part not accounted for by differences in endowments and captures the differences in returns to characteristics, reflecting differences in unobserved characteristics (Jann 2008). It can be used to indicate the expected change in female-owned enterprise innovation outcomes if they had the coefficients of male-owned enterprises. This can be interpreted as the gap arising from the differences in resource utilization.

As a first step, three separate logit regressions were estimated by enterprise ownership type. The logit regressions predict the likelihood of innovation in male-owned enterprises, female-owned enterprises, and in the pooled sample including both male-owned and female-owned enterprises:

$$Innov_i^m = \beta_0^m + \beta_1^m x_i^m + \beta_2^m Controls_i^m + u_i^m \tag{1}$$

$$Innov_i^f = \beta_0^f + \beta_1^f x_i^f + \beta_2^f Controls_i^f + u_i^f \tag{2}$$

$$Innov_i^p = \beta_0^p + \beta_1^p x_i^p + \beta_2^p Controls_i^p + u_i^p \tag{3}$$

$$Innov_i = Innov_i^* \text{ if } Innov_i^* > 0; \; Innov_i = 0 \text{ otherwise}$$

where the superscripts m, f, and p represent the separate equations for male-owned enterprises, female-owned enterprises, and the pooled sample. $Innov_i$ is a binary latent variable that represents innovation for firm i taking the value 1 when the firm reports introducing new or significantly improved products or processes, that is, $innov_i^* > 0$. The vector x_i comprises the determinants of innovation performance, namely firm investment, industry, skills gap, and female manager $Controls_i$ represents the control variables including managerial experience, firm age, firm size, formal R&D, and regional dummies, and u_i is the idiosyncratic error term.

The Blinder–Oaxaca approach assumes that the estimated effects of observed characteristics for female-owned enterprises and male-owned enterprises are identical in the absence of a gender gap. A twofold decomposition of the mean gender innovation gap would therefore be found as follows:

$$Innov^m - Innov^f = \Delta x \beta^m - \Delta \beta x^f \tag{4}$$

where the gap between the mean outcomes in innovation between male-owned enterprises and female-owned enterprises is given by $Innov^m - Innov^f$ and x represents a vector of the determinants of innovation and control variables comprising managerial, firm, and industry characteristics. The first component of the twofold decomposition $\Delta x \beta^m$ represents the gap due to endowments, applying the male coefficients (β^m) to the difference in endowments (Δx). This effect arises when male-owned enterprises and female-owned enterprises differ in terms of characteristics. This gap is positive if female-owned enterprises have worse endowments than male-owned enterprises. The second component $\Delta \beta x^f$ represents the gap in coefficients, applying the difference in coefficients ($\Delta \beta$) to the female endowments (x^f); it also captures the potential effects arising from differences in unobservable factors. This gap represents effects that arise from the characteristics of male-owned enterprises and female-owned enterprises having different effects on innovation. This gap is also negative if female-owned enterprises have worse coefficients than male-owned enterprises; if it is positive that implies that females make better use of their (lower) endowments (so their coefficients are higher).

6.4 Results and discussion

6.4.1 Descriptive statistics

Table 6.1 shows the descriptive statistics and correlation matrix of the data used in the analysis. Only 12 per cent of the firms conducted formal R&D although two-thirds reported innovation. Only 24 per cent of the firms were female owned (but had a similar level of innovation, Table 6.2) and only 10 per cent were female managed. Considering the independent variables, 51 per cent of the firms purchased fixed assets. About 50 per cent of the firms were in the manufacturing industry and just under 10 per cent were in the construction industry. About 26 per cent of the firms reported that employee skills did not meet the firm's requirements. On average, the managers had about fifteen years of experience. Surprisingly perhaps, very few firms were young; almost half the firms were categorized as mature and only a slightly lower share were old (or long-established) firms. This is consistent with relatively few small firms in the sample—almost two-thirds were medium-sized enterprises and almost a quarter were large. The under-representation of small/young firms implies the sample is not representative of the population of firms, which should be kept in mind interpreting results (especially for innovation). About half were located in Dar es Salaam, which is not surprising as this is the largest city in Tanzania.

Table 6.2 shows the differences in means between female-owned and male-owned enterprises. There are few significant differences: female-owned enterprises were more likely to have female managers (a third of firms compared to only 3 per cent of male-owned firms) and were more likely to be in Mbeya, whereas male-owned enterprises were more likely to be in Dar es Salaam. There were no significant differences in any other variables, including innovation performance and investment. Interestingly, contrary to industry choice arguments, there is no difference in the sector composition (even for construction).

6.4.2 Determinants of innovation for female-owned and male-owned enterprises

The likelihood of innovation is modelled using a logit regression, disaggregated by ownership: female-owned enterprises, male-owned enterprises, and a pooled model including both types of ownership. The results are shown in Table 6.3. A number of characteristics were only significant for female-owned enterprises,

Table 6.1 Descriptive statistics and correlation matrix (n = 403)

Variable	Mean	Std Dev	Min	Max	1	2	3	4	5	6	7	8	9	10	11	12	13	14	15	16	17	18	19	20
1 Innovation	0.66		0.00	1.00	1.00																			
2 Female ownership	0.24		0.00	1.00	0.04	1.00																		
3 Firm investment	0.51		0.00	1.00	0.22	-0.04	1.00																	
4 Manufacturing industry	0.50		0.00	1.00	0.05	-0.02	0.04	1.00																
5 Service industry	0.40		0.00	1.00	-0.02	0.03	-0.02	-0.83	1.00															
6 Construction industry	0.09		0.00	1.00	-0.06	-0.02	-0.03	-0.32	-0.26	1.00														
7 Skills gap	25.62	24.84	0.00	100.00	-0.19	0.05	-0.06	0.19	-0.09	-0.18	1.00													
8 Female manager	0.10		0.00	1.00	-0.01	0.45	-0.12	0.01	0.03	-0.08	0.06	1.00												
9 Managerial experience (years)	15.27	9.88	1.00	60.00	0.12	-0.06	0.11	0.08	-0.16	0.13	-0.03	-0.10	1.00											
10 Young firm	0.06		0.00	1.00	0.02	0.02	0.00	-0.02	0.03	-0.01	0.03	-0.02	-0.13	1.00										
11 Mature firm	0.48		0.00	1.00	0.02	-0.01	0.02	0.06	-0.06	0.00	-0.05	-0.02	-0.32	-0.25	1.00									
12 Old firm	0.46		0.00	1.00	-0.03	0.00	-0.02	-0.05	0.05	0.00	0.03	0.03	0.38	-0.24	-0.88	1.00								
13 Small enterprise	0.63		0.00	1.00	-0.04	-0.08	-0.19	0.07	-0.01	-0.11	0.16	0.16	-0.15	0.10	0.12	-0.17	1.00							
14 Medium-sized enterprise	0.24		0.00	1.00	0.06	0.06	0.11	-0.03	-0.03	0.10	-0.08	-0.12	0.16	-0.05	-0.10	0.12	-0.73	1.00						
15 Large enterprise	0.13		0.00	1.00	-0.03	0.03	0.12	-0.06	0.05	0.03	-0.13	-0.09	-0.13	0.00	-0.07	-0.04	-0.51	-0.22	1.00					
16 Formal R&D	0.12		0.00	1.00	0.20	0.07	0.08	-0.09	0.09	-0.01	-0.07	0.08	-0.32	-0.10	0.10	-0.05	-0.12	0.07	0.08	1.00				
17 Arusha	0.11		0.00	1.00	0.13	0.04	-0.08	0.01	-0.06	0.08	-0.18	0.03	0.03	0.03	0.00	-0.02	-0.08	0.04	0.07	-0.01	1.00			
18 Dar es Salaam	0.52		0.00	1.00	0.04	-0.12	0.15	-0.13	0.18	-0.09	0.07	-0.05	-0.05	-0.01	-0.06	0.02	0.23	-0.05	0.00	0.05	-0.37	1.00		
19 Mbeya	0.12		0.00	1.00	-0.06	0.12	-0.22	0.03	-0.02	-0.02	0.09	0.09	-0.01	-0.04	0.00	0.02	-0.11	-0.18	-0.10	0.00	-0.14	-0.39	1.00	
20 Mwanza	0.11		0.00	1.00	-0.24	-0.04	-0.19	0.09	-0.11	0.02	0.02	0.01	-0.04	-0.03	0.03	-0.02	-0.11	0.13	0.00	0.02	-0.13	-0.37	-0.14	1.00
21 Zanzibar	0.13		0.00	1.00	0.12	0.07	0.25	0.06	-0.10	0.06	-0.05	-0.06	0.09	0.05	0.05	-0.08	-0.12	0.10	0.05	-0.09	-0.14	-0.40	-0.14	-0.14

Notes: For all binary variables the mean is the percentage share and standard deviation is not reported (values are either 0 or 1).
Source: Author's calculations based on TFLSS data.

Table 6.2 Differences in means between female-owned enterprises and male-owned enterprises

	Variables	Mean male ownership (n=306)	Mean female ownership (n=97)	Difference
1	Innovation	0.65	0.69	−0.040
2	Firm investment	0.52	0.47	0.045
3	Manufacturing industry	0.51	0.49	0.025
4	Construction industry	0.10	0.08	0.012
5	Skills gap	24.88	27.96	−3.086
6	Female manager	0.03	0.35	−0.324***
7	Managerial experience (years)	2.50	2.43	0.077
8	Mature firm	0.48	0.47	0.006
9	Old firm	0.46	0.45	0.004
10	Medium-sized enterprise	0.65	0.56	0.090
11	Large enterprise	0.23	0.29	−0.063
12	Formal R&D	0.11	0.16	−0.050
13	Arusha	0.11	0.13	−0.026
14	Dar es Salaam	0.56	0.41	0.143**
15	Mbeya	0.10	0.20	−0.095**
16	Mwanza	0.12	0.09	0.028

Note: Significance of difference (male mean minus female mean) based on t-test on equality of means
** $p<0.05$, *** $p<0.01$).
Source: Author's calculations based on TFLSS data.

although the signs were the same for male-owned firms. The likelihood of innovation in the construction industry was 26 percentage points lower when compared to enterprises in the service industry (and manufacturing, which was not different to services). This might be due to the complexities and interdependencies that surround construction processes that are likely to impede innovation (Sambasivan et al. 2017). The likelihood of innovation was 24 percentage points lower for mature firms relative to young firms; old firms were also less innovative than young (with larger coefficients than mature), but the difference was not significant. This should be interpreted with caution given the low proportion of young firms in the sample. Although insignificant, small and medium female-owned firms had positive coefficients (more likely than large to innovate), suggesting that the sample included a few young, small, and especially innovative firms. The likelihood of innovation was higher for female-owned enterprises in Arusha (relative to firms in Zanzibar), but only weakly significant and with no evident implications given the small samples.

Table 6.3 Logit models predicting the likelihood of innovation

Variables	Female ownership		Male ownership		Pooled sample	
	Logit coefficients	Marginal effects	Logit coefficients	Marginal effects	Logit coefficients	Marginal effects
Firm investment	-1.799 (1.873)	-0.206 (0.161)	1.574*** (0.286)	0.219*** (0.038)	0.804*** (0.266)	0.127*** (0.049)
Manufacturing industry	0.541 (0.446)	0.062 (0.056)	0.137 (0.392)	0.019 (0.052)	0.285 (0.323)	0.045 (0.048)
Construction industry	-2.265** (1.003)	-0.259** (0.117)	-0.221 (0.187)	-0.031 (0.028)	-0.740*** (0.172)	-0.117*** (0.025)
Skills gap	-0.019 (0.017)	-0.002 (0.001)	-0.017* (0.010)	-0.002* (0.001)	-0.013*** (0.004)	-0.002*** (0.001)
Female manager	-1.696*** (0.497)	-0.194*** (0.072)	-1.110* (0.631)	-0.155* (0.077)	-0.881*** (0.276)	-0.139*** (0.043)
Managerial experience (log)	1.852** (0.866)	0.212** (0.050)	0.434*** (0.168)	0.061*** (0.021)	0.629*** (0.201)	0.100*** (0.026)
Mature firm	-2.112*** (0.668)	-0.242*** (0.057)	-0.853 (1.017)	-0.119 (0.126)	-0.743* (0.383)	-0.118* (0.052)
Old firm	-2.692 (1.731)	-0.308 (0.112)	-0.132 (0.662)	-0.018 (0.090)	-0.562 (0.518)	-0.089 (0.075)
Small enterprise	2.159 (1.342)	0.247 (0.086)	1.377** (0.561)	0.192** (0.054)	1.641** (0.698)	0.260** (0.089)
Medium-sized enterprise	1.917 (1.350)	0.220 (0.099)	1.626** (0.723)	0.227** (0.086)	1.692** (0.665)	0.268** (0.089)
Formal R&D	1.746 (3.330)	0.200 (0.332)	3.503*** (1.086)	0.488*** (0.083)	2.402*** (0.481)	0.380*** (0.068)
Arusha	5.974* (3.195)	0.684* (0.236)	1.074 (1.573)	0.150 (0.207)	1.621 (1.277)	0.257 (0.187)
Dar es Salaam	0.682 (1.082)	0.078 (0.109)	-1.404 (1.057)	-0.196 (0.140)	-1.020* (0.600)	-0.162* (0.090)
Mbeya	-2.658 (1.700)	-0.304 (0.136)	-1.262 (1.010)	-0.176 (0.136)	-1.615*** (0.583)	-0.256*** (0.079)
Mwanza	0.338 (1.078)	0.039 (0.121)	-5.558** (2.636)	-0.775** (0.255)	-3.146*** (0.658)	-0.498*** (0.072)
Female ownership					0.684*** (0.150)	0.108*** (0.020)
Constant	-1.304 (1.782)		-0.229 (1.005)		-0.904** (0.657)	
Pseudo R-squared	0.46		0.33		0.26	
No. of observations	97		306		403	

Note: Robust clustered standard errors in parentheses (* p<0.10, ** p<0.05, *** p<0.01).
Source: Author's calculations based on TFLSS data.

Some characteristics were only significant for male-owned enterprises, and in most cases the signs were the same for female-owned firms (except investment and Mwanza). The most important of these were firm investment (likelihood of innovation was 22 percentage points higher for firms that purchased assets compared to those that didn't) and R&D (49 percentage points higher likelihood compared to firms with no formal R&D). This is consistent with evidence that acquisition of fixed assets is associated with enhanced innovation (Islam et al. 2018) and the importance of R&D for innovative firms (González et al. 2016; Grimpe et al. 2017). The two are likely to be related and suggest that male-owned firms are more likely (than female) to engage in costly innovation. The likelihood of innovation was marginally lower for firms reporting a high degree of skills gap; although the effect is negligible, perhaps because of how the measure is constructed, this is consistent with the need for skilled labour to make most use of certain forms of innovation (van Uden et al. 2017). The likelihood of innovation was 19 percentage points higher for small enterprises (but recall there are few of these) and 23 percentage points higher for medium-sized enterprises when compared to large enterprises. This at least suggests that medium-sized enterprises are more agile in terms of adapting to market changes and embracing technological innovation as a means of enhancing competitive advantage (Bessant et al. 2002). The only significant regional effect is that the likelihood of innovation was lower for (the 12 per cent of) firms located in Mwanza (compared to firms in Zanzibar).

Two characteristics were significant determinants of innovation for both male- and female-owned firms—managerial experience (positive) and female managers (negative). The likelihood of innovation was 21 percentage points higher for female-owned and 6 per cent higher for male-owned firms with more experienced managers. Managerial experience has been associated with dynamic managerial capabilities that enhance the ability to identify and exploit opportunities for innovation (Helfat and Martin 2015; Helfat and Peteraf 2015), and appears to be more important for females (consistent with those who have survived longer being more capable and better able to overcome constraints so that they are more innovative. The likelihood of innovation was 19 percentage points lower for female-owned and 15 per cent lower for male-owned firms with female managers (but this was only 3 per cent of male-owned firms). Various studies suggest that limited access to social networks and economic networks account for the negative association between female managers and innovation (McAdam et al. 2019; Rutashobya et al. 2009). This may be exacerbated in Tanzania where female managers are far more likely to be in female-owned firms.

Only manufacturing sector and old firms, in addition to some regional locations, were insignificant for both male and female-owned firms; manufacturing and old remain insignificant in the pooled sample, although regions such as Arusha are significant (the other regions appear less innovative than Zanzibar but this may be simply due to small, diverse samples in each location). The results from the pooled sample are generally similar to those by gender. Investment, managerial experience, small and medium-sized enterprises, and formal R&D were positively associated with the likelihood of innovation. In contrast, skills gap, the construction industry, female managers, and mature firms were associated with a lower likelihood of innovation. The pooled model also included female ownership, which was positively associated with innovation. Although female-owned enterprises face gender-based obstacles, *ceteris paribus* they were more innovative (perhaps because this was considered important for survival, given that female owners tended to be experienced). The measure—the female ownership share in capital holdings of not less than 51 per cent—encompasses gender diversity as ownership is not exclusively restricted to women and (some) managers may be male. Gender diversity contributes to gender equality and is associated with innovation because it fosters knowledge sharing between women and men and improves decision-making (Dohse et al. 2019; Ritter-Hayashi et al. 2019).

6.4.3 Decomposition of the gender gap in innovation

Table 6.4 displays the results of the decomposition of the gender innovation gap. These results largely support the hypotheses stated above. Gender differences in the likelihood of innovation were decomposed using female ownership as the reference point, distinguishing the endowments and coefficients effects. Male-owned enterprises had a higher probability of innovation (a 7 per cent difference) and this was due to the endowments effect increasing the probability of innovation by 18 per cent compared to female-owned firms. This implies that male-owned enterprises had more access to innovation resources, and female-owned enterprises would have had better innovation outcomes if they possessed the same characteristics as their male counterparts. Four endowments account for this effect in favour of males: higher firm investment and greater managerial experience, a lower skills gap, and less likely to have a female manager (there were also regional effects associated with location in Mbeya and Mwanza).

The second part of the decomposition, the coefficients effect, represents the returns to resource utilization. The negative and statistically significant coefficients effect means that male returns on their endowments were lower than for females; female-owned enterprises were better able to take advantage of the resources than their male counterparts. Female-owned enterprises would have had an 11 per cent lower likelihood of innovation compared to males if they had the same coefficients as male-owned enterprises. The decomposition of the independent variables reveals that managerial experience is the main factor for higher female coefficients—experienced females are more likely to be innovative than experienced males (females in Mwanza also seem to be more innovative). Male-owned firms, however, are more likely to innovate based on investment (consistent with females being more credit-constrained or risk averse).

Table 6.4 Non-linear decomposition of gender innovation gap

Differential		
Prediction (male)	0.665***	(0.032)
Prediction (female)	0.595***	(0.061)
Difference	0.070**	(0.035)
Decomposition		
Endowments	0.181***	(0.042)
Coefficients	−0.111***	(0.025)
Endowments		
Independent variables		
Firm investment	0.021*	(0.012)
Manufacturing industry	0.001	(0.007)
Construction industry	−0.004	(0.004)
Skills gap	0.027**	(0.014)
Female manager	0.084***	(0.026)
Control variables		
Managerial experience (log)	0.027***	(0.009)
Mature firm	−0.002	(0.007)
Old firm	0.005	(0.009)
Small enterprise	−0.001	(0.017)
Medium-sized enterprise	0.005	(0.016)
Formal R&D	−0.005	(0.009)
Arusha	−0.007	(0.007)
Dar es Salaam	−0.011	(0.014)
Mbeya	0.028**	(0.014)
Mwanza	0.011***	(0.004)
Coefficients		
Independent variables		
Firm investment	0.184***	(0.047)
Manufacturing industry	−0.017	(0.029)
Construction industry	0.011	(0.014)
Skills gap	−0.009	(0.140)
Female manager	0.064	(0.046)
Control variables		
Managerial experience (log)	−0.436**	(0.182)
Mature firm	0.081	(0.070)
Old firm	0.170**	(0.068)
Small enterprise	−0.090	(0.090)
Medium-sized enterprise	−0.006	(0.017)
Formal R&D	0.023	(0.051)
Arusha	−0.054	(0.038)
Dar es Salaam	−0.166	(0.170)
Mbeya	0.031	(0.042)
Mwanza	−0.075*	(0.041)
Constant	0.179	(0.463)
No. of observations	403	

Note: Robust clustered standard errors in parentheses (* p<0.10, ** p<0.05, *** p<0.01).
Source: Author's calculations based on TFLSS data.

The greater coefficient effect for females reflects unobserved differences between female-owned enterprises and male-owned enterprises that affect innovation. Innovation in male-owned enterprises can be improved by better utilization of resources, in particular encouraging experienced owners to innovate. Female-owned enterprises would have higher innovation if they had better endowments (specifically investment, managerial experience and a lower skills gap, having more male managers). This is consistent with the finding in the pooled logit regression of a positive association (*ceteris paribus*) between female ownership and innovation. As previously discussed, better resource utilization by female-owned enterprises might be accounted for in part by gender diversity. Increasing gender diversity in all firms could facilitate access to social and business networks, promoting better utilization of innovation resources (Dohse et al. 2019).

6.5 Conclusions and implications for policy and practice

The main objective of this study was to investigate the factors contributing to the gender innovation gap in Tanzania. This was done within the constraint-driven gaps and preference-driven gaps framework (Klapper and Parker 2011; Sabarwal et al. 2009). A non-linear Blinder–Oaxaca technique was applied to the 2015 TFLSS data to decompose the mean differences in innovation. The results of the decomposition revealed that innovation by female-owned enterprises is lower than for male-owned enterprises because female-owned enterprises have less favourable characteristics. Male-owned enterprises benefit, in terms of endowments associated with innovation, from higher levels of investment (suggesting easier access to credit), a lower skills gap (suggesting better able to recruit suitable workers), and fewer female managers (implying less gender diversity). However, despite having worse endowments, female-owned enterprises had better resource utilization—they made better use, in terms of innovation, of the resources available than males would with similar resources. Specifically, experienced females are more likely to innovate relative to their male counterparts. Innovation in female-owned enterprises could be increased by improving their resources, specifically their ability to finance investment and hire more skilled workers, whilst innovation in male-owned enterprises could be increased by hiring experienced female managers (implying that it is not the number of female managers but their skills and experience that matters).

These findings have implications for policies aimed at reducing gender inequalities in entrepreneurship. Policies that promote access to credit to finance investment can enhance the acquisition of assets by female-owned enterprises and is likely to support innovation. Removing any gender gaps in access to credit could help level the playing field in terms of resources that are available to female-owned enterprises to those of male-owned enterprises. Policies aimed at narrowing the skills gap by improving literacy and quality of the labour force are beneficial for entrepreneurship. Enhancing the provision of, and female participation in, STEM subjects may encourage entrepreneurial activity by providing technical knowledge, computing and numeracy skills to improve the pool of skilled labour, especially managers. Whilst school education is vital, employers also value what are often termed 'soft' skills, such as creativity, inter-personal and communication skills. Such skills are better provided through on-the-job training, internships (work experience), and group networking. Encouraging female participation in private and public business networks would improve the entrepreneurial environment and expose female entrepreneurs and managers to social and business networks that enhance access to economic resources and innovation knowledge.

However, it is important to point out that while female-owned enterprises were disadvantaged in terms of resource endowments, they seemed to have an advantage with regards to resource utilization, at least those with business experience. Indeed, while female-owned enterprises require support in acquiring resources, male-owned enterprises could benefit from training aimed at enhancing resource use, in particular encouraging experienced owners and managers to avail of innovation opportunities. There is a suggestion in the analysis that gender diversity in management can facilitate innovative thinking; this may only have been observed for female-owned firms where male involvement at a senior level is likely. Promoting diversity in male-owned firms may be more challenging to ensure that skilled females can reach senior positions and be engaged with male managers and owners. Policy makers thus need to strike a balance between enhancing resource acquisition by female-owned enterprises and improving resource utilization by their male counterparts to avoid reversals in the gender innovation gaps. These reversals might occur when policies result in imbalances in resource endowments.

Ultimately, the results of this study provide policy insights that can guide policy makers on how to close the gender innovation gap, essentially by making it easier for female entrepreneurs to access finance and innovation opportunities and encouraging gender diversity in management in all firms. This is critical for promoting growth-enhancing female entrepreneurs' participation in private-sector development. Policies that advance ownership of innovation resources by female-owned enterprises will support the achievement of Tanzania's Development Vision 2025, Africa's common policy goal of industrialization, and the global development agenda comprising SDGs.

The COVID-19 pandemic has had adverse effects on sustained growth and development globally but is likely to have disproportionately adverse effects on female entrepreneurs as compared to their male counterparts. Regarding innovation, the pandemic may have put further demands on women's time due to family responsibilities, which is likely to have compromised their resource utilization. In addition, the pandemic may also have limited women's access to resources for innovation including credit and skilled labour. However, Tanzania has taken measures to reduce interest rates and encourage restructuring of loans to shield the economy from the adverse effects of the pandemic. These measures are likely to make firms more resilient to shocks, and to enhance firm productivity for sustained growth and development.

References

African Union (2014). *Science, Technology and Innovation Strategy for Africa 2024 (STISA-2024)*. Addis Ababa: African Union.

Amoroso, S., and A. N. Link (2018). 'Under the AEGIS of Knowledge-intensive Entrepreneurship: Employment Growth and Gender of Founders among European Firms'. *Small Business Economics*, 50(4): 899–915. https://doi.org/10.1007/s11187-017-9920-4.

Bessant, J., D. Knowles, G. Briffa, and D. Francis (2002). 'Developing the Agile Enterprise'. *International Journal of Technology Management*, 24(5–6): 484–97. https://doi.org/10.1504/IJTM.2002.003066.

Beugnot, J., and E. Peterlé (2020). 'Gender Bias in Job Referrals: An Experimental Test'. *Journal of Economic Psychology*, 76: 102209. https://doi.org/10.1016/j.joep.2019.102209.

Blinder, A. S. (1973). 'Wage Discrimination: Reduced Form and Structural Estimates'. *Journal of Human Resources*, 8: 436–55.

Carrasco, I. (2014). 'Gender Gap in Innovation: An Institutionalist Explanation'. *Management Decision*, 52(2): 410–24. https://doi.org/10.1108/MD-07-2012-0533.

Conroy, T., and S. Weiler (2016). 'Does Gender Matter for Job Creation? Business Ownership and Employment Growth'. *Small Business Economics*, 47(2): 397–419. https://doi.org/10.1007/s11187-016-9735-8.

Cropley, D., and A. Cropley (2017). 'Innovation Capacity, Organisational Culture and Gender'. *European Journal of Innovation Management*, 20(3): 493–510. https://doi.org/10.1108/EJIM-12-2016-0120.

Dohse, D., R. K. Goel, and M. A. Nelson (2019). 'Female Owners versus Female Managers: Who Is Better at Introducing Innovations?' *Journal of Technology Transfer*, 44(2): 520–39.

Doss, C. R., C. D. Deere, A. D. Oduro, and H. Swaminathan (2014). 'The Gender Asset and Wealth Gaps'. *Development*, 57(3): 400–09. https://doi.org/10.1057/dev.2015.10.

Doss, C. R., C. D. Deere, A. D. Oduro, H. Swaminathan, Z. Catanzarite, and J. Y. Suchitra (2019). 'Gendered Paths to Asset Accumulation? Markets, Savings, and Credit in Developing Countries'. *Feminist Economics*, 25(2): 36–66. https://doi.org/10.1080/13545701.2019.1566753.

Freel, M. S. (1999). 'Where Are the Skills Gaps in Innovative Small Firms?' *International Journal of Entrepreneurial Behavior and Research*, 5(3): 144–54. https://doi.org/10.1108/13552559910371095.

González, X., D. Miles-Touya, and C. Pazó (2016). 'R&D, Worker Training and Innovation: Firm-level Evidence'. *Industry and Innovation*, 23(8): 694–712. https://doi.org/10.1080/13662716.2016.1206463.

Grimpe, C., W. Sofka, M. Bhargava, and R. Chatterjee (2017). 'R&D, Marketing Innovation, and New Product Performance: A Mixed Methods Study'. *Journal*

of Product Innovation Management, 34(3): 360–83. https://doi.org/10.1111/jpim.
12366.

Helfat, C. E., and J. A. Martin (2015). 'Dynamic Managerial Capabilities: Review and
Assessment of Managerial Impact on Strategic Change'. *Journal of Management*,
41(5): 1281–312. https://doi.org/10.1177/0149206314561301.

Helfat, C. E., and M. A. Peteraf (2015). 'Managerial Cognitive Capabilities and the
Microfoundations of Dynamic Capabilities'. *Strategic Management Journal*, 36(6):
831–50. https://doi.org/10.1002/smj.2247.

Hillesland, M. (2019). 'Gender Differences in Risk Behavior: An Analysis of Asset Allocation Decisions in Ghana'. *World Development*, 117: 127–37. https://doi.org/10.
1016/j.worlddev.2019.01.001.

Idris, A. (2009). 'Management Styles and Innovation in Women-owned Enterprises'.
African Journal of Business Management, 3(9): 416–25. https://doi.org/10.5897/
AJBM09.131.

Islam, A., S. Muzi, and J. Meza (2018). 'Does Mobile Money Use Increase Firms' Investment? Evidence from Enterprise Surveys in Kenya, Uganda, and Tanzania'. *Small
Business Economics*, 51(3): 687–708. https://doi.org/10.1007/s11187-017-9951-x.

Jann, B. (2008). 'The Blinder–Oaxaca Decomposition for Linear Regression Models'.
The Stata Journal, 8(4): 453–79.

Klapper, L. F., and S. C. Parker (2011). 'Gender and the Business Environment for
New Firm Creation'. *World Bank Research Observer*, 26(2): 237–57. https://doi.org/
10.1093/wbro/lkp032.

Kuada, J. (2009). 'Gender, Social Networks, and Entrepreneurship in Ghana'. *Journal
of African Business*, 10(1): 85–103.

Marvel, M. R., I. H. I. Lee, and M. T. Wolfe (2015). 'Entrepreneur Gender and Firm
Innovation Activity: A Multilevel Perspective'. *IEEE Transactions on Engineering
Management*, 62(4): 558–67. https://doi.org/10.1109/TEM.2015.2454993.

McAdam, M., R. T. Harrison, and C. M. Leitch (2019). 'Stories from the Field: Women's
Networking as Gender Capital in Entrepreneurial Ecosystems'. *Small Business Economics*, 53(2): 459–74. https://doi.org/10.1007/s11187-018-9995-6.

Nziku, D. M., and J. J. Struthers (2018). 'Female Entrepreneurship in Africa: Strength
of Weak Ties in Mitigating Principal-Agent Problems'. *Journal of Small Business and
Enterprise Development*, 25(3): 349–67.

Oaxaca, R. (1973). 'Male–Female Wage Differentials in Urban Labor Markets'. *International Economic Review*, 14: 693–709.

OECD (2005). *Oslo Manual: Proposed Guidelines for Collecting and Interpreting
Innovation Data* (3rd edn). Paris: OECD Publishing.

OECD/Eurostat. (2018). *Oslo Manual 2018: Guidelines for Collecting, Reporting
and Using Data on Innovation* (4th edn). Paris: OECD Publishing, Luxembourg:
Eurostat.

Osabutey, E. L. C., and Z. Jin (2016). 'Factors Influencing Technology and Knowledge Transfer: Configurational Recipes for Sub-Saharan Africa'. *Journal of Business
Research*, 69(11): 5390–5. https://doi.org/10.1016/j.jbusres.2016.04.143.

Ravazzini, L., and J. Chesters (2018). 'Inequality and Wealth: Comparing the Gender Wealth Gap in Switzerland and Australia'. *Feminist Economics*, 24(4): 83–107.
https://doi.org/10.1080/13545701.2018.1458202.

Ritter-Hayashi, D., P. Vermeulen, and J. Knoben (2019). 'Is This a Man's World? The
Effect of Gender Diversity and Gender Equality on Firm Innovativeness'. *PLoS ONE*,
14(9). https://doi.org/10.1371/journal.pone.0222443.

Rutashobya, L. K. (2001). 'Female Entrepreneurship in Tanzania: Constraints and Strategic Considerations'. *Business Management Review*, 7(1): 22–32.

Rutashobya, L. K., I. S. Allan, and K. Nilsson (2009). 'Gender, Social Networks, and Entrepreneurial Outcomes in Tanzania'. *Journal of African Business*, 10(1): 67–83. https://doi.org/10.1080/15228910802701387.

Sabarwal, S., K. Terrell, and E. Bardasi (2009). 'How Do Female Entrepreneurs Perform: Evidence from Three Developing Regions'. *Small Business Economics*, 37(4): 417–41.

Sambasivan, M., T. J. Deepak, A. N. Salim, and V. Ponniah (2017). 'Analysis of Delays in Tanzanian Construction Industry: Transaction Cost Economics (TCE) and Structural Equation Modeling (SEM) Approach'. *Engineering, Construction and Architectural Management*, 24(2): 308–25. https://doi.org/10.1108/ECAM-09-2015-0145.

Sospeter, N. G., P. D. Rwelamila, M. Nchimbi, and M. Masoud (2014). 'Review of Theory and Practice Literature on Women Entrepreneurship in the Tanzanian Construction Industry: Establishing the Missing Link'. *Journal of Construction in Developing Countries*, 19(2): 75–87.

Strohmeyer, R., V. Tonoyan, and J. E. Jennings (2017). 'Jacks-(and Jills)-of-all-Trades: On Whether, How and Why Gender Influences Firm Innovativeness'. *Journal of Business Venturing*, 32(5): 498–518. https://doi.org/10.1016/J.JBUSVENT.2017.07.001.

United Nations (2015). *Transforming our World: The 2030 Agenda for Sustainable Development (A/RES/70/1)*. New York: United Nations.

van Uden, A., J. Knoben, and P. Vermeulen (2017). 'Human Capital and Innovation in Sub-Saharan Countries: A Firm-level Study'. *Innovation: Organization and Management*, 19(2): 103–24.

Weiler, S., and A. Bernasek (2001). 'Dodging the Glass Ceiling? Networks and the New Wave of Women Entrepreneurs'. *Social Science Journal*, 38(1): 85–103.

World Bank (2016). *Tanzania Enterprise Skills Survey, 2015*. Available at: https://microdata.worldbank.org/index.php/catalog/2578 (accessed 15 July 2019).

Yun, M.-S. (2004). 'Decomposing Differences in the First Moment'. *Economics Letters*, 82(2): 275–80. https://doi.org/10.1016/j.econlet.2003.09.008.

7

Labour diversification by households
2008–2013

Rumman Khan and Oliver Morrissey

7.1 Introduction

This chapter contributes to research on sustainable livelihoods by analysing the diversification of sources of household incomes and the association with household welfare using three waves of the Tanzania National Panel (household) Surveys (TNPS 2008/09, 2010/11, and 2012/13) (NBS 2010, 2011, 2013). Household welfare is measured using consumption of food (including an imputed value for consumption out of own production for farm households) and non-food items per adult equivalent, adjusted for regional and time price variation (including temporal differences associated with the fieldwork as each survey spanned over 12 months).[1] As the focus is on household welfare, and household size is included as a control in the analysis, the adult equivalent measure is more appropriate than per capita consumption.

Household income sources are separated into four labour categories that can be consistently measured at the national level within each wave and can be tracked accurately across waves given the changes in the underlying questionnaires: wage employment or self-employment and agricultural or non-agricultural employment.[2] Agricultural self-employment, or agriculture (farm) income, includes all self-employed activities in agriculture and fisheries. Non-agricultural self-employment (NAS) includes all individuals operating a business or engaged in any self-employed activity outside of agriculture. Agricultural wage (AW) employment includes all private and public agricultural employment, while non-agricultural wage (NAW) employment includes all private and public non-agricultural work. In the first wave, individuals can only list one form of wage employment for the last year while the other waves allow for up to two wage jobs. Consequently, even

---

[1] Information about the surveys and construction of the consumption measures can be found in the Tanzania National Bureau of Statistics TNPS report (URT 2011). Consumption is consistent for each wave but not across waves (so year fixed effects are included in the analysis in Section 7.4); the TNPS reports suggest consumption has fallen in real terms since the first wave and poverty slightly increased.

[2] In their study of diversification in Uganda, Khan and Morrissey (2019) included remittances as a source of income. However, the recording of remittances in TNPS is inconsistent and incomplete so this source is omitted.

Rumman Khan and Oliver Morrissey, *Labour diversification by households 2008–2013*. In: *Sustaining Tanzania's Economic Development*. Edited by: Oliver Morrissey, Joseph Semboja, and Maureen Were, Oxford University Press.
© UNU-WIDER (2024). DOI: 10.1093/oso/9780192885746.003.0007

if an individual has work in two off-farm wage categories, we only include the one reported as the main wage job. The analysis of diversification considers changes in the number and type of labour activity by members of the household.

Diversified sources of income are an important component of household liveli-hood strategies in low-income countries (Asfaw et al. 2019; Van den Broeck and Kilic 2019) by increasing total income and spreading risk. Much of the literature addresses engagement of farming households in non-farm activities (e.g. Reardon et al. 2007; Davis et al. 2017). These studies do not investigate household diver-sification at a national level or relate diversification to a measure of household welfare. Van den Broeck and Kilic (2019) consider diversification into non-farm employment measured at the individual level for self-employment (distinguishing industry and services) or wage (agriculture, industry, and services) employment, for five sub-Saharan Africa (SSA) countries including Tanzania (with only the 2011 and 2013 survey rounds). Drivers of diversification vary across countries and by gender—for example, women are less likely to participate in any type of wage employment and when females gain any wage employment it is most likely to be casual wage work in agriculture. This chapter provides a more in-depth analysis for Tanzania.

Section 7.2 provides a brief overview of related literature on diversification. Section 7.3 discusses the data and how income diversification is measured, with some descriptive statistics of the evolution of relative household welfare over the period of study. Ideally one could identify certain activities as welfare-increasing (associated with higher earnings) and others as welfare-maintaining (low earn-ing opportunities but allow the household to maintain consumption levels). The data are limited, but sufficient to consider the association between engaging in additional activities and household welfare (relative to the average household). Section 7.4 presents estimates of the relationship between income diversification and household welfare. Three issues are addressed: correlations between types of diversification and household welfare, distinguished by gender and rural or urban; identification of which activities are likely to be welfare-improving; and identification of household characteristics associated with types of diversification. Section 7.5 concludes by considering implications for employment policy.

7.2 Diversification of sources of income

Existing literature on income diversification tends to have a specific focus, such as increases in non-farm activities in rural areas (e.g. Reardon et al. 2007), household enterprises in urban areas (e.g. Fox and Sohnesen 2012), or on-farm crop diver-sification (e.g. McNamara and Weiss 2005). Davis et al. (2017) consider patterns of household engagement in agricultural wage, non-agricultural self-employment, and non-agricultural wage for twenty-two countries, focusing on SSA where richer households are more likely to engage in non-agricultural activities (suggesting that diversification is welfare enhancing). For Tanzania, more than half of households get three-quarters of income from farming, and one-third of households are classified as diversified (Davis et al. 2017: 160). However, the analysis is restricted to the primary source of household income for rural households; household welfare is not addressed; and Tanzanian data are only for 2009.

The analysis by Van den Broeck and Kilic (2019) is closely related to our analysis as they use similar categories of off-farm employment for five SSA countries. In the case of Tanzania, they find that women are less likely than men to participate in off-farm wage employment by at least ten percentage points, and the gap is largest in urban areas; females in off-farm employment are more likely than males to be in AW and far less likely to be in NAW; and almost half of women never engage in off-farm employment, compared to about one-third of males (Van den Broeck and Kilic 2019: 85–90). The analysis is based on individual-level data over 2011–13 and does not relate diversification to a measure of household welfare. In contrast, we analyse diversification at a household level over 2008–13 and relate this to relative household consumption.

Asfaw et al. (2019) consider both crop and income diversification for farming households in Malawi, Niger, and Zambia (data for various years between 2010 and 2015) and find that poorest households tend to benefit most from diversification. Although 'income diversification is a welfare enhancing strategy in all the three countries', crop diversification has no effect on welfare in Niger and is positive in Malawi but 'a welfare-decreasing strategy in Zambia' (Asfaw et al. 2019: 286). Thus, our expectation is that households with more sources of income will tend to have higher welfare, and we investigate this for Tanzania.

7.3 Data and measuring income diversification

The TNPS are part of the series of surveys released by the World Bank for its Living Standards Measurement Study (LSMS-ISA) project. In this chapter we use three waves of the panel. The 2008/09 wave started with an initial sample of 3,265 households. Of these, 3,168 households were re-sampled in 2010/11 alongside another 756 new or split-off households, producing a combined sample of 3,924. The 2012/13 wave re-sampled 3,786 households from the previous wave and had a total sample size of 5,010 after including new and split-off households. We exclude households that reported an income diversification (ID) value of 0 (had no farm or off-farm income), and once households with missing data are excluded we have a panel dataset of 10,141 observations taken from 3,676 households that appear in at least two waves, of which 2,789 appear in all three waves. Household income sources are separated into four labour categories that can be consistently measured at the national level within each wave and can be tracked accurately across waves given the changes in the underlying questionnaires. The labour activities are wage employment or self-employment and agricultural or non-agricultural employment.

Agricultural self-employment, or agriculture (farm) income, includes all self-employed activities in agriculture and fisheries. Although the surveys contain an agriculture module, to keep the analysis consistent between farming and non-farming households we do not consider the type of farming (cash crops or food crops) or crop diversification as part of our measure, unlike many of the studies focusing on rural household diversification. Non-agricultural self-employment includes all earnings activities for which the individual is not listed as an employee (such as being an own account worker, helping in a household enterprise, or being an employer) that is done outside of agriculture. Agricultural wage employment includes all private and public agricultural employment, while non-agricultural wage employment includes all private and public non-agricultural work.

Income diversification can be measured in various ways. If only concerned with two sources, shares are appropriate. If it is necessary to allow for many sources, either because household adults each engage in more than one activity or because activities can be sub-divided (different types of non-farm activity or diversifying crops grown), two approaches are common. One is to construct discrete indicator variables based on numbers of sources or categories of types of income (Abdulai and CroleRees 2001). An alternative is to construct a Herfindahl index measure based on earning shares of multiple sources (Asfaw et al. 2019). This is not feasible with the TNPS: the way in which earnings from NAS and household enterprises were recorded was changed between the second and third waves; farm earnings are not measured in a manner consistent with other income sources; and earnings from wage employment were limited to the primary source of wage employment for each individual in the first wave but the primary and secondary sources in the other two waves. Furthermore, the income data from household surveys is not reliable (Carletto et al. 2022).

Creating a measure of diversification at the individual level using earning shares also proves difficult given the inconsistent way wage earnings are recorded and, more importantly, earnings from self-employment are only available at the household level (given multiple members work on the family farm or business). However, which types of employment (AW, NAS, NAW) each worker engaged in can more reliably be calculated. As such, it is possible to classify each worker in each type of employment as a different source of income. Although two workers in wage jobs are two distinct income sources, this separation is harder to justify for household activities so employment on household farm or enterprise is treated as one (family labour) income source.

We measure diversification as a simple count of how many of the four different income sources households received. The simplicity of count assures consistency across waves given the different underlying questionnaires. This does not account for how much each activity contributes to overall incomes; for households engaged in multiple activities, those where almost all income is from one or two activities are less diversified than households with the same number of activities and shares are spread fairly evenly across all activities. However, the count is indicative and mainly used for descriptive purposes—the main analysis is for types of activities. At the national level, Khan and Morrissey (2020: Table 1) show the rise in the relative importance of off-farm work (especially NAW) and the decline in importance of farm incomes over the three surveys.[3] The most pronounced relative increases have been for the share of households with a member engaged in NAW (from 23 to 32 per cent) and AW (17 to 22 per cent);[4] NAS increased slightly from 41 to 44 per cent so most of the growth in off-farm labour was in wage employment. There was a decline from 85 to 78 per cent in the proportion of households relying on farm income.

Household size in terms of potential workers (adults) is quite stable although the average number of wage workers increased by almost half while the average number of NAS increased by 20 per cent; the fastest growth was in AW employment. Although the overall increase in ID from 1.87 to 2.06 appears small, it compares favourably with a decline from 1.72 to 1.66 in Uganda between 2005 and 2012 (Khan and Morrissey 2019). Furthermore, the increase in ID masks compositional changes where the fall in farm income has been offset by rises in off-farm, particularly wage, employment. There has been sustained growth in both male and female off-farm employment over the five-year period, more pronounced for females (whose off-farm participation increased by 41 per cent compared to 24 per cent for males, closing the participation gap. Consequently, by 2013 almost half of all households have at least one female off-farm worker compared to around one-third in 2008.

The trends in diversification for rural and urban areas separately are shown in Table 7.1. Over 90 per cent of rural households remained engaged in farming (Panel A), despite a decline of five percentage points, showing a similar pattern to eight other African countries (Davis et al. 2017). The proportion of urban households engaged in farming declined but remained over 40 per cent. Off-farm employment involves a much larger share of urban (over 90 per cent) than rural (under 70 per cent) households but has grown much faster in rural areas. Over half of urban households gain NAW income compared to about one-fifth in rural areas, although NAW has grown by about one-third in rural areas compared to 15 per cent in urban areas. Unsurprisingly, AW is very low in urban areas (but increased to 7 per cent of households) and increased by 38 per cent in rural areas to a share of 29 per cent of households, remaining the more common form of

---

[3] For convenience throughout, we refer to 2008/09 as 2008, 2010/11 as 2010, and 2012/13 as 2013.
[4] Some caution in the shares is warranted as the classification of wage workers is based on whether their main wage job is NAW or AW (however, it appears that fewer than 10 per cent of wage workers had two wage jobs).

Table 7.1 Rural-urban and gender distribution of income sources, 2008–13

Panel A: Percentage of households with each income source

	Rural			Urban		
	2008/09	2010/11	2012/13	2008/09	2010/11	2012/13
Population %	74	69	68	26	31	32
N	2,063	2,629	3,219	1,202	1,295	1,791
Farm income	99	95	94	47	45	42
Off-farm work	55	66	68	87	92	92
• NAS	35	38	38	59	60	58
• Wage	34	45	47	51	60	60
• NAW	14	21	21	47	55	54
• AW	21	26	29	4	5	7

Panel B: Average number of workers per household

Off-farm work	0.79	1.03	1.09	1.27	1.40	1.46
• NAS	0.42	0.48	0.52	0.76	0.76	0.82
• Wage	0.46	0.65	0.71	0.60	0.77	0.78
• NAW	0.17	0.25	0.25	0.56	0.71	0.68
• AW	0.29	0.40	0.46	0.04	0.06	0.09
Potential workers	2.87	2.94	2.84	2.82	2.75	2.65

Panel C: Average income diversification count score

ID	1.81	1.99	2.01	2.03	2.20	2.15
ID off-farm	0.83	1.04	1.06	1.57	1.75	1.73

Panel D: Average number of male workers per household

Off-farm work	0.47	0.60	0.60	0.72	0.77	0.80
• NAS	0.22	0.24	0.24	0.36	0.34	0.37
• Wage	0.30	0.42	0.42	0.42	0.52	0.51
• NAW	0.13	0.19	0.19	0.40	0.49	0.46
• AW	0.17	0.24	0.23	0.02	0.03	0.05
Potential workers	1.38	1.42	1.37	1.30	1.26	1.22

Panel E: Average number of female workers per household

Off-farm work	0.33	0.43	0.50	0.55	0.63	0.66
• NAS	0.21	0.25	0.28	0.41	0.42	0.44
• Wage	0.16	0.23	0.29	0.18	0.25	0.27
• NAW	0.03	0.07	0.06	0.16	0.22	0.22
• AW	0.12	0.16	0.23	0.02	0.03	0.05
Potential workers	1.49	1.51	1.46	1.48	1.45	1.39

Notes: N is number of households; data population weighted using survey weights. 'Potential workers' shows the average number of working-age adults (15 years or above) per household. ID is income diversification; ID off-farm is a count of the three types of off-farm work (includes AW); 'percentage' refers to the percentage of households containing at least one member of each type; 'average' is the average number across all households. Percentages in Panel A need not add up as households can have multiple activities.
Source: Authors' calculations based on Tanzania National Panel Surveys (NBS 2010, 2011, 2013).

wage employment in such areas. The share of households with NAS changed only slightly, remaining around 60 per cent in urban areas and increasing to almost 40 per cent in rural areas. The steady increase in wage employment over the five-year period has resulted in wage employment becoming more prevalent than NAS in both urban and rural locations.

Panel B shows that the average number of wage workers has increased significantly in rural and urban households (although the AW number is very low in urban areas). The growth rates in the average number of off-farm workers in rural households have been over twice the rates for urban households (except AW, which more than doubled in urban areas but only to an average of 0.09, compared to a 58 per cent increase to 0.46 workers in rural households). The average number of NAW workers in rural households increased by almost half (and one-fifth for urban) while NAS increased by over one-fifth (less than one-tenth for urban). This suggests some dynamism in rural employment.

Panel C shows that both urban and rural households have on average two of the four income sources, and rural households are less diversified than their urban counterparts for off-farm jobs. The average off-farm ID for rural households rose by 28 per cent (to 1.06), although it is still well below the level for urban households (which increased by 10 per cent to 1.73). Much of the increase in diversification came during the first two waves. Panel D shows that the average number of male off-farm workers in rural households increased by 28 per cent to 0.60; more than one-third of this in 2013 is NAS (grew by 10 per cent), AW is over one-third (and increased by one-third), and NAW is less than one-third (increased by half). In urban households the increase was about 10 per cent to 0.80 (most of the increase was NAW to 0.46). The fastest growth in female off-farm employment has been in rural areas (Panel E), where the average number increased by 50 per cent to 0.50 (and AW almost doubled). In rural areas, women have come to be predominant in NAS and equal the number of men engaged in AW, but participation in NAW still remains far lower. The average number of female off-farm workers in urban households is higher than in rural but only increased by 10 per cent to 0.66 (about half the growth was NAW, which accounts for about one-third of the total, with most of the rest in NAS). Overall, although off-farm employment grew faster in rural areas it remains more widespread in urban areas, particularly non-agricultural activities.

Khan and Morrissey (2020: Figure 1) show how income sources differ by quintiles of adult equivalent consumption. Richer quintiles are more diversified, especially for off-farm ID, and diversification increased for all quintiles (specifically between 2008 and 2010). The percentage of households with a farm was stable for the poorest (with almost all engaged in farming) but declined sharply for the richest. The share with off-farm employment increased for all quintiles, but at a faster rate for richer households. The poorest households are predominantly in farming with the lowest shares in off-farm employment and hence are least diversified. Just over half of the richest households but only a third of the poorest have a member in NAS; shares with NAW increase consistently for richer quintiles while the reverse is the case for AW.

Diversification increased over the five years: the average number AW and NAW workers in households has increased by almost half, with faster growth for females. For rural households, most of the additional female wage jobs are AW, whereas for males the additional jobs are more evenly split between AW and NAW; farming and AW predominate for the poorest households, whereas a majority of the richest households have NAW.

7.4 Empirical analysis and discussion

The relationship between income diversification and household welfare is explored using a standard reduced form model of household consumption (Glewwe 1991; Appleton 1996). Consumption (our measure of household welfare) is explained by a variety of household characteristics, to which measures of income diversification are added:

$$logCons_{it} = \alpha_i + \beta ID_{it} + \lambda X_{it} + \delta Z_{it} + \gamma_t + \varepsilon_{it} \tag{1}$$

The dependent variable is the log of adult equivalent household consumption; ID is the count of income sources for the household; and X is a vector of dummy variables capturing the main labour activity of the household head (farm, AW, NAS, NAW, or not employed). Vector Z is a set of controls including household size, wealth index, and a number of characteristics of the household head including their age and its square, education, and marital status. The region the household is from and whether it is urban or rural are included as fixed effects. We include household fixed effects to account for unobserved time invariant factors, such as household attitudes towards risk or innate ability of members, being correlated with diversification (or more generally with selection into type of employment). The inclusion of these fixed effects may cause many of the other controls to drop out, but we include them as the panel contains households that have moved to a new location or split off. The γ_t captures time effects with a survey-year variable. In (1), i indexes households and t indexes time (survey), and estimation is for the panel of all three waves (except Table 7.5, which has estimates for each wave).

7.4.1 Diversification and welfare correlations

Estimating (1) indicates if measures of diversification (ID and off-farm ID) are correlated with household welfare. A positive coefficient indicates that diversification is greater for households with *relatively* higher consumption spending, suggesting it is welfare enhancing. A negative coefficient indicates correlation with *relatively* lower consumption spending; this does not mean welfare is reduced as the measure is relative but is consistent with welfare-maintaining activities.

Results using fixed effects are in Table 7.2 (with 1 the omitted category for ID and 0 for ID off-farm). Columns (1) and (2) show a strong positive correlation between either ID measure and household welfare, indicating that for Tanzania it is households that are involved in earnings from multiple employment categories who are better off in terms of consumption/welfare. Columns (3) and (4) split the diversification variables into separate dummies for the number of sources and show that relative welfare is significantly higher for households with two (off-farm) or more income sources, irrespective of the ID measure used. The positive association between welfare and income diversification remains, even accounting for household-level factors, but does not permit any inference regarding causality. The positive correlation indicates that diversified income sources are an attribute of higher welfare households. This is consistent with household diversification being driven more by pull factors or opportunity-led diversification where the availability of jobs allows households to increase income. Columns (5) and (6) use lagged values of the diversification measures to partially address the contemporaneous correlation between welfare and diversification. The coefficients remain positive and are larger, indicative of a positive effect of diversification on welfare, although we interpret the results with caution given the short time between the waves and likely high degree of autocorrelation for both variables.

The results also give some indicative evidence that the type of job matters: having a household head whose main sector of employment is NAW offers the highest returns, closely followed by NAS (although both are insignificant in the IV regressions, suggesting persistence). Having a household head engaged in AW employment (or not employed) has no significant effect on household consumption compared to having a head whose main income is from farming (the excluded category). Although 'absent head' is significantly associated with lower consumption, one should not read too much into this as there are very few observations. Note that the coefficient on household size is negative and significant; larger households have lower consumption and effects for income diversification control for household size. Consumption is higher for richer households (in terms of wealth index) but lower for female-headed households. Coefficients for year dummies (capturing the increase in nominal consumption over time)

Table 7.2 Income diversification and household consumption

	FE				IV	
	(1)	(2)	(3)	(4)	(5)	(6)
ID [ID off-farm]	0.041***	[0.042***]			0.055**	[0.059***]
	(0.008)	(0.008)			(0.022)	(0.022)
ID=2 [ID off =1]			0.015	[0.034*]		
			(0.017)	(0.018)		
ID=3 [ID off =2]			0.082***	[0.094***]		
			(0.020)	(0.022)		
ID=4 [ID off =3]			0.120***	[0.118***]		
			(0.025)	(0.025)		
Head NAS	0.069**	0.064**	0.069**	0.066**	0.051	0.044
	(0.028)	(0.028)	(0.028)	(0.028)	(0.034)	(0.035)
Head AW	0.014	0.011	0.022	0.013	−0.061	−0.066
	(0.065)	(0.065)	(0.064)	(0.064)	(0.085)	(0.085)
Head NAW	0.092***	0.084**	0.094***	0.082**	0.060	0.048
	(0.035)	(0.036)	(0.035)	(0.036)	(0.043)	(0.045)
Absent	−0.208***	−0.234***	−0.207***	−0.229***	−0.025	−0.088
	(0.040)	(0.039)	(0.042)	(0.040)	(0.536)	(0.535)
Not employed	0.051	0.048	0.051	0.048	0.015	0.010
	(0.040)	(0.040)	(0.040)	(0.040)	(0.051)	(0.051)
Wealth index	0.059***	0.058***	0.059***	0.058***	0.040***	0.040***
	(0.006)	(0.006)	(0.006)	(0.006)	(0.009)	(0.009)
HH size	−0.064***	−0.064***	−0.065***	−0.064***	−0.069***	−0.069***
	(0.006)	(0.006)	(0.006)	(0.006)	(0.007)	(0.007)
Head age	−0.000	−0.000	−0.001	−0.000	−0.011	−0.011
	(0.006)	(0.006)	(0.006)	(0.006)	(0.009)	(0.009)
Head age^2	−0.000	−0.000	−0.000	−0.000	0.000	0.000
	(0.000)	(0.000)	(0.000)	(0.000)	(0.000)	(0.000)
Female head	−0.111**	−0.112**	−0.113**	−0.111**	−0.168***	−0.169***
	(0.050)	(0.050)	(0.050)	(0.050)	(0.062)	(0.062)
Married head	−0.185***	−0.184***	−0.187***	−0.184***	−0.176***	−0.173***
	(0.035)	(0.035)	(0.035)	(0.035)	(0.043)	(0.043)
Head education	0.012**	0.012**	0.012**	0.012**	0.001	0.001
	(0.005)	(0.005)	(0.005)	(0.005)	(0.006)	(0.006)
Observations	10,141	10,141	10,141	10,141	6,437	6,437
Households	3,676	3,676	3,676	3,676	3,648	3,648
R-squared	0.815	0.815	0.815	0.815		

Notes: Dependent variable is the log of adult equivalent consumption. Estimators are fixed effects (FE), and instrumental variable (IV). ID (ID off-farm) is the count of household sources of income, and ID=2, etc., are dummies for the given number of sources (ID = 1 is the omitted category for ID and ID off-farm = 0 is the omitted category ID off-farm). HH size refers to the number of members of the household. The IV regressions use lagged ID as an instrument. *** p<0.01, ** p<0.05, * p<0.1.
Source: Authors' calculations based on Tanzania National Panel Surveys (NBS 2010, 2011, 2013).

and other household characteristics are all significant with the expected sign (available on request).[5]

Khan and Morrissey (2020: Table 4) present results interacting the ID measures with survey year and urban or rural location. The association between ID and welfare is positive and significant in all cases (with one exception), and the coefficients are similar in all years for urban location but increasing for rural location, which has a larger coefficient than urban in 2010 and 2013. Khan and Morrissey (2020) also show that the positive association of welfare and diversification can be found across the whole income range, and the size of the effect remains largely the same.

7.4.2 Types of employment and welfare

Given the limitations of the simple count measure, to assess how employment in the different income sources is associated with household welfare, ID is replaced with a set of dummies for whether the household receives farm income (*farms*), any off-farm income (*off-farm*), and NAS, NAW, or AW (Table 7.3). All regressions use the full set of controls and household fixed effects. We exclude the household head's main activity as for many households the head is the sole income earner, which causes collinearity issues. Moving into any form of off-farm employment is associated with a 6 per cent increase in household welfare while engaging in farming has no correlation with welfare (Table 7.3, column 1). Column 2 splits off-farm employment into three dummies for each of AW, NAS, and NAW. The positive association for off-farm employment seen in (1) is shown to arise because of employment in the non-agricultural sectors; AW is not significantly related to welfare whilst engagement in NAS or NAW is associated with an 8 per cent increase in welfare.

Column 3 in Table 7.3 interacts AW, NAS, and NAW with rural and urban dummies, and the associations hold in both urban and rural locations: AW is insignificant while NAS and NAW are positive and significant, although the relationship is slightly weaker in urban areas particularly for NAW. Having NAW employment in rural areas has the strongest association with household welfare (10 per cent increase), followed by rural NAS (9 per cent), and then urban NAS and NAW (6 and 5 per cent). Column 4 interacts the employment sources

---

[5] The standard adult equivalence scale understates the welfare of female-headed households and households with relatively many adult females. Khan and Morrissey (2020: Appendix Table A4) calculated welfare using revised scales with higher weights on adult women (which gives lower mean real consumption). Using the revised scale has no substantive effect on the results.

Table 7.3 Off-farm employment and household consumption

	(1)	(2)	(3)	(4)		
	-	-	-	2008	2010	2012
Off-farm	0.061***					
	(0.017)					
NAS		0.083***				
		(0.016)				
Rural			0.087***	0.011	0.106***	0.135***
			(0.018)	(0.027)	(0.025)	(0.026)
Urban			0.063**	0.097***	0.031	0.070**
			(0.027)	(0.035)	(0.033)	(0.032)
AW		−0.024				
		(0.017)				
Rural			−0.025	−0.048	−0.004	−0.034
			(0.019)	(0.032)	(0.028)	(0.028)
Urban			−0.008	0.009	−0.037	0.015
			(0.046)	(0.074)	(0.065)	(0.067)
NAW		0.088***				
		(0.018)				
Rural			0.102***	0.126***	0.111***	0.066**
			(0.022)	(0.036)	(0.030)	(0.029)
Urban			0.050*	0.032	0.066**	0.067**
			(0.028)	(0.037)	(0.033)	(0.033)
Farms	−0.003	0.002	0.001		−0.000	
	(0.032)	(0.032)	(0.032)		(0.032)	
FE	Yes	Yes	Yes	Yes		
Observations	10,141	10,141	10,141	10,141		
Households	3,676	3,676	3,676	3,676		
R-squared	0.814	0.816	0.815	0.816		

Notes: As for Table 7.2, all regressions use the full sample, and estimates by rural/urban location or for different time periods are obtained by interacting with the main regression variables.
Source: Authors' calculations based on Tanzania National Panel Surveys (NBS 2010, 2011, 2013).

with time dummies as well as the rural/urban dummy (to see how the associations have changed across the three panel waves. In all locations and survey waves AW remains insignificant. In rural areas the coefficient on NAS has been increasing (to a significant 13.5 per cent effect by the third wave) while the positive association with NAW has been falling (roughly halved to 7 per cent), and in urban areas the trends are the reverse with the NAW coefficients increasing and NAS decreasing, both with about 7 per cent in 2012/13. None of the agricultural activities are significant in any of the specifications in Table 7.3, while most of the non-agricultural activities are positive and significant, and there are differing time trends in rural and urban areas even over a relatively short time period.

The lack of significance for AW in all regressions where it was included is noteworthy given the negative correlation of AW with household consumption (Khan and Morrissey 2020: Figure 1). This suggests that after accounting for factors that may 'push' households into such employment out of necessity, the negative association with welfare disappears. We extend this analysis to distinguish employment by gender in Table 7.4. The positive benefit of a male with off-farm employment is more than twice that for a female (column 1), but this male effect is only significant in rural areas whereas the effect is positive and significant for females in urban areas only (column 2). The coefficients on farms and male AW are always insignificant, but female AW is negatively associated with consumption (column 3), suggesting distress especially in rural areas as this is the only case where AW is significant (column 4). The gender differential favouring males applies to NAS, but this is driven by rural areas (female NAS is larger and significant in urban areas). The gender differential benefit is minimal for NAW

Table 7.4 Off-farm employment and household consumption by gender

	(1)	(2)		(3)	(4)	
	-	Rural	Urban	-	Rural	Urban
Male off-farm	0.078***	0.088***	0.045			
	(0.017)	(0.019)	(0.035)			
Female off-farm	0.030**	0.014	0.078***			
	(0.015)	(0.017)	(0.025)			
Male NAS				0.094***	0.115***	0.021
				(0.018)	(0.020)	(0.030)
Male AW				0.013	0.018	−0.017
				(0.021)	(0.022)	(0.061)
Male NAW				0.087***	0.110***	0.021
				(0.020)	(0.024)	(0.029)
Female NAS				0.046***	0.041**	0.053**
				(0.016)	(0.020)	(0.025)
Female AW				−0.048**	−0.056**	0.004
				(0.024)	(0.025)	(0.057)
Female NAW				0.084***	0.082**	0.085**
				(0.027)	(0.038)	(0.035)
HH farms	−0.000	0.001		−0.000	−0.000	
	(0.032)	(0.032)		(0.032)	(0.032)	
FE	Yes	Yes		Yes	Yes	
Observations	10,141	10,141		10,141	10,141	
Households	3,676	3,676		3,676	3,676	
R-squared	0.815	0.815		0.816	0.816	

Notes: As for Table 7.2, all regressions use the full sample, and estimates by rural/urban location are obtained by interacting with the main regression variables.
Source: Authors' calculations based on Tanzania National Panel Surveys (NBS 2010, 2011, 2013).

overall but is greater for males in rural areas and only significant for females in urban areas.

7.4.3 Influences on diversification

The increased diversification shown in Section 7.3 appears in general to have been associated with higher welfare if into non-agricultural, especially wage, activities (although there is no clear evidence of causality). These could be considered as pull activities where individuals are attracted into higher-earning activities. In contrast, agricultural wage employment is a push activity that tends to be associated with lower relative welfare (but may be welfare maintaining). A significant number of individuals, especially females, moved into AW—17 per cent of rural households in 2010 and 2012 and even 5 per cent of urban households—although exit rates were also high. Table 7.5 shows that NAS and NAW exhibited the highest entry (and exit) rates for urban households, but AW had typically the highest entry for rural households.

Khan and Morrissey (2020: Table 8) present estimates of household entry into a new employment type, overall and separately for urban and rural areas. Few determinants are significant: poorer households are more likely to enter AW and NAS in rural areas, as are households with a less-educated head; however, in rural areas, households with an educated head are more likely to enter NAW. Table 9 in Khan and Morrissey (2020) reports results for continuing employment into each of the three types of off-farm work. Poorer and less-educated households are more likely to continue working in AW as well as those that may have experienced some distress and had to obtain a loan to meet consumption needs. In rural areas, wealthier and more-educated households continue in NAS, whilst in urban

Table 7.5 Off-farm employment entry and exit rates (%)

	Non-agricultural self				Agricultural wage				Non-agricultural wage			
	Rural		Urban		Rural		Urban		Rural		Urban	
	2010	2013	2010	2013	2010	2013	2010	2013	2010	2013	2010	2013
None	49	48	25	25	62	57	91	89	73	69	39	34
Exit	12	15	12	12	11	14	3	3	7	11	8	16
Continue	22	23	44	49	10	13	1	2	7	9	39	40
Entry	17	14	19	14	17	17	5	5	12	11	14	11

Notes: Data population weighted and show the percentage of households not engaged in each activity in the current or previous wave (none), left the activity since the previous wave (exit), engaged in the activity in both the current and previous waves (continue), or engaged in the current wave but not the previous (entry).
Source: Authors' calculations based on Tanzania National Panel Surveys (NBS 2010, 2011, 2013).

areas more-educated households are more likely to exit NAS. The rural informal sector is welfare increasing: poorer households are more likely to enter, and this increases income, so they continue in NAS. In urban and rural areas richer and more-educated households are more likely to continue in NAW.

7.5 Conclusion

The chapter investigated the role of income diversification on household welfare using three waves of Tanzanian National Panel Surveys (TNPS 2008/09, 2010/11, and 2012/13) to construct a panel with 10,141 observations from 3,676 households that appear in at least two waves. Household income sources are separated into four labour categories that can be consistently measured at the national level within each wave and can be tracked accurately across waves given the changes in the underlying questionnaires. These labour activities are agriculture (farming), non-agricultural self-employment (NAS), and agricultural (AW) and non-agricultural (NAW) wage employment. Household welfare is measured in terms of food consumption (adult equivalent expenditure). Income diversification is captured by the number and types of sources of income for household workers.

Households in Tanzania have increased diversification of sources of income even over the five-year period from 2008 to 2013, and this has been associated with higher household welfare. There has been significant growth in agricultural wage (especially for rural females) and non-agricultural wage employment, while the percentage of households with any member with income from non-agricultural self-employment increased only slightly. The average number of wage workers in households has increased by almost half (although the average number of working-age members per household has fallen), and growth has been faster for females so that gender participation gaps in wage employment are declining. For rural households, most of the additional female wage jobs are in (low-skilled) agricultural wage employment, whereas for males the additional jobs are more evenly split between agricultural and non-agricultural wage employment. Farming and agricultural wage employment predominate for the poorest households, whereas almost 60 per cent of the richest households have non-agricultural wage employment. In rural areas it is additional non-agricultural opportunities that are associated with increased welfare, consistent with rural economic diversification contributing to a reduction in rural poverty (Aikaeli et al. 2021: 1883).

There is an association between labour diversification and higher household welfare, but not all types of off-farm employment are equally beneficial, and there are significant gender differences. Non-agricultural self-employment is beneficial, irrespective of gender, but has grown relatively slowly; policies that support informal opportunities, especially in rural areas, would facilitate gender-inclusive welfare-improving diversification. As could be expected, non-agricultural wage employment is beneficial for both genders, so the relatively high growth is a good sign (although may not have continued beyond 2013). Continuing to support increased education and wage employment opportunities is worthwhile. Although agricultural wage employment has been an important source of new employment opportunities for females, especially in rural areas, it is not a good diversification strategy insofar as disadvantaged females are pushed into low-earning employment. Increased support to improve productivity seems essential to increase potential earnings from agriculture (wage or farming) and will tend to benefit women. For the poorest rural households, employment opportunities will remain limited and public support will be required. There is evidence that public work projects are successful at targeting women and the poor with earnings probably at least comparable to agricultural wage work.[6]

A number of the findings for Tanzania in Van den Broeck and Kilic (2019) are consistent with or complementary to our analysis: women are less likely to participate in off-farm wage employment, and when they do it is most likely to be agriculture; the majority of those working report only one job; and women are significantly less likely than men to be in non-agricultural wage employment. The broad findings are consistent with evidence from the literature on the importance of off-farm employment for rural households but goes further in including urban households and distinguishing effects, in terms of welfare, of the type of employment. Non-agricultural self- and wage employment are associated with higher welfare, and growth of non-agricultural wage employment in Tanzania has helped to raise welfare for households. Agricultural wage employment has also increased, but this does not deliver a benefit in terms of higher consumption (especially for females). Income diversification does matter for household welfare, but there are differences by gender and activities where opportunities are available that have important implications for the effect of diversification.

These findings contrast with those of Khan and Morrissey (2019) for Uganda where non-agricultural wage employment grew more slowly and the general finding is that engaging in more labour activities is primarily because of push factors: lower-income households need to engage in more activities to meet their consumption needs, and these are primarily in agricultural wage employment where jobs are, especially for females, associated with lower consumption. In Uganda it appears that diversifying income sources is a sign of distress and driven by push factors or what Loison (2015) classifies as 'survival-led' as opposed to 'opportunity-led' diversification. Poorer households in Uganda diversified into

---

[6] An assessment report of the TASAF Public Works Programme finds that the scheme targets the poor and has a 70 per cent female participation rate with potential to scale up (see http://ispatools.org/tools/ISPA-Country-Report-Tanzania-PWP.pdf).

low-return activities in order to ensure survival and reduce vulnerability to shocks. We do not find this to be the case in general for Tanzania over 2008–13.

At the outset of the COVID-19 pandemic in 2020, Tanzania avoided lockdown measures, sustained school closures, or bans on large public gatherings; the measures put in place have been less restrictive than those adopted by neighbouring countries. When President Samia Suluhu Hassan assumed power following the death of President Magufuli in March 2021, some measures were put in place, such as recommending the use of masks in public and a vaccination campaign, but the government avoided restrictions that would significantly disrupt economic activity (Aikaeli et al. 2021: 1886). Nevertheless, economic effects of the global pandemic, such as loss of exports and tourist earnings and disruptions in the supply of imported inputs, were associated with employment losses in the formal sector and income losses among the self-employed that may have pushed more than half a million people below the poverty line (World Bank 2021).

Given the household characteristics associated with vulnerability to poverty—low education, employment in agriculture, large households, and living in rural areas (Aikaeli et al. 2021: 1872)—inferences can be drawn on the sustainability of welfare improvements due to diversification since 2020. The indirect effects of COVID-19 appear to have been less severe in rural areas. The positive association between diversification and welfare for rural households with males in non-agricultural employment is likely to persist (although those in tourism-related activities will have suffered losses). The challenge remains how to improve the prospects of rural females, who fared less well than males. Females in poorer households (lower wealth or less-educated head and more dependents) are more likely to enter and remain in agricultural wage employment (negatively associated with household welfare), consistent with diversification motivated by push factors as this may be the only option for less-educated females to help maintain household consumption. Females in non-agricultural employment work fewer hours (as there are more dependents in the household or females are also working on the farm), although this does appear to be a welfare-increasing diversification strategy.

Females in non-agricultural self-employment have benefited compared to males in urban areas, a gender-inclusive welfare-increasing diversification strategy (as it is associated with richer and more-educated households). However, this is the sector where income losses have been most common during COVID-19, especially in urban areas, so any gains from diversification may have been lost in recent years. As the economy begins to recover, households should be able to re-establish self-employment activities. Households who experienced job losses in non-agricultural wage employment, mostly in urban areas, will be the most severely affected and may take longest to recover because firms need to start hiring workers again.

References

Abdulai, A., and A. CroleRees (2001). 'Determinants of Income Diversification amongst Rural Households in Southern Mali'. *Food Policy*, 26(4): 437–52. https://doi.org/10.1016/S0306-9192(01)00013-6

Aikaeli, J., D. Garcés-Urzainqui, and K. Mdadila (2021). 'Understanding Poverty Dynamics and Vulnerability in Tanzania: 2012–2018'. *Review of Development Economics*, 25: 1869–94, https://doi.org/10.1111/rode.12829

Appleton, S. (1996). 'Women-Headed Households and Household Welfare: An Empirical Deconstruction for Uganda'. *World Development*, 24(12): 1811–27. https://doi.org/10.1016/S0305-750X(96)00089-7

Asfaw, S., A. Scognamillo, G. Di Caprera, N. Sitko, and A. Ignaciuk (2019). 'Heterogeneous Impact of Livelihood Diversification on Household Welfare: Cross-Country Evidence from Sub-Saharan Africa'. *World Development*, 117: 278–95. https://doi.org/10.1016/j.worlddev.2019.01.017

Carletto, G., M. Tiberti, and A. Zezza (2022). 'Measure for Measure: Comparing Survey-Based Estimates of Income and Consumption for Rural Households'. *World Bank Research Observer*, 37(1): 1–28. https://doi.org/10.1093/wbro/lkab009

Davis, B., S. Di Guiseppe, and A. Zezza (2017). 'Are African Households (Not) Leaving Agriculture? Patterns of Households' Income Sources in Rural Sub-Saharan Africa'. *Food Policy*, 67: 153–74. https://doi.org/10.1016/j.foodpol.2016.09.018

Fox, L., and T. P. Sohnesen (2012). 'Household Enterprises in Sub-Saharan Africa: Why They Matter for Growth, Jobs, and Livelihoods'. Policy Research Working Paper WPS6184. Washington, DC: World Bank. https://doi.org/10.1596/1813-9450-6184

Glewwe, P. (1991). 'Investigating the Determinants of Household Welfare in the Côte d'Ivoire'. *Journal of Development Economics*, 35: 307–37. https://doi.org/10.1016/0304-3878(91)90053-X

Khan, R., and O. Morrissey (2019). 'Income Diversification and Household Welfare in Uganda 1992–2013'. CREDIT Research Paper 19/05. Nottingham: University of Nottingham, School of Economics.

Khan, R., and O. Morrissey (2020). 'Income Diversification and Household Welfare in Tanzania 2008–2013'. WIDER Working Paper 2020/110. Helsinki: UNU-WIDER. https://doi.org/10.35188/UNU-WIDER/2020/867-2

Loison, S. A. (2015). 'Rural Livelihood Diversification in Sub-Saharan Africa: A Literature Review'. *The Journal of Development Studies*, 51(9): 1125–38. https://doi.org/10.1080/00220388.2015.1046445

McNamara, K., and C. Weiss (2005). 'Farm Household Income and On- and Off-Farm Diversification'. *Journal of Agricultural and Applied Economics*, 37: 37–48. https://doi.org/10.1017/S1074070800007082

National Bureau of Statistics (NBS) [Tanzania] (2010). 'Tanzania National Panel Survey 2008–2009 (Round 1)'. Ref. TZA_2008_NPS-R1_v03_M. Dar es Salaam, Tanzania: NBS. Available at: http://microdata.worldbank.org (accessed 14 February 2014).

NBS [Tanzania] (2011). 'Tanzania National Panel Survey Report (NPS)—Wave 2, 2010–2011'. Dar es Salaam, Tanzania: NBS. Available at: www.nbs.go.tz (accessed 16 September 2015).

NBS [Tanzania] (2013). 'Tanzania National Panel Survey Report (NPS)—Wave 3, 2012–2013'. Dar es Salaam, Tanzania: NBS. Available at: www.nbs.go.tz (accessed 16 September 2015).

Reardon, T., J. Berdegué, C. Barrett, and K. Stamoulis (2007). 'Household Income Diversification into Rural Nonfarm Activities'. In P. Hazel, S. Haggblade, and T. Reardon (eds), *Transforming the Rural Nonfarm Economy* (pp. 115–40). Baltimore: Johns Hopkins University Press.

URT (2011). *Basic Information Document*: *National Panel Survey (NPS 2010–2011)*. Dar es Salaam: National Bureau of Statistics.

Van den Broeck, G., and T. Kilic (2019). 'Dynamics of Off-Farm Employment in Sub-Saharan Africa: A Gender Perspective'. *World Development*, 119: 81–99. https://doi.org/10.1016/j.worlddev.2019.03.008.

World Bank (2021). *Tanzania Economic Update (February 2021): Raising the Bar—Achieving Tanzania's Development Vision*. Washington, DC: World Bank.

8

Long-run rural livelihood diversification in Kagera

Ralitza Dimova, Sandra Kristine Halvorsen, Milla Nyyssölä, and Kunal Sen

8.1 Introduction

Income diversification is one of the most established resilience-building characteristics of a typical rural household in developing countries (Banerjee and Duflo 2007). It has consistently proved to play a crucial role in achieving sustained growth and development, especially in the face of major shocks such as those associated with a global pandemic. The literature has identified two main strategies of resilience building via income diversification, namely risk reduction as an ex ante or ex post response to shocks, and asset accumulation that tends to originate from movement into non-farm activities and migration to cities (Barrett et al. 2001a; Ellis 1998; 2000a; 2000b). Household income diversification can thus be seen as either necessity and survival, where diversification is born out of desperation and driven primarily by the household's poverty status (Ellis 1998), or 'as a matter of choice and opportunity, involving proactive household strategies for improving living standards' (Ellis 1998: 7). The aims of household income diversification driven by survival motives could be:

> risk reduction, response to diminishing factor returns in any given use, such as family labour supply in the presence of land constraints driven by population pressure and fragmented landholdings, reaction to crisis and liquidity constraints, high transaction costs that induce households to self-provision in several goods and services, etc.
>
> (Barrett et al. 2001a: 315–16)

Household income diversification due to accumulation strategies can involve the 'realization of strategic complementarities between activities such as crop–livestock integration' or 'local engines of growth such as commercial agriculture or proximity to an urban area (that) create opportunities for income

Ralitza Dimova et al., *Long-run rural livelihood diversification in Kagera*. In: *Sustaining Tanzania's Economic Development*. Edited by: Oliver Morrissey, Joseph Semboja, and Maureen Were, Oxford University Press. © UNU-WIDER (2024). DOI: 10.1093/oso/9780192885746.003.0008 diversification in productivity and expenditure-linkage activities' (Barrett et al. 2001a: 316).[1]

We make two contributions to this discussion. First, by examining the pattern of income diversification revealed by the Kagera Health and Development Survey (KHDS), we address the question of whether the income diversification behaviour of a panel of predominantly agricultural[2] households in the Kagera region of Tanzania during the 1991–94 period was characterized by survival or accumulation motives. One strong manifestation of the 'diversification for survival' view is that poor households diversify more than richer households, while the opposite is true under the 'diversification for accumulation' view. Whether household income diversification is a matter of necessity or choice is of considerable policy importance. If poor households diversify out of necessity but moving into higher-return yet higher-risk livelihoods endangers their long-term survival, the policy priority should be to reduce the risk of opting for high-return choices. Alternatively, if diversification is a route out of poverty that is mostly undertaken by wealthier households due to high entry costs, it would be more important from a policy point of view to emphasize public investments in infrastructure (e.g. public transport or electricity), along with the removal of impediments to access to finance and to engaging in high-value agricultural activities by relatively poor households. Earlier literature has failed to provide an unambiguous answer to the 'diversification as survival' versus 'diversification as accumulation' puzzle (Djido and Shiferaw 2018; Ellis 2000b). Moreover, much of earlier literature focuses on diversification within agriculture, examining different crop mixes for example, whereas we also consider other sources of income. The evidence provided in this chapter supports the diversification-as-accumulation hypothesis, after accounting for the endogeneity problem stemming from the fact that wealthier households tend to have more diversified income sources.

Second, we use the extension of the 1991–94 KHDS to 2004 not only to examine how livelihood diversification changed over this ten-year period, but also to discuss the motivations behind these changes and whether the changes benefited the poor. Our main focus is on policy-relevant determinants of diversification, with special interest in how these differ across the different portions of the income distribution. While our results based on data from the 1990s give support to the accumulation hypothesis and inequality in diversification is found to persist in the long run (the rich continued to diversify more than the poor in 2004), there

---

[1] This a is a significantly modified version of Dimova and Sen (2010). The authors would like to thank the editors and an anonymous reviewer for valuable comments on earlier versions of this chapter. The usual disclaimer applies.

[2] The clusters are predominantly rural, even though some are classified as urban in the KHDS. Using agricultural income as a proxy for rural living, only 3 per cent of households in urban clusters in our sample do not have any agricultural income in the study period and 58 per cent have agricultural income as their main source of income.

is evidence to suggest that the rural–urban divide in diversification has narrowed. We also find that improvements in public transport and daily markets are related to more diversification, especially among poorer households. Households that were situated in either the poorest or the richest percentile diversified more in 2004 than they did before. This trend was mainly driven by higher return opportunities in non-agricultural employment and non-agricultural self-employment.

The Kagera region in Tanzania is a particularly pertinent context for this analysis, as it tends to be seen as emblematic of a remote, landlocked African rural setting and Tanzania was for long among the poorest countries in the world (De Weerdt 2010; Litchfield and McGregor 2008).[3] The 1990s were characterized by the apparent stagnancy of the rural Tanzanian economy due to slippages in macroeconomic policies and the absence of an enabling environment for households to pursue dynamic strategies of income diversification (Sen 2002). A new wave of reforms started to take place in the 2000s. Although diversification of incomes within rural settings and rural–urban migration can be seen as powerful mechanisms of poverty alleviation in Kagera, there is no unambiguous answer to the questions of whether the government needs to prioritize rural diversification and, if so, precisely how this should be done, or whether rural–urban migration should be a goal in itself (Beegle et al. 2011; De Weerdt 2010; Khan and Morrissey 2020). Access to credit and access to infrastructure are seen as promising routes out of poverty. Yet, there is evidence that granting access to certain types of infrastructure, for instance roads, could in some situations be problematic (Dumas and Játiva 2020).

The rest of the chapter is organized as follows. In the next section, we discuss how we measure income diversification. Section 8.3 discusses the empirical strategy, the econometric methodology, and the data used in the empirical analysis. Section 8.4 presents patterns of income diversification evident in the data and other relevant descriptive statistics. Section 8.5 presents the results of the short- and long-term regression analyses and provides some further analyses that characterize the findings. Section 8.6 concludes.

8.2   Measuring household income diversification

A diversified household is generally seen as a household that moves away from only growing crops (that is, being pure cultivators) into non-farm labour such as rearing livestock or into off-farm activities through migration of some members of the household to cities. A variation of this approach makes an additional distinction between crops grown for pure subsistence and commercial (both traditional and high-value) crops. In these studies, diversification is measured using discrete

---

[3] https://data.worldbank.org/?locations=XO-TZ (accessed 25 September 2020).

indicator variables for different types of income portfolio that may exist among households (e.g. an income portfolio with no diversification—pure cultivators—will get a value of 1, a mixed income portfolio with both cultivation and livestock rearing will get a value of 2, a mixed income portfolio of both farming and non-farming income will get a value of 3, and so on).

Other studies measure income diversification as the proportion of income derived from non-farm sources (Davis et al. 2010; Reardon et al. 1992). While the move from farm activities to non-farm activities would be clearly beneficial to the household in most contexts, measuring diversification only as a transition to more rewarding sources of income or a move away from subsistence agriculture is problematic. First, it becomes a tautological matter that diversification is associated with accumulation if the former is measured as a movement from less productive to more productive sources of income. Second, it is not obvious why a household that derives, say, most of its income from one source should be seen as being more diversified than another household that derives equal shares of income from different sources. For this reason, the use of indicator variables to denote the degree of diversification in different income portfolios is problematic: the construction of such indicator variables is sensitive to the assumptions made about the precise thresholds of income shares used to assign different households to different income portfolio categories.

Two measures of income diversification have been popularly used in literature: the Herfindahl-Simpson (HS) index and the Shannon-Weiner index. Despite the differences in their emphasis, they both measure the richness of used income sources and consider the evenness in their distribution (Barrett and Reardon 2000; Johny et al. 2017; Joshi et al. 2004). In this chapter we choose to employ the normalized HS index, as it emphasizes evenness and dominance of a certain strategy rather than rare events or the variety of the strategies available, as in Shannon-Weiner index. The HS index also does not necessitate the arbitrary assignment of households to different income diversification categories (Ellis 2000b).[4] An advantage of the HS measure is that it makes no assumption that a higher degree of diversification is necessarily related to greater household engagement in more remunerative non-farm activities, so by construction, higher values of the measure do not mean greater income accumulation. To explain the used measure with clarity, we begin by presenting the traditional measure of concentration, the Herfindahl index (HI):

$$HI_{i,t} = \sum_{k=1}^{n} IS_{k,i,t}^2 \tag{1}$$

---

[4] The logic of this income diversification index is broadly similar to those of the income diversification indices used by Davis et al. (2010), which have been constructed at the country level, but unlike these indices, it allows us to measure diversification at the level of the household, which is our unit of analysis, as opposed to the country level.

The HI measure is constructed of the sum of income shares $IS_{k,i,t}$ of household i from income source k in wave t:

$$IS_{k,i,t} = \frac{I_{k,i,t}}{I_{i,t}} \qquad (2)$$

where $I_{k,i,t}$ is household income from a given source k, and $I_{i,t}$ is the total household income from all income sources. In this chapter the income diversification index is based on all seven broad categories of income that are present in the data: income from agricultural production (sales and consumption of unprocessed and home-processed crops and livestock); farm employment; non-farm employment; non-farm businesses (self-employment); rents; transfers and remittances; and other non-labour income (pension, insurance, lottery, bride price, and inheritance). This set of income categories is fairly representative of the categories used in the literature (e.g. Davis et al. 2010; Dedehouanou and McPeak 2020).

The HS index is then the complement of the HI, calculated as:

$$HS_{i,t} = 1 - \sum_{k=1}^{n} IS_{k,i,t}^2 \qquad (3)$$

A higher value of the index indicates higher levels of diversification. Normalizing the index will render the maximum value to 1. Without the normalization, the maximum value would be $1-(1/n)$. The normalized index is calculated simply[5] as:

$$NHS_{i,t} = \frac{HS_{i,t}}{1 - \frac{1}{n}} \qquad (4)$$

8.3 Data and empirical strategy

We use data from the first five waves of the KHDS, a longitudinal household survey conducted in the Kagera region of Tanzania. There were six waves of the KHDS: 1991/92, 1992, 1992/93, 1993/94, 2004, and 2010. The sixth wave (2010) is not used in this chapter, because it omitted the detailed income questions previously included. This region of approximately 1.9 million people is located on the western shore of Lake Victoria, bordering Uganda to the north and Rwanda and Burundi to the West. The population is overwhelmingly rural and mainly engaged in the production of bananas and coffee in the north and rain-fed annual crops (maize, sorghum, and cotton) in the south. The survey was conducted in fifty-one

---

[5] This form is the one used in Smith and Wilson (1996). It is a simplified form of the ones presented in some recent literature (e.g. Dedehouaunou and McPeak 2020; Djido and Shiferaw 2018).

communities in all eight districts of Kagera: Bukoba urban, Bukoba rural, Missenyi, Karagwe, Kyerwa, Muleba, Biharamulo, and Ngara.[6] Of the 912 original households, 759 completed all waves in the 1990s and 832 were re-interviewed in 2004. The household questionnaire is based on the World Bank's Living Standards Measurement Survey, assuring representativeness and quality of the data.

8.3.1 Empirical strategy

To reiterate, the first step of our empirical analysis, based on a four-year panel from the 1990s, focuses on testing whether income diversification is driven by survivalist or accumulation motives. To answer this question, we estimate a regression of the following generic form for the 1991–94 panel:

$$NHS_{ivt} = \alpha + \rho Y_{it} + \sum_k \gamma_k R_{vt} + \sum_k \beta_k X_{it} + d_t + u_i + e_{it} \tag{5}$$

where i designates the household, v designates the village in which the household resides, t designates time, NHS is the normalized HS index of household diversification (larger values imply more income diversification), Y is the logarithm of real household income[7] per adult equivalent (PAE), and R_{vt} and X_{it} are vectors of standard control variables at the village and household level, respectively. The error terms d_t and u_i capture the time-invariant and household-invariant components of the error term, while is the white noise component of the error term. The year effects d_t have been included to capture year-specific national-level shocks, such as weather and other macroeconomic shocks that may affect diversification behaviour for all households in a given year. Knowing that agricultural income often varies from season to season, we also control for the season, because the interviews were not done every year at the same time.[8] The household-specific effect u_i captures unobserved household characteristics that are time-invariant and, most importantly from our perspective, unobserved household attitudes to risk. Because the households were drawn from a stratified random sample of households, the standard errors are clustered at village level to account for village-level unobservables.

A positive sign of the coefficient of the income variable indicates that the diversification-as-accumulation hypothesis holds, while a negative sign indicates that the diversification-as-survival hypothesis holds. Given the plausible assumption that the income portfolios of the richest and poorest strata of the population

---

[6] After the last wave of the KHDS, the district borders were redrawn, so that two new districts were formed in Kagera (namely Kyerwa and Missenyi) and an area from Bukoba rural was reallocated to Muleba. This chapter uses the pre-2010 definition of districts in the empirical analysis.

[7] Inflation adjustments are based on the World Bank Consumer Price Index for Tanzania (https://data.worldbank.org/country/tanzania?view=chart, accessed 16 May 2020).

[8] There are three seasons: Masika (heavy rain), Vuli (light rain), and Kiangazi (dry).

may be more diversified than those of the middle-income strata (Anderson and Deshingkar 2005), we also test the U-hypothesis, where the relationship between income diversification and income may be characterized by a U-shape pattern, with high levels of diversification at both ends (at low and high levels of income) but a low level in the middle of the distribution. However, this hypothesis was not supported by our data.[9]

Our control variables at the village level are a set of dummy variables that capture whether the village is categorized as urban (such as some villages in the district of Bukoba and Muleba); has access to any formal or informal credit institutions; is electrified; has access to a post office and telecommunications; has public transport; has a daily market; has at least one secondary school; has a health facility. Infrastructure is expected to have a positive effect on household income diversification, as households in villages that have these infrastructural facilities would be more able to diversify by taking advantage of non-farm employment opportunities or trade, or by migrating to cities. The effect of credit facilities on household income concentration could be positive or negative, depending on whether household income diversification is driven by survival or accumulation concerns. If income diversification is driven by survival concerns, then greater access to credit will enable poor households to smooth consumption inter-temporally, rather than by diversifying their income portfolios. In that case, the relationship between access to credit facilities in the village and household income diversification will be negative. On the other hand, if income diversification is mostly a means of accumulation, access to credit will provide households with an easier route into non-farm activities or livestock rearing, which have high entry costs. In that case, the relationship between access to credit facilities in the village and household income diversification will be positive.

Our control variables at the household level are standard demographic variables such as the age, education (dummy equal to 1 if the head has at least completed primary school), and gender of the head of household; the proportion of members of the household who are dependants; and the size of the household. Previous research has found that male-headed households and households with more children are associated with more diversified income portfolios (Dercon and Krishnan 1996). With respect to household size, we expect that larger households diversify more, given that there are more individuals in the household.

We use an Instrumental Variables (IV) method of estimation along with household fixed effects and year effects. The reliance on an IV methodology is driven by the possibility of reverse causality between household income and income diversification. For example, using a Q-squared methodology combining ten-year panel

---

[9] We tested the hypothesis using centred quadratic regression. The results did not give support to the U-hypothesis, but rather gave an indication of a positive linear relationship between log-income and diversification.

data with qualitative life histories for Tanzania, De Weerdt (2010) finds that households that moved out of poverty were those that diversified their farming activities, growing food crops for their own consumption and cash crops for sale, and keeping livestock. It is not clear whether the positive correlation between diversification away from food crops and movement out of poverty is due to income diversification, or whether household income status drives the diversification behaviour. Our data set provides a large number of variables that are exogenous in the household income regression and could serve as credible instruments. There is no credible econometric way of assuring the quality of our instruments. Most tests for endogeneity available in the literature assume ex ante that the instrument chosen is at least conceptually appropriate. We experimented with instrumentation (without simultaneously correcting for fixed or random effects) and our final set of instruments passed the Sargan overidentification test. The set of instruments that we finally selected includes different types of village-level shocks (e.g. refugee inflow, epidemic, or natural disaster), the rainfall variability in the district over the preceding year, and an indicator of whether a working member of the household died during the preceding year. These variables impact on diversification via their effects on income and not directly, while also satisfying the exclusion criteria of being included as instruments.

Additionally, we use household fixed effects to account for unobserved household attitudes to risk, which may explain household diversification behaviour, independent of income. For instance, the classical literature invariably conditions income diversification strategies to household (or head of household's) attitude towards risk taking (Dercon 1996; 2002). Yet, the more recent behavioural literature finds high levels of risk preference heterogeneity among households across the different portions of the income distribution (Basu and Dimova 2020; Basu et al. 2020). This suggests that empirical analysis of income diversification must disentangle household innate characteristics, such as attitudes to risk, from those of other households, alongside community and macro variables that may impact on household income diversification. We also include random effects instead of fixed effects in several of the estimates as robustness checks. Given the short time variation in our panel, and the large cross-sectional dimension, random effects estimation may be more efficient than fixed effects, and we experiment with both random and fixed effects in the estimation of equation (5). Since certain variables are often fixed over time in the short run, we follow the two-step procedure suggested in Pesaran and Zhou (2018) to correct for collinearity between the time-invariant variables in fixed effects models.

In the second part of the empirical analysis we take advantage of the fact that we have a 2004 wave of the KHDS data. The ten-year gap between the last wave in the 1990s and the 2004 wave provides an ideal opportunity for us to examine the long-run patterns and correlates of income diversification for both poor and rich households. First, we examine whether actual income diversification of households in 2004, as captured by the HS index of household diversification, is closely correlated with the predicted measure of income diversification that we obtain from the panel regressions using the 1990s data across the income distribution. This allows us to assess how the actual income diversification patterns differ vis-à-vis the synthetic scenario of the socio-economic situation of the 1990s remaining unchanged. These differences are explored separately for poor and rich households and between those living in rural and in urban areas.

We next examine whether and to what extent the observed differences between the actual and predicted income diversification patterns are related to households gaining access to infrastructural factors (credit institutions, electricity, telephone and postal service, public transport, daily market, secondary school, and health facility) for different portions of the income distribution through correlation analysis. Following households over long periods is problematic, as household members grow older and enter or exit the labour force, or move in or out of the household, possibly changing the household composition. To link households from the 1991–94 panel with households in 2004, we identify and follow the household head and include only household members who live with the household head. In 38 per cent of the households, the person who was the head in Waves 1–4 is not interviewed in Wave 5, because the person is either no longer alive or has moved out and can no longer be traced. In these cases, we follow the household in which most of the family members remain and where the spouse, son, or parent has taken over as the household head.

Finally, we use a difference-in-differences approach to examine whether entering different types of income activities is motivated by income accumulation or survival. The model follows the standard generic form:

$$Y_{ivt} = \alpha + \beta_1 enter_s + \beta_2 W_{t=5} + \beta_3 (enter_s \cdot W_{t=5}) + \sum_k \gamma_k R_{vt} + \sum_k \delta_k X_{it} + e_{ivt} \quad (6)$$

where i indicates the household, v indicates the village, t indicates the wave (0 if Waves 1–4 and 1 if Wave 5), and s indicates an income source. The model is run for each income source separately. Y_{it} is the equivalized log-income, $enter_s$ is a dummy indicating whether a household entered into a certain income activity (for example, it takes the value 1 if a household had no income from employment in Waves 1–4 but had employment income in Wave 5), $W_{t=5}$ is a dummy indicating Wave 5, and R_{vt} and X_{it} are vectors of standard control variables at the village and household level, respectively (head age, female head, household head completed primary school, dependence ratio, household size, season, urban area, district, and log of total household assets). The parameter β_3 is the coefficient of interest and measures the effect of a household's entering a new income-generating activity in Wave 5.

8.4 Descriptive statistics and patterns of income diversification

Table 8.1 presents the descriptive statistics of the pooled sample of the first four waves and the fifth wave separately. First, the mean of the normalized index of diversity is roughly 0.30 when pooling all waves with a median of 0.24 and range of 0–0.88.[10] Diversification is not increasing over time on average. The household characteristics have remained quite similar across the waves. The age of household head has increased by only five years in a decade, as some household heads have died between the waves and a younger head has taken over. Households have experienced fewer deaths and disasters in Wave 5 than on average in Waves 1–4. Notable improvements have taken place when it comes to access to infrastructure and facilities. In 2004 almost all villages have a health facility, secondary school, and bank.

Table 8.1 Descriptive statistics

	Waves 1–4 (n = 3,328)		Wave 5 (n = 725)	
	Mean	SD	Mean	SD
Diversification index	0.297	0.241	0.294	0.241
HH income (PAE)	200,036	320,719	216,358	526,706
Age of head	49.314	17.107	54.421	16.853
Female head	0.274	0.446	0.309	0.462
Proportion of dependants	0.483	0.243	0.459	0.253
Household size	5.725	3.109	5.266	2.928
Head no education	0.207	0.405	0.258	0.438
Head elementary school	0.741	0.438	0.666	0.472
Head secondary school	0.046	0.210	0.065	0.246
Head university	0.005	0.069	0.010	0.098
Death in family (6–12 months)	0.125	0.331	0.072	0.258
Access to:				
Urban areas	0.212	0.408	0.211	0.408
Credit	0.521	0.500	0.971	0.168
Post and telephone	0.098	0.298	0.760	0.427
Electricity	0.269	0.444	0.684	0.465
Daily market	0.592	0.492	0.472	0.500
Public transport	0.255	0.436	0.699	0.459
Secondary school	0.080	0.271	1.000	0.000
Health facility	0.365	0.481	1.000	0.000
Disaster (last 6–12 months)	0.609	0.488	0.166	0.372

Note: Income is reported in real Tanzanian shillings PAE.[11]
Source: Authors' calculations based on KHDS data.

[10] This is comparable to that of Dedehouanou and McPeak (2020) for Nigeria.
[11] This chapter uses a gender-neutral version of the Tanzanian adult equivalence scale (AES), as in Nyyssölä et al. (forthcoming). The model results are robust to using the official Tanzanian AES as well.

The main variable of interest for the diversification as a means of accumulation or survival hypothesis is household income. Figure 8.1 provides a plot of the household diversification index in each year against the household income percentiles. The relationship between income diversification and level of income is positive. This provides some preliminary support for the diversification as a means of accumulation hypothesis. The level of income diversification is lower in Wave 1 than the level of diversification across all income groups in later waves. In our empirical analysis in Section 8.5, we control for various types of year-specific shocks that may influence diversification behaviour on a year-to-year basis using a year dummy.

The type of income source varies by income status and over time. Figure 8.2 presents the income diversification strategies by grouping the households into categories of income portfolios. Among the poorer half, the majority is engaged only in agriculture, whereas the richer half tends to have more than one income source. Dependence on agriculture has decreased over time among the richer half, and more households are diversifying in 2004. The poorer half has not become more diversified over time when it comes to the number of income sources.

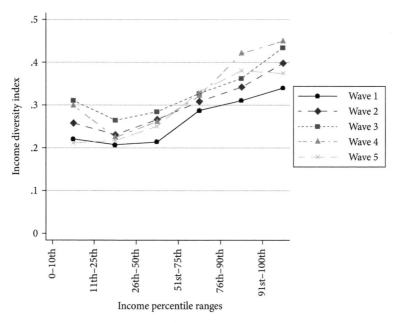

Figure 8.1 Mean income diversification index by income percentiles
Source: Authors' illustration based on KHDS data.

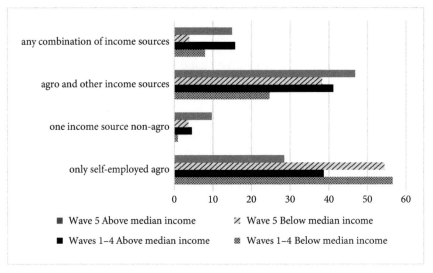

Figure 8.2 Income diversification by wave and income strata

Source: Authors' illustration based on KHDS data.

8.5 Results

8.5.1 Income diversification in the short run

Table 8.2 presents the estimates of equation (5), where the key explanatory variable is the equivalized real household log-income using Waves 1–4. Columns 1–3 give the simple ordinary least squares estimates without household fixed effects (FE). Columns 2–3 include household-level controls and year effects, using first fixed effects and then random effects (RE). Columns 4–5 present the estimates using the IV method of estimation with household-level controls and year effects and with fixed and random effects. Finally, columns 6–7 give estimates of the full specification including all village level controls.

The results are fairly consistent across the different specifications. The estimates of the main models (4–7) indicate a strong positive impact of the income variable on the degree of diversification, which provides support for the accumulation hypothesis. While age and education of the household head and dependency ratio do not affect household income diversification in the main models, female-headed households tend to diversify more than male-headed households (only significant in RE models). Household size is positively correlated with income diversification across all specifications.

There are also seasonal effects on diversification. In all specifications, there seems to have been more diversification when the month prior to the interviews was in the dry season, compared with the base season of heavy rain (Masika). This

Table 8.2 Impact of household income on diversification index, Waves 1–4

	(1) OLS	(2) FE	(3) RE	(4) FE + IV	(5) RE + IV	(6) FE + IV	(7) RE + IV
Log HH income (PAE)	0.037***	0.008	0.026***	0.192***	0.220***	0.197***	0.221***
	(0.008)	(0.009)	(0.008)	(0.074)	(0.060)	(0.074)	(0.056)
Head age	−0.000	−0.001	−0.000	0.001	0.000	0.001	0.000
	(0.000)	(0.001)	(0.000)	(0.001)	(0.000)	(0.001)	(0.000)
Female head	0.047***	0.021	0.041***	0.068	0.071***	0.070	0.070***
	(0.013)	(0.031)	(0.013)	(0.045)	(0.021)	(0.045)	(0.020)
Head has primary educ.	0.032**	−0.001	0.024*	0.008	−0.000	0.008	−0.002
	(0.015)	(0.018)	(0.014)	(0.023)	(0.018)	(0.023)	(0.018)
Proportion of dependants	−0.051**	−0.025	−0.050**	−0.037	−0.005	−0.034	−0.002
	(0.021)	(0.039)	(0.022)	(0.045)	(0.035)	(0.045)	(0.033)
Household size	0.012***	0.010**	0.012***	0.025***	0.019***	0.026***	0.019***
	(0.002)	(0.004)	(0.002)	(0.007)	(0.003)	(0.007)	(0.003)
Season: Vuli (light rain)	0.019	0.026*	0.018	0.021	0.018	0.016	0.016
	(0.014)	(0.015)	(0.015)	(0.017)	(0.017)	(0.017)	(0.016)
Season: Kiangazi (dry)	0.031**	0.038**	0.030**	0.042**	0.041**	0.040**	0.042**
	(0.015)	(0.016)	(0.015)	(0.018)	(0.017)	(0.018)	(0.016)
Urban	0.110***	0.148***	0.135***	0.158***	0.065**	0.125***	0.054*
	(0.023)	(0.015)	(0.024)	(0.015)	(0.030)	(0.019)	(0.030)
Credit	0.005					0.032**	0.023*
	(0.017)					(0.015)	(0.013)
Electricity	0.027					0.071***	0.021
	(0.020)					(0.020)	(0.021)
Post and telephone	0.059*					0.027	0.051
	(0.031)					(0.027)	(0.039)
Public transport	−0.003					0.036*	−0.026
	(0.017)					(0.019)	(0.025)
Daily market	0.021					0.003	0.004
	(0.015)					(0.017)	(0.015)
Secondary school	0.065					0.077***	−0.013
	(0.050)					(0.023)	(0.061)
Health facility	0.009					0.010	0.004
	(0.023)					(0.026)	(0.023)
Overall R²	0.141	0.036	0.121	0.062	0.069	0.063	0.072

Note: Number of observations is 3,328 in all models. Number of households is 915 in all models. All models include year effects, which appear statistically significant at 1 per cent level. Log household income is the log of real household income PAE. Season indicates the season prevailing during the month (self-reported by the households) prior to the months when the interviews took place. The omitted season is Masika (heavy rain). Some of the village-level covariates were reported only in Wave 1 and are therefore omitted in the FE regressions. The figures in brackets are cluster robust standard errors. ***, **, * indicate significance at the 1 per cent, 5 per cent, and 10 per cent levels.
Source: Authors' calculations based on KHDS data.

positive finding could be evidence that diversification undertaken during the dry season is based on accumulation motives rather than survival motives. During the dry season farmers tend to engage in different activities than in rainy seasons (de Bont et al. 2019). Using the dry season as the base category, we find that the estimates for Masika are significant and negative for all the models, suggesting that the farmers who choose to diversify during the heavy rain season may do so out of necessity.

To make sure that the regression results are not driven by potential differences between rural and urban areas, an indicator variable was included for urban communities.[12] Not surprisingly, this coefficient is positive, indicating higher diversification in urban areas. Among the infrastructural variables only access to credit has a significant (positive) effect on household income diversification in the main models. This positive effect would support the hypothesis that access to credit in the 1990s may have provided households with opportunities to diversify rather than only allowing them to smooth consumption.

8.5.2   Income diversification in the long run

To explore long-term changes in diversification and their policy drivers, we first compare the predicted values based on the 1991–94 sample, and the actual 2004 index values and then look at the policy determinants of both the gap between predicted and actual values and of actual long-term diversification patterns. The actual index averages in 2004 and predicted values of the diversification index, as well as their differences, are reported in Table 8.3 for all empirical specifications underlying the empirical analysis in Table 8.2. The predicted values are calculated using the estimated coefficients in Table 8.2 on the 2004 data. The differences are all statistically significant at the 1 per cent level and positive in models 2–5 and 7 and negative in models 1 and 6. There is more variation in the prediction models that include instrumental and infrastructural variables. Models 2–5 and 7 suggest that the actual level of diversification is higher than it would have been if nothing in the economy had changed in the ten-year period. However, models 1 and 6 suggest the opposite: when we include the significant changes in infrastructural factors, actual diversification is higher than it would have been if nothing in the economy had changed in the ten-year period.

Figure 8.3 illustrates both the actual (2a, light grey bar) and predicted (dark grey bar) diversification index values using model 6[13] and changes (2b) over the ten-year period by income percentile in 1991–94. Although the actual levels of diversification in 2004 are somewhat higher among richer households, relatively

---

[12] We also estimated the equations controlling for district fixed effects but this did not affect our results significantly.

[13] Model 6 is the most plausible as it controls for endogeneity, considers unobserved household attitudes (household fixed effects), and incorporates crucial infrastructural improvements.

Table 8.3 Comparing predicted and actual income diversification index values

		Income diversification index					Conf. intervals	
		Mean	SD	Predicted	SD	Diff.	Lower	Upper
Model 1	OLS + Inf.	0.294	0.241	0.339	0.107	−0.045	0.331	0.347
Model 2	FE	0.294	0.241	0.261	0.074	0.032	0.256	0.267
Model 3	RE	0.294	0.241	0.228	0.086	0.066	0.221	0.234
Model 4	FE + IV	0.294	0.241	0.143	0.364	0.151	0.116	0.169
Model 5	RE + IV	0.294	0.241	0.089	0.495	0.204	0.060	0.119
Model 6	FE + IV + Inf.	0.294	0.241	0.337	0.378	−0.043	0.310	0.365
Model 7	RE + IV + Inf.	0.294	0.241	0.125	0.406	0.169	0.095	0.154

Note: Number of observations (households) is 725. Mean income diversification index is calculated using data from Wave 5 and the predicted income diversification index values are calculated using the estimated coefficients in Table 8.4 on data from Wave 5, where models 1–7 refer to columns 1–7. Inf. stands for infrastructural variables.
Source: Authors' calculations based on KHDS data, Waves 1–4 and 5.

poorer households are characterized by very similar actual diversification levels when compared with their 'intrinsic' counterparts. Households above the median, however, are characterized by lower levels of 'real' diversification than the model predicted, given the improvements in observed infrastructure. For this group we observe negative values in the actual changes, while the predicted changes are positive. In sum, and keeping in mind that our baseline analysis indicated a diversification pattern consistent with the accumulation hypothesis, we observe very similar levels of both 'real' and 'intrinsic' livelihood diversification among poorer households, while we observe a failure to fulfil the 'intrinsic' potential in diversification among richer households.

Figures 8.4a and 8.4b show diversification patterns over time and income group and across rural and urban areas. The figures show that inequality in diversification across the income distribution has increased. Simultaneously, however, the diversification patterns in rural areas have become more similar to those in urban areas. In general, the agricultural income share has decreased over time, while off-farm employment and self-employment have increased. In the 1990s, higher-income households in urban areas engaged considerably more in private non-farm businesses and non-farm employment than rural households or lower percentiles in urban areas. In 2004, in both urban and rural areas, the better-off half and the poorest tenth percentile were further diversifying into private non-farm businesses. The increase in this respect is noteworthy among the top and bottom percentiles: income share coming from private businesses more than doubled in a decade for the top tenth percentile (for rural areas the growth was 32 percentage points (from 21 per cent to 53 per cent) compared with a 16 percentage point increase in urban areas (from 23 per cent to 39 per cent)), while for the bottom

8.3.a: Absolute value comparison

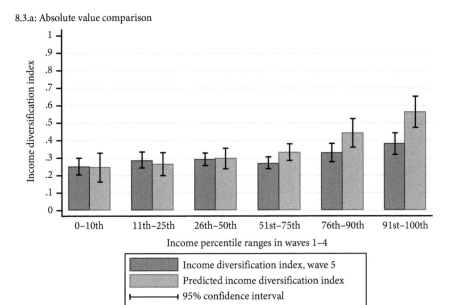

8.3.b: Change in value comparison

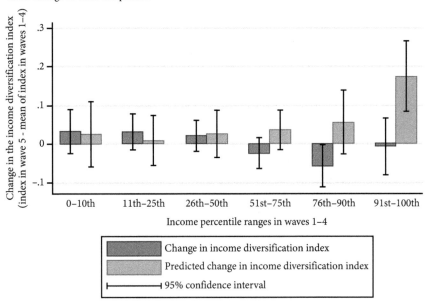

Figure 8.3 Comparing predicted (model 6) and actual income diversification index values by income percentiles

Source: Authors' illustrations based on KHDS data, Waves 1–4 and 5.

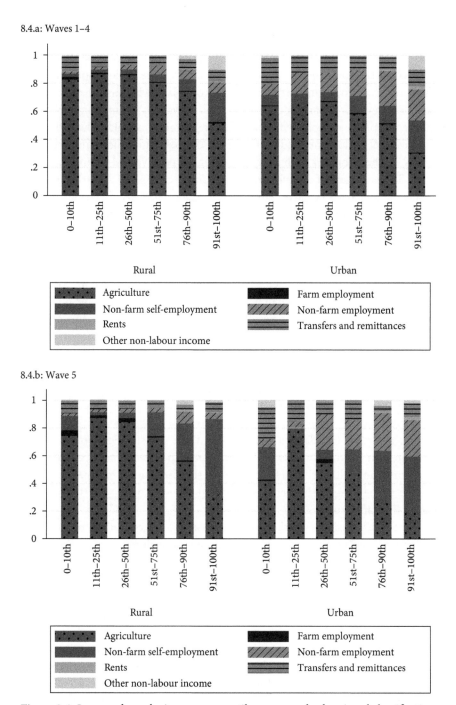

Figure 8.4 Income shares by income percentile ranges and urban/rural classification

Source: Authors' illustrations based on KHDS data

percentile it quadrupled (for rural areas the share grew from 2 per cent to 10 per cent and for urban areas from 7 per cent to 25 per cent).

Second, from a policy perspective it is most interesting to consider the factors over which the government has control. In Table 8.4 we explore how a positive change in access to key infrastructural factors correlates with diversification, number of income sources, and household income in Wave 5. The results are reported for the sample as a whole and separately for poorer households (those that had income levels below the median in the 1990s panel) to understand better the effects on the poor. For both samples, we find a positive and significant correlation between levels of diversification and gaining access to public transport and a daily market, and a negative significant correlation between diversification and gaining access to credit, and secondary school. Access to public transport and a daily market may have facilitated diversification into off-farm employment or self-employment. The negative relationship observed for the pooled sample between income diversification and improved access to credit facilities can be interpreted as evidence of credit being a factor that enables households to smooth consumption inter-temporally, rather than helping them diversify their income portfolios. A possible explanation for the negative correlation between access to secondary school and income diversification (columns 1 and 4) is that the school reform in Tanzania that happened just a few years before Wave 5 may have decreased household child labour and the number of available income sources (columns 2 and 5). Based on these results, infrastructural development appears to have had some effect on household income diversification strategies in the Kagera region over the survey period.

Last, regarding correlations with income, there is a significant positive relationship with improved access to electricity, post and telecommunication, public transport, and health facility. This correlation suggests that the income-generating abilities of the surveyed households improved simultaneously with the introduction of this infrastructure.

Third, we consider whether the increase in diversification observed in Figure 8.4—and particularly entrance into non-agricultural self-employment—among the poorer half of the households was driven by higher return opportunities or out of necessity (pull or push factors). Tables 8.5a and 8.5b present the results from a difference-in-differences estimation for both the poorer (a) and richer (b) halves, aiming to measure the effect of changes in diversification strategies. For each income activity a dummy variable indicates whether a household entered a new activity that generates income in Wave 5. In other words, the dummy is equal to 1 if in Waves 1–4 a household had on average no or less than 10 per cent of its income from a given source and in Wave 5 more than 10 per cent of its income from this source, and 0 otherwise. While this 'treatment' is endogenous, we do not claim causal inference but instead interpret the estimates as indications of a

Table 8.4 Correlations between household diversification measures and income and positive change in infrastructural factors

	Pooled sample			Poor households (income < median)		
	Income diversification index	No. of income sources	Log of household income PAE	Income diversification index	No. of income sources	Log of household income PAE
	(1)	(2)	(3)	(4)	(5)	(6)
Gained access to						
Credit	-0.051**	-0.063	0.106	-0.011	0.042	-0.014
	(0.025)	(0.066)	(0.187)	(0.041)	(0.107)	(0.294)
Electricity	0.005	-0.004	-0.134	0.014	0.030	-0.104
	(0.019)	(0.050)	(0.142)	(0.027)	(0.072)	(0.198)
Post and telecom	0.002	0.010	0.079	0.025	0.040	-0.153
	(0.020)	(0.054)	(0.151)	(0.031)	(0.080)	(0.221)
Public transport	0.064***	0.172***	0.277**	0.070**	0.183**	0.109
	(0.019)	(0.050)	(0.140)	(0.028)	(0.073)	(0.201)
Daily market	0.098*	0.304**	-0.109	0.072	0.190	-0.072
	(0.052)	(0.139)	(0.392)	(0.090)	(0.236)	(0.651)
Secondary school	-0.053**	-0.160***	-0.479***	-0.097***	-0.259***	-0.284
	(0.022)	(0.057)	(0.161)	(0.033)	(0.087)	(0.241)
Health facility	-0.010	-0.009	0.094	-0.005	0.025	0.078
	(0.018)	(0.049)	(0.137)	(0.027)	(0.070)	(0.194)
Observations	725	725	725	345	345	345

Note: Columns 1–3 show correlations for the full sample and columns 4–6 for the households below median income in the sample. Standard errors in parentheses.
*** p<0.01, ** p<0.05, * p<0.1.
Source: Authors' estimations based on KHDS data.

Table 8.5a Impact of households with below-median incomes changing their diversification strategies from 1990s to 2004 on their PAE income using DID

	(1)	(2)	(3)	(4)	(5)
Wave 5	-0.379***	-0.424***	-0.503***	-0.374***	-0.415***
	(0.058)	(0.058)	(0.061)	(0.058)	(0.057)
Enter	-0.110	-0.119	-0.012	0.118	0.247
	(0.137)	(0.102)	(0.067)	(0.106)	(0.262)
Wave 5 * **Enter**	-0.594**	0.328	0.590***	-0.510**	1.155**
	(0.288)	(0.221)	(0.145)	(0.227)	(0.536)
Observations	2,009	2,009	2,009	2,009	2,009
Controls	Yes	Yes	Yes	Yes	Yes
R-squared	0.075	0.072	0.080	0.073	0.075
Enter =	Entered agricultural employment	Entered non-agricultural employment	Entered non-agricultural self-employment	Started receiving transfers and remittances income	Started receiving other non-labour income
% share entering new activity (Enter=1)	3.27	5.62	14.4	5.18	0.83

Note: Outcome variable: Log of household income PAE. Changes to diversification in activities where there were less than fifteen observations (rents and agriculture) are not significant and not presented. Standard errors in parentheses. *** p<0.01, ** p<0.05, * p<0.1.
Source: Authors' calculations using DID regression based on KHDS data, Waves 1–5.

Table 8.5b Impact of households with above-median incomes changing their diversification strategies from 1990s to 2004 on their PAE income using DID

	(1)	(2)	(3)	(4)	(5)	(6)
Wave 5	-0.776***	-0.812***	-0.776***	-0.887***	-0.779***	-0.790***
	(0.060)	(0.061)	(0.060)	(0.063)	(0.062)	(0.060)
Enter	-0.185	0.087	-0.124	-0.014	0.070	0.257
	(0.200)	(0.132)	(0.292)	(0.081)	(0.103)	(0.201)
Wave 5 * **Enter**	-0.425	0.577**	-0.878	0.843***	-0.086	0.227
	(0.443)	(0.285)	(0.622)	(0.178)	(0.221)	(0.416)
Observations	1,986	1,986	1,986	1,986	1,986	1,986
R-squared	0.169	0.170	0.169	0.179	0.167	0.169
Enter =	Entered agricultural employment	Entered non-agricultural employment	Entered agricultural self-employment	Entered non-agricultural self-employment	Started receiving transfers and remittances income	Started receiving other non-labour income
Share entering	1.50	3.59	0.85	10.0	6.08	1.74

Note: Outcome variable: log of household income PAE. Standard errors in parentheses. *** p<0.01, ** p<0.05, * p<0.1.
Source: authors' calculations using DID regression based on KHDS data, Waves 1–5.

positive or negative relationship between entering different income activities and household income.

The first row in both tables shows that there is a significant negative time effect in all regressions, indicating that real incomes were lower in 2004 than in the 1990s. The second row ("Enter") indicates the selection bias, that is the income difference of households choosing to enter the various income activities. In Table 8.5a, column (2) the selection bias is negative. This estimate indicates that households that entered non-agricultural employment were on average poorer than those that did not; whereas, among the wealthier half (Table 8.5b), columns (2), (5) and (6) have a positive estimate: households entering farming and other non-labour income were on average richer than those that did not enter these activities. The third row ("Wave 5 * Enter") is the difference-in-differences estimate. This estimate is negative and significant in Table 8.5a for columns (1) and (4), indicating that households that entered agricultural employment or started receiving transfers or remittances had on average lower income in Wave 5 than other households among the population below the median income.

For the other income-generating activities, there are positive effects, but they are only significant in columns (3) and (5), meaning that households that entered non-agricultural self-employment (private businesses) or received non-labour income such as a pension, inheritance, or marriage payments were on average better off in Wave 5 than other households. For the wealthier half in Table 8.5b, columns (2) and (4) give a positive significant estimate, suggesting that households entering non-agricultural employment and starting a private business outside agriculture were on average better off than others.

Hence, it seems that for households that diversified their income source portfolio over time, there were two types of trajectory. There were those who were most likely pushed into employment or had to rely on transfers from migrated family members. These households did not experience income improvements over time from diversifying their portfolio on average. The other trajectory resulted (on average) in success stories among those who managed to enter non-farm self-employment (among both the richer and poorer halves) or start new enterprises outside agriculture (among the richer half).

8.6 Conclusion

Most rural households in developing countries, and especially in sub-Saharan Africa, have highly diversified portfolios. While several studies have examined the determinants of household income diversification in developing economies, the causes of household income diversification remain unclear. In particular, it remains an empirical issue whether household income diversification is driven by survival or accumulation motives. In this chapter, we first examined the determinants of income diversification for a panel of rural households in Tanzania for the period 1991–94. We then described diversification patterns in the long run and showed how improved access to certain infrastructure is linked with more income diversification and higher incomes. Then we looked at the effect of entrance into specific income-generation activities on changes in prosperity, using a difference-in-difference analysis.

One of our core findings is that that the diversification behaviour of households in rural Tanzania is on average driven by accumulation motives rather than by survival concerns. In other words, richer households are in a better position to diversify their incomes than relatively poor households. Although the greater income diversification capacity of relatively richer households observed in the 1990s persists in 2004, there are also positive impacts among poorer households. Not only did relatively richer households perform worse compared to their potential, based on predicted values, but also poorer households benefited more from entering off-farm self-employment and from relying on transfers and remittances. We further find that gaining access to infrastructure such as public transport is positively correlated with income diversification as well as with the improvement of income levels.

Our results call into question the pessimistic view of rural Africa that has shaped the academic discourse and policy discussions on household income diversification for many decades (for example, see Bryceson 2005: 48–61). In contrast to the widely held belief that household income diversification is a symptom of African de-peasantization and of a failing agricultural sector, our analysis suggests that household income diversification may well be a choice, and not a necessity, as both poorer and richer rural households use the capital that they have generated from agriculture to move into profitable non-agricultural activities. However, our study also suggests that asset and poverty traps may develop among those rural households that are not able to make the transition into such activities. In this case, specific policy measures may be needed to allow rural poor households to generate agricultural income and make the transition to diversified portfolios, including public investment in infrastructure and easier access to rural financial institutions and rural markets. This should be a particularly important consideration in a context where policy makers work on an equitable exit from the COVID-19 crisis.

References

Anderson, E., and P. Deshingkar (2005). 'Livelihood Diversification in Rural Andhra Pradesh, India'. In F. Ellis and H. A. Freeman (eds), *Rural Livelihoods and Poverty Reduction Policies*. London: Routledge, 55–74.

Banerjee, A. V., and E. Duflo (2007). 'The Economic Lives of the Poor'. *Journal of Economic Perspectives*, 21(1): 141–68. https://doi.org/10.1257/jep.21.1.141

Barrett, C. B., and T. Reardon (2000). 'Asset, Activity, and Income Diversification among African Agriculturalists: Some Practical Issues'. Working Paper 14734. Ithaca, NY: Cornell University, Department of Applied Economics and Management. https://doi.org/10.2139/ssrn.257344

Barrett, C. B., T. Reardon, and P. Webb (2001). 'Nonfarm Income Diversification and Household Livelihood Strategies in Rural Africa: Concepts, Dynamics and Policy Implications'. *Food Policy*, 26: 315–31. https://doi.org/10.1016/S0306-9192(01)00014-8

Basu, A., and R. Dimova (2020). 'Household Behavioral Preferences and the Child Labor–Education Trade-off: Framed Field Experimental Evidence from Ethiopia'. IZA DP 13011. Bonn: Institute of Labour Economics.

Basu, A., R. Dimova, M. Gbakou, and R. Viennet (2020). 'Parental Behavioural Preferences and Educational Progressions of Girls and Boys: Lab-in-the-Field Evidence from Rural Côte d'Ivoire'. Mimeo. Ithaca, NY: Cornell University; Manchester: Manchester University.

Beegle, K., J. De Weerdt, and S. Dercon (2011). 'Migration and Economic Mobility in Tanzania: Evidence from a Tracking Survey'. *Review of Economics and Statistics*, 93(3): 1010–33. https://doi.org/10.1162/REST_a_00105

Bryceson, D. (2005). 'Rural Livelihoods and Agrarian Change in Sub-Saharan Africa: Processes and Policies'. In F. Ellis and H.A. Freeman (eds), *Rural Livelihoods and Poverty Reduction Policies* (pp. 48–61). London: Routledge.

Davis, B., P. Winters, G. Carletto, K. Coarrubias, W. Quinones, A. Zezza, K. Stamoulis, C. Azzarri, and S. DiGiuseppe (2010). 'A Cross-country Comparison of Rural Income-Generating Activities'. *World Development*, 38(1): 48–63. https://doi.org/10.1016/j.worlddev.2009.01.003

de Bont, C., H. Komakech, and G. Veldwisch (2019). 'Neither Modern Nor Traditional: Farmer-led Irrigation Development in Kilimanjaro Region, Tanzania'. *World Development*, 116: 15–27. https://doi.org/10.1016/j.worlddev.2018.11.018

Dedehouanou, S. F. A., and J. McPeak (2020). 'Diversify More or Less? Household Income Generation Strategies and Food Security in Rural Nigeria'. *The Journal of Development Studies*, 56(3): 560–77. https://doi.org/10.1080/00220388.2019.1585814

Dercon, S. (1996). 'Risk, Crop Choice and Savings: Evidence from Tanzania'. *Economic Development and Cultural Change*, 44(3): 484–513. https://doi.org/10.1086/452229

Dercon, S., and P. Krishnan (1996). 'Income Portfolios in Rural Ethiopia and Tanzania: Choices and Constraints'. *Journal of Development Studies*, 55: 1–42.

De Weerdt, J. (2010). 'Moving out of Poverty in Tanzania: Evidence from Kagera'. *Journal of Development Studies*, 46(2): 331–49. https://doi.org/10.1080/00220380902974393

Dimova, R., and K. Sen (2010). 'Is Household Income Diversification a Means of Survival or a Means of Accumulation? Panel Data Evidence from Tanzania'. BWPI Working Paper 122. Manchester: Brooks World Poverty Institute, University of Manchester. https://papers.ssrn.com/sol3/papers.cfm?abstract_id=1688433 (accessed 21 December 2020).

Djido, A., and B. Shiferaw (2018). 'Patterns of Labor Productivity and Income Diversification: Empirical Evidence from Uganda and Nigeria'. *World Development*, 105: 416–27. https://doi.org/10.1016/j.worlddev.2017.12.026

Dumas, C., and X. Játiva (2020). 'Better Roads, Better Off? Evidence on Improving Roads in Tanzania'. FSES Working Paper 518. Faculty of Economics and Social Sciences, University of Freiburg/Fribourg, Switzerland.

Ellis, F. (1998). 'Household Strategies and Rural Livelihood Diversification'. *Journal of Development Studies*, 35(1): 1–38. https://doi.org/10.1080/00220389808422553

Ellis, F. (2000a). 'The Determinants of Rural Livelihood Diversification in Developing Countries'. *Journal of Agricultural Economics*, 51(2): 289–302. https://doi.org/10.1111/j.1477-9552.2000.tb01229.x.

Ellis, F. (2000b). *Rural Livelihoods and Diversity in Developing Countries*. Oxford: Oxford University Press.

Dercon, S. (2002). 'Income Risk, Coping Strategies, and Safety Nets'. In *The World Bank Research Observer* (17/2: pp. 141–66). Oxford: Oxford University Press.

Johny, J., B. Wichmann, and B. Swallow (2017). 'Characterizing Social Networks and their Effects on Income Diversification in Rural Kerala, India'. *World Development*, 94: 375–92. https://doi.org/10.1016/j.worlddev.2017.02.002

Joshy, P., A. Gulati, P. Birthal, and L. Tewari. (2004). 'Agriculture Diversification in South Asia: Patterns, Determinants and Policy Implications'. *Economic and Political Weekly*, 39(24): 2457–67.

Khan R., and O. Morrissey (2020). 'Income Diversification and Household Welfare in Tanzania 2008–2013'. WIDER Working Paper 2020/110. Helsinki: UNU-WIDER. https://doi.org/10.35188/UNU-WIDER/2020/867-2.

Litchfield, J., and T. McGregor (2008). 'Poverty in Kagera, Tanzania: Characteristics, Causes and Contributions'. PRUS Working Paper 42. Brighton: University of Sussex, Poverty Research Unit. http://citeseerx.ist.psu.edu/viewdoc/download?doi=10.1.1.177.4777&rep=rep1&type=pdf (accessed 14 December 2020).

Nyyssölä, M., P. Rattenhuber, G. Wright, E. Kisanga, and H. Barnes (forthcoming). 'A gendered analysis of the welfare impact of the tax–benefit systems in three sub-Saharan Africa countries'. WIDER Working Paper. Helsinki: UNU-WIDER.

Pesaran M. H., and Q. Zhou (2018). 'Estimation of Time-Invariant Effects in Static Panel Data Models'. *Econometric Reviews*, 37(10): 1137–71. https://doi.org/10.1080/07474938.2016.1222225

Reardon, T., C. Delgado, and P. Matlon (1992). 'Determinants and Effects of Income Diversification amongst Farm Households in Burkina Faso'. *Journal of Development Studies*, 28(2): 264–96. https://doi.org/10.1080/00220389208422232

Sen, K. (2002). 'Economic Reforms and Rural Livelihood Diversification in Tanzania'. LADDER Working Paper 12. London: Department for International Development. https://assets.publishing.service.gov.uk/media/57a08d4440f0b652dd001884/Ladder-wp12.pdf (accessed 14 December 2020).

Smith, B., and J. B. Wilson (1996). 'A Consumer's Guide to Evenness Indices'. *Oikos*, 76(1): 70–82. https://doi.org/10.2307/3545749

9

Gender disparities in financial inclusion in Tanzania

Maureen Were, Maureen Odongo, and Caroline Israel

9.1 Introduction

The role of financial inclusion in reducing poverty and promoting economic growth and development is increasingly acknowledged. The belief that access to quality financial services can lift the poor out of poverty and promote sustainability of household welfare in developing countries has motivated widespread adoption of policies and measures aimed at increasing financial inclusion (Ardic et al. 2011; Pande et al. 2012; World Bank 2014). These include leveraging digital financial technology to promote access to affordable financial services such as payments, transfers, savings, credit, and insurance. Furthermore, financial empowerment has been proven to increase female participation in community decision-making, improve well-being and combat socio-economic marginalization (World Bank 2015; 2020a).[1]

Digital financial services (DFS) have been the main driver of financial inclusion. Modern technological developments and adoption of DFS such as mobile money, Internet or mobile banking, and electronic payment systems have increased efficiency in service delivery and lowered transactions, thereby increasing outreach to the poor (Sahay et al. 2020; World Bank 2020a). In particular, mobile financial services enabled by mobile phone technology and financial innovations have tremendously transformed the financial landscape in Africa, leading to increased outreach to rural areas, where the majority of the population not only live but were previously excluded (Nguena 2019; Pazarbasioglu et al. 2020).

Despite these developments, there still exist gender gaps in financial inclusion. Unequal social relations and unequal opportunities create gender-specific barriers to financial access, which in most cases have resulted in missed opportunities for growth and persistent inequalities (Sahay et al. 2020; World Bank 2008). The shift towards digital technology following the outbreak of COVID-19 pandemic in 2020 has provided fundamental lessons regarding the role of DFS in promoting

[1] The authors are grateful to Isaac Mwangi, Oliver Morrissey, and Joseph Semboja for their insightful and valuable comments.

Maureen Were, Maureen Odongo, and Caroline Israel, *Gender disparities in financial inclusion in Tanzania.*
In: *Sustaining Tanzania's Economic Development.* Edited by: Oliver Morrissey, Joseph Semboja, and Maureen Were,
Oxford University Press. © UNU-WIDER (2024). DOI: 10.1093/oso/9780192885746.003.0009

economic resilience during crises. However, it has also exposed the deep digital divide and missed opportunities, particularly for women and rural populations (Agur et al. 2020; GSMA 2020b; OECD 2020; World Bank 2020a). Going forward, DFS and digital technologies will play a more prominent role not only in accessing a variety of financial products and services, but as a strategy for promoting a digital economy and enhancing economic resilience of households and businesses. Although Tanzania's state of digitalization is still low by global standards, it is evolving rapidly, propelled by the relatively strong momentum (Chakravorti et al. 2020).[2]

Tanzania has witnessed a notable expansion in access to formal financial services, from about 58 per cent in 2013 to 65 per cent by 2017, largely driven by mobile money services. The latest FinScope Tanzania 2023 survey report that was launched recently shows access to formal financial services increased to 76 per cent in 2023.[3] The proportion of the rural adult population living within a five-kilometre radius of a financial access point increased from 66 per cent in 2017 to 78 per cent in 2017. However, despite concerted efforts to enhance financial inclusion in Tanzania, women still lag behind in both access to and use of formal financial services. This is in spite of the important role women play in poverty alleviation and household welfare. Although women account for slightly over 50 per cent of Tanzania's population, challenges regarding their access to and use of financial services still remain. Yet, there is a paucity of in-depth studies focusing on gender disparities in financial services in Tanzania. There is need for a better understanding of gender dynamics and barriers to financial inclusion in the context of the changing dynamics and technological innovations.

This chapter analyses gender disparities in access to formal financial services, focusing on the traditional bank-based and mobile money services as the main modes of formal financial inclusion in Tanzania. Furthermore, we also analyse gender disparities in saving and borrowing, which are key indicators of the extent of utilization of financial services. Both descriptive and regression analyses are employed. The main source of data is Tanzania's FinScope surveys,[4] complemented by other sources such as the World Bank's Global Findex data.

The analysis shows 60.7 per cent of women compared with 70.1 per cent of men had access to formal financial services in 2017, leading to a gender gap of 9.4 percentage points. 30.3 per cent of women were financially excluded, while 9.0 per cent relied on informal financial services. However, according to the recent FinScope Tanzania 2023 report, the gender gap narrowed in 2023, with

---

[2] Based on the Digital Intelligence Index scores for 2020, Tanzania was ranked number 82 and 31 under current state and momentum of digitalization respectively, out of the ninety countries sampled.

[3] The analysis in this chapter is, however, largely based on FinScope Tanzania 2017 survey, since by the time FinScope Tanzania 2023 survey report was being launched the chapter had already been completed and the final steps of publishing the the book commenced.

[4] The findings and conclusions expressed in this chapter are entirely those of the authors and do not necessarily represent the views of FinScope Tanzania. The analysis is largely based on FinScope Tanzania survey for 2017.

the proportion of women who are financially excluded declining to 19.4 per cent. Mobile-based financial services remain the most widely used and preferred mode of access to and use of formal financial services across genders. The uptake of mobile financial services increased from 50 per cent in 2013 to 60 per cent in 2017. The empirical results show that even after controlling for a variety of factors such as education, income, and employment, women—especially married women—are less likely to access mobile-based and bank-based financial services compared with men. Additionally, women are less likely to save and borrow compared with men. Constraints on financial inclusion include insufficient income, limited financial literacy, and limited access to digital financial facilities such as smartphones. The persistent gender disparities reflect underlying inequalities and constraints in both access to and use of digital financial channels such as mobile phones, electronic cards, and Internet, by which DFS are enabled. As Tanzania continues to embrace a digital economy, these disparities are likely to hamper women's ability to tap into opportunities or maximize benefits arising from the digital revolution and increased adoption of DFS, which could in turn worsen gender inequalities. Measures to close gender gaps in access to and use of DFS are therefore vital in boosting financial inclusion and enhancing the resilience of the economy to withstand shocks and future crises, especially at the household level.

The rest of the chapter is organized as follows. Section 9.2 provides an overview of the relevant literature, while Section 9.3 describes the empirical strategy and data. Section 9.4 provides an exploratory analysis of financial inclusion in Tanzania. Section 9.5 presents and discusses the empirical findings. Section 9.6 provides conclusions and policy insights.

9.2 Literature overview

Theories of development economics suggest that financial development is an integral component of poverty alleviation and economic growth. The link between finance and growth is mainly through saving and capital accumulation (Goldsmith 1969; McKinnon 1973), as well as technological innovation (Grossman and Helpman 1991). According to Levine (2005), financial systems facilitate economic growth through mobilization of savings and pooling resources, facilitation of information-sharing, diversification, management of risks and the exchange of goods and services.

Economic agents continuously engage in stimulative innovative activities and make technological advances to gain a profitable market niche (King and Levine 1993). However, Geenwood and Jovanovic (1990) showed that in the initial stages of financial sector development, there exists a high level of income inequality, which declines as more people gain access to the system. The main constraints include financial market frictions such as credit constraints and asymmetric information, which restrict the poor's access to investment opportunities (Berger and

Udell 2006). In addition, lack of a legal and regulatory framework, information and infrastructure undermines the scale and efficiency of finance systems (Honohan 2004). These constraints not only prevent the poor from exploiting investment opportunities, but also slow down aggregate growth by keeping capital from flowing to its highest-value use (Greenwood and Jovanovic 1990; Honohan, 2004).

Earlier empirical research focusing on traditional banking services mainly relied on supply-side bank-level indicators, such as the number of bank branches and automated teller machines (ATMs), loan and account deposits, the requirements and charges for opening a bank account, and the credit to the private sector, among other variables, as measures of financial outreach (Beck et al. 2006; 2007; Honohan 2004; 2007). Findings from these studies revealed that barriers to financial inclusion arose mainly from banks' rational decisions based on their business models, the regulatory environment, as well as economic policies. However, these indicators had limited gender-disaggregated information on the extent of financial inclusion of the poor and other marginalized populations (World Bank 2014).

With increased availability of financial inclusion surveys, empirical analyses that use demand-side survey databases such as the Global Findex Database, FinScope, and FinAccess surveys to assess demand-side drivers of financial inclusion have been on the rise (Allen et al. 2016; Aterido et al. 2013; Demirguc-Kunt and Klapper 2012; Demirguc-Kunt et al. 2014, 2018; Ellis et al. 2010; Fanta and Mutsonziwa 2016). Some of the findings from these studies have shown that access to and use of financial services is not gender neutral. There exist disparities between men and women, influenced by both demand-side and supply-side constraints. These include legal and regulatory constraints (Chakraborty 2014; Delechat et al. 2018; Demirguc-Kunt et al. 2013), sociocultural and institutional barriers (Chakraborty 2014; Coleman 2002), and socio-economic factors (Botric and Broz 2017; Delechat et al. 2018; Naidoo and Hilton 2006; Ouma et al. 2017).

Studies undertaken in the context of Africa include one by Fanta and Mutsonziwa (2016), who analysed the financial inclusion of women in Southern African Development Community (SADC) countries based on panel data, with ownership of a bank account as a proxy for access to financial inclusion, and access to credit and saving as proxies for usage. The findings showed that a gender gap prevailed even in countries with the highest levels of financial inclusion, with a wider gender gap in account usage than in account ownership. The main barriers to women's financial inclusion included remote bank branches, lack of finances and financial literacy. Aterido et al. (2013) analysed gender differences in the use of formal and informal financial services using FinScope and FinAccess surveys for the period 2004–09 across nine countries in Southern and East Africa, including Tanzania. Oaxaca-Blinder decomposition was used to assess gender dynamics in the use of financial services, in an addition to multivariate panel data and univariate country-specific regressions. The findings revealed that barriers to financial inclusion arose more from demand-side constraints than supply-side constraints. In particular, the lower use of formal financial services among women was explained by their lower levels of income, education, and employment status. Furthermore, women were found to be 5.8 per cent more likely on average to use informal financial services than men.

The gender gap in education and literacy levels affects women's financial knowledge and their uptake of technological skills that can boost awareness and use of modern financial technology (GSMA 2019; 2020a). In 2017, the primary education completion rate for women in sub-Saharan Africa (SSA) was 66.7 per cent, four percentage points lower than for men, while women's literacy rate was 52.1 per cent compared with 69.4 per cent for men. International Labour Organization (ILO) (2018) revealed lower labour force participation for women in SSA at 64.7 per cent, compared with 74 per cent for men, mainly due to lower education and therefore, lower earnings (Botric and Broz 2017; Kabubo-Mariara 2003). All these factors hinder the usage of formal financial services, such as savings, which is lower for women at 11 per cent compared to 19 per cent for men (Demirguc-Kunt et al. 2018). Legal barriers and regulatory requirements for opening and operating a formal account, including the need for proper identification documents and collateral can also act as a deterrent (Maina 2018). Similarly, social-cultural barriers that hinder account ownership, inheritance, and limited labour force participation limit women's access and use of financial services (Demirguc-Kunt et al. 2013).

Ellis et al. (2010) examined the relationship between financial inclusion, household investment, and growth in Kenya and Tanzania. Their study found that key barriers to the access of financial services included both supply-side and demand-side constraints, such as exorbitant bank charges, inaccessibility of financial services, qualifying requirements, and documentation. Similarly, focusing on Tanzania, studies by Alliance for Financial Inclusion (2016) and Idris (2018a; 2018b) revealed that inappropriate services and inefficiencies in delivery channels were the main supply-side constraints, while information asymmetries, lack of documentation, irregular income patterns, women's relatively lower incomes, and low financial literacy were the main demand-side constraints. In addition, lack of a legal and regulatory framework, and delays in rolling out a national identification system hindered contract enforcement. Ndanshau and Njau (2021) empirically assessed demand-side determinants of financial inclusion in Tanzania without specifically analysing gender dynamics. Based on FinScope Tanzania survey for 2013, Mndolwa and Alhassan (2020) found a lower likelihood of women saving at a formal financial institution. However, the role of DFS was not considered.

More recent studies following the COVID-19 global pandemic show increased dependence on digital platforms for a variety of activities such as work, learning, healthcare, shopping, and entertainment. Yet various hurdles including limited access, affordability, lack of education, and inherent biases and socio-cultural norms still curtail women's ability to benefit from the opportunities offered by the digital transformation (GSMA 2020a; 2020b; OECD 2020). According to the OECD (2018), girls' low enrolment rates in science, information and communication technologies, coupled with their limited use of digital tools, may widen gender gaps and inequalities. While digital technology provided an armoury for the COVID-19 response in Tanzania, the affordability of smartphones, electricity connectivity, and transaction fees remained a hindrance to women's access and use (World Bank 2020b).

Although the number of studies that examine demand-side factors using financial inclusion survey databases is growing, few studies have delved into analysing gender gaps, especially in DFS in the context of Tanzania. This study makes a contribution to the literature not only by utilizing relatively more recent databases to analyse gender disparities in financial inclusion in Tanzania, but also uses multiple indicators that encompass access to and use of both the traditional bank-based financial services, and DFS such as mobile money.

9.3 Methodology and data

9.3.1 Data

The main source of data is Tanzania's FinScope surveys, complemented by the World Bank's Global Findex Database on financial inclusion and Global Systems for Mobile Association (GSMA) data. The FinScope surveys are national surveys representative of individuals aged sixteen years or older. They were conducted in 2006, 2009, 2013, and 2017.[5] These surveys provide a rich set of information regarding financial services, including demand indicators for formal and informal financial services, as well as key information on individual characteristics such as age, sex, marital status, and education. The empirical analysis was conducted using data from the FinScope survey of 2017. The survey comprised a sample of 9459 respondents.

The FinScope surveys use four 'access strands' to denote respondents' levels of financial inclusion: (i) use banks; (ii) have or use non-bank formal products; (iii) use only informal mechanisms; (iv) are excluded. Respondents are ranked according to their highest level of usage. Formal bank institutions are those supervised by a financial services regulator. Non-bank formal financial institutions are those with some formal supervision, but not by a financial services regulator. This category includes savings and credit cooperative societies, microfinance institutions, remittance companies, and mobile money. The informal segment includes small, usually community-based organizations, such as saving or credit groups. The totally unserved or excluded category covers everyone else and includes people who may use non-monetary means to save, borrow, or transfer money, that is, friends and family, or saving at home or in-kind.

People who are formally financially included are individuals who have or use financial products and services provided by a financial service provider that is

---

[5] The latest survey was conducted and launched recently in 2023.

regulated or officially supervised. Individuals considered to be informally included are those who use financial mechanisms not provided by a regulated or supervised financial institution. The financially excluded are individuals who use no financial mechanisms and rely only on themselves, family, or friends for saving, borrowing, and remitting, with their transactions being cash-based or in-kind.

The Global Findex Database is compiled by the World Bank using surveys of adults aged fifteen and above in over 140 economies worldwide based on a sample of 1,000 respondents. The database has additional information on how people make and receive payments, and constraints on account ownership. This information was used to complement our analysis of the FinScope surveys.

The GSMA has a mobile money programme, which collects and analyses industry data based on annual surveys and a range of quantitative information about the performance of mobile financial services. The data is used to track progress and provide insights into the performance of mobile financial service deployments that target unbanked and underserved customers globally. We largely utilized this database when assessing gender disparities in access to digital platforms that facilitate access to DFS.

9.3.2 Methodology

Both exploratory and regression analyses are employed to examine gender disparities in financial inclusion. Descriptive analysis was used to explore gender variations, based on various indicators of financial services. In line with similar studies, a binary regression model was used to empirically assess the role of gender in influencing one's likelihood of being financially included. Specifically, a logistic regression model enabled us to establish the relationship between whether one is financially included or not, and a set of predictor variables modelled on a logit-transformed probability.

The logistic regression model is specified by the following function:

$$logit\,(\pi_i) = log\left(\frac{\pi_i}{1 - \pi_i}\right) = \alpha_0 + \alpha_1 x_{i1} + \alpha_2 x_{i2} + \dots + \alpha_p x_{ip} + \varepsilon_i \tag{1}$$

Let

$$f_i = \alpha_0 + \alpha_1 x_{i1} + \alpha_2 x_{i2} + \dots + \alpha_p x_{ip} + \varepsilon_i \tag{2}$$

Equation (1) can be transformed into probabilities by the following:

$$\pi_i = \frac{e^{f_i}}{1 + e^{f_i}} \tag{3}$$

where π_i is the probability that the ith person is financially included; f_i is the binary outcome for the ith person, that is, 1 if financially included, and 0 otherwise; $x_{i1,}$ $x_{i2}...x_{ip}$ is a set of explanatory variables including the gender variable; p is the number of explanatory variables; and e is the exponential term.

The logistic regression model estimates the parameter values α_0, $\alpha_1...\alpha_p$ via the maximum likelihood method. The model was used to assess the likelihood of women being financially included or excluded, while controlling for a variety of other factors that are likely to determine access to financial services. These include education, age, income, marital status, and mobile phone ownership. The dependent variable was defined using access indicators for the two main forms of formal financial services in Tanzania, that is, access to bank-based services and mobile phone financial services. For robustness, the estimations were conducted separately for each. Furthermore, we also analysed factors that influence the extent of usage of financial services based on two key indicators, that is, saving and credit access through borrowing.

The dependent variables are defined as follows. Access to banking services is a binary variable coded 1 for all respondents who had taken up or indicated that they used banking services, for example, making payments, borrowing, and saving—also classified as banked—and 0 otherwise. Access to mobile financial services takes the value of 1 for all respondents who indicated that they had or used mobile money services such as receiving and sending money, making payments, etc. The saving variable is coded as 1 if the respondent indicated having saved or put money aside for this purpose in the previous twelve months, and 0 otherwise. Access to credit equals 1 if the respondent had borrowed in the previous twelve months, and 0 otherwise.

The explanatory variables are defined as follows:

- Gender, which is the key variable of interest, equals one if the respondent is female, and zero otherwise (i.e. if the respondent is male). We hypothesize that women are less likely to access or use financial services, especially formal financial services, compared with men.
- Education equals one if the respondent completed primary education or above, and zero otherwise. The latter includes respondents with no formal education, only pre-primary education, or only some primary education.
- Age is the number of years of age of each respondent. As a standard practice, age squared is included to capture the non-linear relationship between age and financial inclusion.
- Income is a dummy variable, equal to one if the respondent reports having an income of their own that they can spend as they wish, and zero otherwise. This variable was used as a proxy in the absence of a suitable variable capturing actual income.

- Employment status describes whether a respondent is formally employed, that is, receives a salary, in which case the variable equals one, and zero otherwise.
- Household size is the number of dependants aged sixteen years or older in a household.
- Marital status equals one if the respondent is married and zero if single or divorced.
- Access to mobile phone equals one if the respondent indicated owning or having access to a mobile phone. Ownership of, or some form of access to a mobile handset is the first step towards accessing mobile financial services. Access to a mobile phone, especially a smartphone, also influences one's use of banking services as more and more banks incorporate Internet banking.

9.4 Exploratory analysis

There has been a notable expansion in financial inclusion, largely as a result of the increase in demand for non-bank financial services, particularly mobile phone-based financial services. FinScope Tanzania surveys data show access to formal financial services increased from about 16 per cent in 2009 to 65.4 per cent in 2017, mainly driven by the uptake of mobile money services, which increased from 50 per cent to 60 per cent between 2013 and 2017 (Figure 9.1). The recently released FinScope Tanzania 2023 report indicates formal financial inclusion increased to 76 per cent in 2017. On the other hand, the penetration of traditional banking remained low, with only 16.7 per cent and 22.2 per cent of the adult population having access to commercial bank services in 2017 and 2023, respectively.

Mobile money has evolved beyond the simple money transfer, to services such as payments, online deposits, savings, and access to credit, among other services. Access to banking services can be made conveniently without a physical visit to the bank or utility service provider. The expansion of mobile money services is consistent with the observed increase in the number of mobile money agents, which more than doubled from 238,461 in 2014 to 560,043 in 2019, while active mobile phone users increased from 13.5 million to 24.0 million over the same period (Bank of Tanzania 2020). Access to mobile phone handsets provided the impetus to financial inclusion through mobile money, thereby enabling the majority of the population to access formal financial services and products. The proportion of the adult population that relied on informal financial services declined to 6.7 per cent in 2017, down from 16 per cent in 2013, while that of the financially excluded increased marginally to 28 per cent from 27 per cent over the same period.

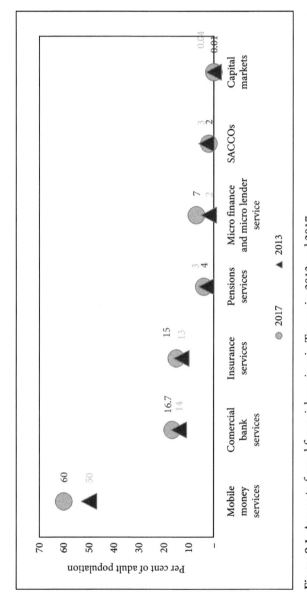

Figure 9.1 Access to formal financial services in Tanzania, 2013 and 2017

Source: Authors' illustration based on data from FinScope Tanzania (2017).

Increased adoption of DFS is a phenomenon observed not only in Tanzania but generally across the other East Africa Community (EAC) countries.[6] However, there are still gender gaps in access to and use of financial services, though for countries like Kenya, the gap has been narrowing—85.6 per cent of men had access to formal financial services compared with 80.4 per cent of women in 2019. The gender gap narrowed further to 4.2 per cent in 2021 (for a comparison across EAC countries see Were et al. 2021). Based on Tanzania's FinScope survey for 2017, 60.7 per cent of women compared with 70.1 per cent of men had access to formal financial services, leading to a gender gap of 9.4 percentage points (Figure 9.2). Nine per cent of women had access to informal financial services, while nearly a third (30.3 per cent) were financially excluded. However, the latter is noted to have declined to 19.4 per cent in 2023,which implies a narrower gender gap. The gap between rural and urban access to formal financial services was 25 percentage points in 2017, with 57 per cent of the rural adult population accessing formal financial services compared with 82 per cent of the urban population. Thus, the financially excluded were mainly women and those residing in rural areas. In terms of age distribution, the majority of those accessing formal financial services fell into the 25–65 age bracket (Figure 9.2). This age group is considered to be of working age, and therefore able to afford formal financial services.

Gender disparities in access to formal financial services are reflected in gender gaps in ownership and use of digital platforms. For instance, GSMA (2019) report shows Tanzania's gender gap in mobile ownership was 11 percentage points, with 77 per cent of women compared with 86 per cent of men owning mobile phones. The gender gap was lower in Kenya, with mobile phone penetration among women at 86 per cent compared with 91 per cent among men. Tanzania's gender gap in mobile Internet was 18 percentage points, with only 17 per cent of women compared with 35 per cent of men using mobile Internet. The Global Findex data for 2017 depicts a similar pattern. The percentage of men and percentage of women who reported having used a mobile phone or the Internet to access an account among the EAC countries was higher in Kenya (77 per cent and 68 per cent), followed by Uganda (57 per cent and 38 per cent), Tanzania (40 per cent and 33 per cent), and Rwanda (34 per cent and 24 per cent).

FinScope Tanzania (2017) shows mobile money agents were the most important or preferred financial services provider for both men and women. However, fewer women (52.8 per cent) compared with men (63.4 per cent) relied on mobile money agents. Saving groups were the second most important source for women to meet their financial needs: 23.1 per cent of women preferred this source, compared with only 9.9 per cent of men. Moreover, only 7.9 per cent of women relied on banks as

---

[6] The EAC is comprised of Kenya, Rwanda, Tanzania, Uganda, Burundi, and South Sudan, which joined much later in 2016. The Republic of Congo joined recently in July 2022. Reference to EAC is mainly with respect to the first four countries.

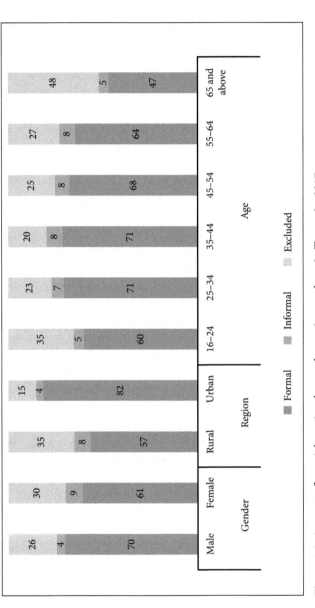

Figure 9.2 Access to financial services by gender, region, and age in Tanzania, 2017

Source: Authors' illustration based on data from FinScope Tanzania (2017).

a key provider of financial services, compared with almost double that figure for men at 14.2 per cent.

Despite the notable progress in access to financial services, usage especially by women is comparatively low. For instance, based on Global Findex databases, the proportion of people who saved in a financial institution in Tanzania was not only low but also decreased between 2011 and 2017, particularly for women—from 11 per cent in 2011 to 4 per cent in 2017 (Demirguc-Kunt et al. 2018).

There are various factors that still constrain access to and effective utilization of financial services. Global Findex data for 2017 shows lack of sufficient income was the main obstacle for not having a financial account, as indicated by at least 80 per cent of respondents (Table 9.1). Other constraints included affordability (financial services are too expensive) of financial institutions, and the lack of necessary documentation. The main reasons for not having a financial account were more or else similar across EAC countries, and hence not necessarily unique to Tanzania (Table 9.1). The results are not surprising, given that nearly 70 per cent of the population reside in rural areas and engaged in either agricultural activities or other informal work, with low or irregular returns.

Figure 9.3 provides a summary of various barriers with specific reference to the use of mobile money services, based on the 2017 FinScope survey. The topmost reason for not using mobile money services among both men and women was that they did not need those services, with a slightly higher proportion of men (38.2 per cent) compared with women (35.3 per cent). The second was lack of access to a smartphone, with a higher percentage of women (24.1 per cent) compared with

Table 9.1 Reasons for not having an account (% of respondents without a financial institution account), 2017

	Kenya, %	Rwanda, %	Tanzania, %	Uganda, %
Financial institutions are too far away	33	6	35	42
Financial services are too expensive	40	12	39	53
Lack of necessary documentation	30	10	30	28
Lack of trust in financial institutions	22	3	11	25
Religious reasons	4	2	3	6
Insufficient funds	81	94	80	83
Someone in the family has an account	12	6	6	14
No need for financial services	2	0	1	1

Source: authors' compilation based on Global Findex Database (Demirguc-Kunt et al. 2018).

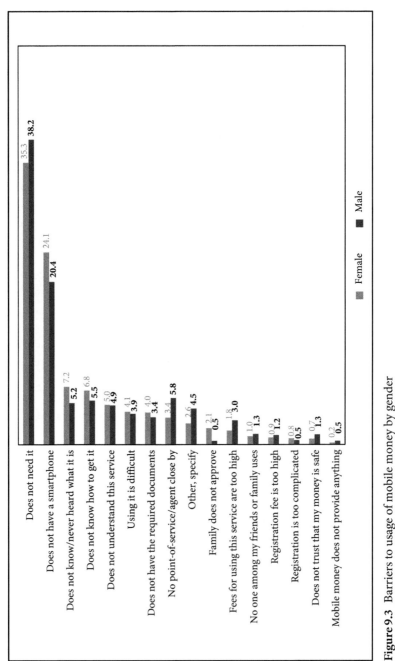

Figure 9.3 Barriers to usage of mobile money by gender

Source: Authors' illustration based on data from FinScope Tanzania (2017).

men (20.4 per cent). Other barriers to access, particularly for women, included lack of financial literacy or access to financial information (they did not know or had never heard about mobile money, and they did not know how to get it), required documents, and lack of approval by the family, which points to women's relatively limited (financial) independence. Although the proportion of women who did not understand the service or found it difficult to use was slightly higher, there was little difference between women and men in this regard. The proportion of respondents who reported a lack of family approval was higher among women (2.1 per cent) compared with men (0.5 per cent).

Given that mobile-phone-based financial services are the main gateway to formal financial services, lack of access to mobile phones, especially smartphones, is a key constraint (GSMA 2019; 2020b). The use of smartphones allows access to a variety of services such as mobile banking, Internet banking, and other DFS including savings, credit, and deposits. Internet use on a smartphone is typically much richer, but affordability remains a key barrier, especially among women, due to their relatively lower incomes and limited financial autonomy to purchase smartphones of their own (FinScope Tanzania 2017; GSMA 2020b; World Bank 2020b). In rural Tanzania, where the majority of the population reside, access to smartphones is relatively lower compared with urban areas (World Bank 2020b). Moreover, the gender gap in access to smartphones is persistent across income groups, with fewer women having access to smartphones. Given the strong link between smartphone ownership and digital inclusion, this limits women's access to formal financial services.

The affordability of mobile Internet data also matters. Costly mobile Internet data limits the use of DFS, including Internet-based financial services, credit, and savings services. The use of the Internet via mobile data is relatively expensive in Tanzania compared to other EAC countries (World Bank 2020b). In addition, education and financial literacy skills may also reduce women's ownership of smartphones, since women tend to use fewer services than men, and prefer to make and receive video calls. Literacy skills remain a major challenge: 72 per cent of Tanzanians can read and write in Kiswahili, compared with only 27 per cent who can read and write in English, yet English remains the main mode of communication for most formal financial products, and indeed for digital applications (FinScope Tanzania 2017). Women are often less confident about independently acquiring the digital skills required to use a mobile phone and are more concerned about the consequences of making mistakes (GSMA 2019). This hinders both the uptake and use of formal financial services. Video calling for example, not only presents lower hurdles to women, who are less confident in using the Internet, but is also more socially accepted as a means of remaining in touch with family members. Men on the other hand are conversely more likely to browse the Internet, download and use apps (GSMA 2017). More recent digital technologies, such as digital identification, biometrics, and big data analytics have factored in end-user information, giving rise to new business models and customized products, which have lowered the costs and increased the speed, transparency, security, and availability of more tailored financial services. However, adoption in Tanzania is still low (World Bank 2020a; 2020b).

The outbreak of the COVID-19 pandemic in 2020 posed many challenges that continue to be felt. Although Tanzania did not impose lockdown measures, there were adverse effects on various groups, especially on micro, small and medium enterprises (MSMEs), and other vulnerable groups such as women and communities in the rural areas (AFI 2021). Most MSMEs depend on imported goods from countries that imposed restrictions. Furthermore, the pandemic had a negative impact on the tourism sector, which has interlinkages with other domestic sectors such as air transport, hotel business, beverages and food, and retail trade. Consequently, both rich and poor households suffered a significant decrease in income (Henseler et al. 2022). Moreover, at the onset of the pandemic, the government temporarily imposed some basic measures to slow down the spread of the virus, such as restrictions on physical movements and gatherings, which had an impact on business activities. For instance, women-owned businesses experienced greater loss of profit and income, given their informal nature. While the restrictions on movement limited the usage of conventional banking institutions, DFS via mobile money transactions increased (Bank of Tanzania 2021). Thus, most households and businesses including MSMEs have continued using mobile phones to make payments for goods and services, access microloans and transfer money, among others.

The COVID-19 crisis intensified the need to promote innovations in financial technologies in order to increase access to and usage of financial services in Tanzania. These measures present great potential, especially to the MSMEs and the unbanked households (the majority being women), to embrace DFS and promote resilience to shocks. That notwithstanding, women risk being left out due to the various constraints including limited use of and access to digital financial platforms.

9.5 Empirical analysis and discussion

The empirical results of the estimated logit model for access to formal financial services, that is, mobile financial services and banking services, are reported in columns 1 and 2 respectively in Table 9.2. Columns 1a and 2a show the basic results without interaction terms, while columns 1b and 2b show the findings when the gender variable is brought into interaction with marital status. The results are

Table 9.2 Empirical results for financial access to mobile money and bank services

Variable	Mobile money		Bank services	
	1a	1b	2a	2b
Constant	−3.51***	−3.57***	−7.11***	−7.13***
	(−9.50)	(−10.9)	(−16.0)	(−16.1)
Age	0.066***	0.060***	0.057***	0.052***
	(8.22)	(7.48)	(4.51)	(4.51)
Age squared	−0.0008***	−0.0008***	−0.0006***	−0.0006***
	(−8.82)	(−8.38)	(−3.88)	(−3.88)
Marital status	−0.187***	0.143*	−0.026	0.172
	(−3.70)	(1.75)	(−0.35)	(1.59)
Education	1.25***	1.25***	2.08***	2.08***
	(24.0)	(24.0)	(15.5)	(15.5)
Female	−0.431***	−0.083	−0.47***	−0.221*
	(−9.0)	(−1.02)	(−6.89)	(−1.83)
Income	0.21***	0.21***	0.62***	0.62***
	(4.15)	(3.98)	(7.09)	(7.01)
No. of dependants	−0.053**	−0.052**	0.029	0.029
	(−2.74)	(−2.71)	(1.08)	(1.09)
Mobile phone access	2.14***	2.14***	1.89***	1.89***
	(17.7)	(17.6)	(5.88)	(5.86)
Salaried	1.53***	1.51***	2.49***	2.48***
	(10.7)	(10.6)	(24.9)	(24.8)
Female*marital status		−0.535***		−0.380***
		(−5.20)		(−2.53)
Pseudo R squared	0.16	0.17	0.22	0.22
No. of observations	9,456	9,456	9,456	9,456

Note: Statistical z-values in brackets. ***, **, and * denote p-values of <1 per cent, <5 per cent, and <10 per cent respectively.
Source: authors' analysis based on data from FinScope Tanzania (2017).

based on a robust estimate of variance.[7] The coefficient for the gender variable is negative and highly statistically significant for both mobile money services and banking services (columns 1a and 2a). In other words, females are less likely to use formal financial services compared with their male counterparts. However, the highly significant interaction term between being female and marital status implies that married women are the most likely to be excluded from access to formal financial services (columns 1b and 2b).[8] This may be due to a variety of factors, such as

[7] A robust variance estimator is used to ensure that results are robust to model misspecification errors and heteroscedasticity.

[8] Although we do not report the results here, for further analysis we examined the impact of the gender variable when it is brought into interaction with education, and we found a positive but insignificant effect. In other words, the fact that one is female and has primary school education or above does not

having limited resources of their own amidst numerous family demands such as childcare, as well as other intra-household relations which the data do not allow us to explore. Furthermore, the now positive coefficient for marital status suggests that unlike married women, married men are more likely to utilize mobile money services (column 1b). Thus, the empirical results provide further evidence of gender disparities in access to formal financial services in Tanzania. The results are consistent with similar findings in the literature (e.g. Demirguc-Kunt et al. 2013; 2014; Lotto 2018).

The other variables have the expected signs. In particular, education, mobile phone access, and formal employment (i.e. whether one is salaried) have a highly significant positive and bigger impact on the use of both mobile and bank financial services. The impact of education on banking services is nearly twice the impact on use of or access to mobile financial services. Similarly, income proxied by whether one has money for one's own use is a key determinant of financial inclusion. For robustness, estimating the equations using ownership of property as a proxy for income yielded similar results. Given that women rank lower in both education and income, this further constrains their access to formal financial services. While the number of adult dependants in a household has a statistically significant negative impact on the use of mobile financial services, the impact on banking services is not statistically significant.

The logit model results for the likelihood of saving and borrowing are reported in Table 9.3. The results show that women are less likely to save and borrow relative to men, even after we control for a variety of factors. Employment, education, income, mobile phone access, age, and marital status are the key factors that determine the likelihood of saving and borrowing. On the other hand, the higher the number of adult dependants, the lower the likelihood of saving or borrowing.

The main reasons respondents gave for borrowing were to cater for medical expenses (24.1 per cent), living expenses (23.1 per cent), emergencies other than medical (14 per cent), starting or expanding a business (10.1 per cent), farming expenses (8.6 per cent), education or school fees (6.1 per cent), and others (14 per cent). The main reasons given for saving were mainly to cater for living expenses when one did not have an income (46.7 per cent), emergencies other than medical (18.5 per cent), medical expenses (9.1 per cent), education or school fees (5.5 per cent), and others (20.2 per cent). Thus, it is clear from the analysis that very few people borrow or save for business purposes; they largely do so to cater for living and medical expenses.

The majority of the adult population still prefer to use informal saving methods. The preferred options that best serve their saving needs are keeping cash at home or in a secret hiding place (36.6 per cent), mobile phones (20.6 per cent),

in itself significantly influence one's likelihood of using mobile financial services. However, the coefficient for education, which in this case was the effect of education when female (with value zero, versus value one when male), was statistically significant and positive.

Table 9.3 Empirical results for saving and borrowing

Variable	Saved	Borrowed
Age	0.042***	0.074***
	(5.72)	(9.37)
Age squared	−0.0005***	−0.000***
	(−6.23)	(−10.1)
Marital status	0.12***	0.26***
	(2.53)	(5.42)
Education	0.50***	0.41***
	(9.87)	(8.21)
Female	−0.17***	0.21***
	(−3.77)	(−4.62)
Income	0.64***	0.20***
	(13.1)	(4.09)
No. of dependants	−0.053***	−0.035**
	(−2.91)	(−1.99)
Mobile phone access	0.62***	0.56***
	(6.89)	(6.24)
Salaried	1.04***	0.35***
	(10.3)	(3.96)
Constant	−2.18***	−2.47***
	(−12.1)	(−13.1)
Pseudo R squared	0.07	0.05
No. of observations	9,456	9,456

Note: Statistical z-values in brackets. *** and ** denote p-values of <1 per cent and <5 per cent respectively.
Source: authors' analysis based on data from FinScope Tanzania (2017).

saving groups (13.5 per cent), and banks (11 per cent). Responses by gender show some variations: higher proportions of men use mobile phones (25.2 per cent) and banks (14.3 per cent) to save, compared with 16.3 per cent and 8 per cent of women respectively. On the other hand, a higher proportion of women keep cash at home or in secret places (41.1 per cent) or save with saving groups (19.4 per cent), compared with 31.8 per cent and 7 per cent of men respectively. Thus, policies to promote financial access and savings should be cognizant of these gender differences in preferences. For instance, to encourage more women to save, policies and programmes should be geared more towards the promotion of saving groups, as bank-based saving products or initiatives mainly benefit men.

9.6 Conclusions and policy insights

Tanzania has made notable progress in the expansion of access to formal financial services. Nevertheless, a gender gap in financial access persists, despite the growing recognition of the role of financial inclusion in alleviating poverty and promoting inclusive development. This chapter analyses gender disparities in financial inclusion in Tanzania, using indicators that encompass access to and use of traditional bank-based and digital financial services, particularly mobile money services.

Based on Tanzania's FinScope survey for 2017, formal financial inclusion increased to 65 per cent in 2017, largely driven by mobile phone money services, which enabled more people who were previously excluded to access formal financial services. A more recent survey report shows access to formal financial services increased to 76 per cent in 2023. However, penetration of banking services is still low. Furthermore, women still lag behind in both access to and use of formal financial services. The gender gap in financial inclusion is reflected in gender disparities in access to and use of digital financial facilities such as mobile phones, especially smartphones that enable a variety of DFS. For instance, the gender gap in mobile phone ownership was 11 percentage points, while that for mobile Internet use was much higher at 18 percentage points in 2019.

The empirical results indicate that women, particularly married women, are less likely to access mobile phone and bank-based financial services compared with men. These results were obtained after controlling for a variety of factors such as education, income, marital status, employment, and mobile phone access. The impact of education on the likelihood of accessing banking services is nearly twice the impact on access to mobile financial services, which suggests the relative significance of education in the utilization of traditional banking services. Additionally, factors such as income, mobile phone ownership, and formal employment significantly increase financial inclusion. Given that women rank lower with regard to such factors, this places further constraints on their access to formal financial services.

Empirical analysis was further conducted to assess gender disparities in saving and borrowing, which are key indicators of the extent of utilization of financial services. The results show that women are less likely to save and borrow compared with men. Both men and women largely borrow and save to cater for living and medical expenses, and not for business purposes; this may suggest that access to medical services in Tanzania is a major concern that deserves attention. While a relatively higher proportion of men use mobile phones and banks to save, a higher percentage of women prefer to keep cash at home or save with a saving group.

Barriers to formal financial inclusion especially by women include lack of income, limited access to digital financial facilities such as smartphones, and lack of financial literacy. DFS are expected to play a more fundamental role, particularly in light of the challenges posed by the COVID-19 pandemic. As the economy continues to embrace digital transformation, it is important to put in place policies, measures, and strategies that are inclusive and gender-sensitive, so that digitally constrained population groups including women can effectively participate and benefit fully. Thus, the promotion of equal access to and usability of digital financial facilities, including mobile phones and smartphones is critical not only for enhancing financial inclusion and closing the gender gap, but also for enhancing the resilience of households and businesses. Furthermore, there is a need for enhancing financial literacy, especially among women. Policies to promote financial inclusion should also be cognizant of gender differences in preferences. For instance, policies and initiatives to increase financial inclusion and the use of formal financial services by women should be geared towards promoting saving groups to reach out to more women, as bank-based products and initiatives largely benefit men. The provision of safety nets for extremely needy cases should be considered.

References

Agur, I., S. M. Peria, and C. Rochon (2020). 'Digital Financial Services and the Pandemic: Opportunities and Risks for Emerging and Developing Economies'. IMF Special Series on COVID-19. Washington, DC: IMF. https://doi.org/10.1596/1813-9450-5537

Allen F., A. Demirguc-Kunt, L. Klapper, and M. Peria (2016). 'The Foundations of Financial Inclusion: Understanding Ownership and Use of Formal Accounts'. *Journal of Financial Intermediation*, 27: 1–30. https://doi.org/10.1016/j.jfi.2015.12.003

Alliance for Financial Inclusion (2016). 'Tanzania Narrows the Financial Inclusion Gender Gap: A Case Study of Policy Change to Support Women's Financial Inclusion'. Kuala Lumpur: Alliance for Financial Inclusion.

Alliance for Financial Inclusion (2021). 'Mitigating the Impact of Covid-19 on Gains in Financial Inclusion: Early Lessons from Regulators and Policy Makers'. Kuala Lumpur: Alliance for Financial Inclusion.

Ardic, O., H. Maximilien, and M. Nataliya. (2011). 'Access to Financial Services and the Financial Inclusion Agenda around the World: A Cross-Country Analysis with a New Data Set'. Policy Research Working Paper 5537. Washington, DC: World Bank.

Aterido, R., T. Beck, and L. Iacovone (2013). 'Access to Finance in Sub-Saharan Africa: Is There a Gender Gap?' *World Development*, 47: 102–20. https://doi.org/10.1016/j.worlddev.2013.02.013.

Bank of Tanzania (2020). *Annual Report 2019/2020*. Dar es Salaam: Bank of Tanzania.

Bank of Tanzania (2021). *Financial Sector Supervision Annual Report 2021*, 25th Edition. Dar es Salaam: Bank of Tanzania.

Beck, T., A. Demirguc-Kunt, and R. Levine (2007). 'Finance, Inequality, and the Poor'. *Journal of Economic Growth*, 12: 27–49. https://doi.org/10.1007/s10887-007-9010-6

Beck, T., A. Demirguc-Kunt, and M. S. Martinez Peria (2006). 'Banking Services for Everyone? Barriers to Bank Access around the World'. Policy Research Working Paper 4079. Washington, DC: World Bank. https://doi.org/10.1596/1813-9450-4079

Berger, A. N., and G. F. Udell (2006). 'A More Complete Conceptual Framework for SME Finance'. *Journal of Banking & Finance*, 30(11): 2945–66. https://doi.org/10.1016/j.jbankfin.2006.05.008

Botric V., and T. Broz (2017). 'Gender Differences in Financial Inclusion: Central and South-Eastern Europe'. *South-Eastern Europe Journal of Economics*, 2: 209–27.

Chakraborty, S. (2014). 'Laws, Attitudes and Financial Inclusion of Women: A Cross-Country Investigation'. *Economics Bulletin*, 34(1): 333–53.

Chakravorti, B., R.S. Chaturvedi, C. Filipovic, and G. Brewer (2020). 'Digital in the Time of COVID: Trust in the Digital Economy and its Evolution across 90 Economies as the Planet Paused for a Pandemic'. Boston, MA: The Fletcher School at Tufts University.

Coleman, S. (2002). 'Constraints Faced by Women Small Business Owners: Evidence from the Data'. *Journal of Developmental Entrepreneurship*, 7(2): 51–174.

Delechat, C. C., M. Newiak, R. Xu, F. Yang, and G. Aslan (2018). 'What Is Driving Women's Financial Inclusion across Countries?' IMF Working Paper 18/38. Washington, DC: IMF. https://doi.org/10.5089/9781484344460.001

Demirguc-Kunt, A., and L. Klapper (2012). 'Measuring Financial Inclusion: The Global Findex Database'. Policy Research Working Paper 6025. Washington, DC: World Bank. https://doi.org/10.1596/1813-9450-6025

Demirguc-Kunt, A., L. Klapper, and D. Singer (2013). 'Financial Inclusion and Legal Discrimination against Women'. Policy Research Working Paper 6416. Washington, DC: World Bank. https://doi.org/10.1596/1813-9450-6416

Demirguc-Kunt, A., L. Klapper, D. Singer, S. Ansar, and J. Hess (2018). 'The Global Findex Database 2017: Measuring Financial Inclusion and the Fintech Revolution'. Washington, DC: World Bank.

Demirguc-Kunt, A., L. Klapper, D. Singer, and P. Van Oudheusden (2014). 'The Global Findex Database 2014: Measuring Financial Inclusion around the World'. Policy Research Working Paper 7255. Washington, DC: World Bank. https://doi.org/10.1596/1813-9450-7255

Ellis, K., A. Lemma, and J. Rud (2010). 'Financial Inclusion, Household Investment and Growth in Kenya and Tanzania'. Project Briefing 42. London: Overseas Development Institute.

Fanta, A. B., and K. Mutsonziwa (2016). 'Gender and Financial Inclusion: Analysis of Financial Inclusion of Women in the SADC Region'. Policy Research Paper 01/2016. Johannesburg: FinMark Trust.

FinScope Tanzania (2017). 'Insights That Drive Financial Inclusion'. Dar es Salaam: FinScope Tanzania. Available at: www.fsdt.or.tz/wp-content/uploads/2017/09/FinScope-Tanzania-2017-Insights-that-Drive-Innovation.pdf (accessed 10 May 2021).

Goldsmith, W. (1969). *Financial Structure and Development*. New Haven, CT: Yale University Press.

Greenwood, J., and B. Jovanovic (1990). 'Financial Development, Growth, and the Distribution of Income'. *Journal of Political Economy*, 98(5): 1076–107. https://doi.org/10.1086/261720

Grossman, G. M., and E. Helpman (1991). 'Quality Ladders in the Theory of Growth'. *Review of Economic Studies*, 58(1): 43–61. https://doi.org/10.2307/2298044

GSMA (2017). '2017 State of the Industry Report on Mobile Money'. London: GSMA.

GSMA (2019). 'Connected Women: The Mobile Gender Gap Report 2019'. London: GSMA. Available at: www.gsma.com/mobilefordevelopment/wp-content/uploads/2019/02/GSMA-The-Mobile-Gender-Gap-Report-2019.pdf (accessed 10 May 2021).

GSMA (2020a). 'Connected Women: The Mobile Gender Gap Report 2020'. London: GSMA. Available at: www.gsma.com/mobilefordevelopment/wp-content/uploads/2020/05/GSMA-The-Mobile-Gender-Gap-Report-2020.pdf (accessed 10 May 2021).

GSMA (2020b). *Mobile Money Recommendations to Central Banks in Response to COVID-19*. London: GSMA.

Henseler, M., H. Maisonnave, and A. Maskaeva (2022). 'Economic Impacts of COVID-19 on the Tourism Sector in Tanzania'. *Annals of Tourism Research Empirical Insights*, 3(1). https://doi.org/10.1016/j.annale.2022.100042.

Honohan, P. (2004). 'Financial Development, Growth and Poverty: How Close Are the Links?' In C. Goodhart (ed.), *Financial Development and Economic Growth: Explaining the Links*. London: Palgrave Macmillan.

Honohan, P. (2007). 'Cross-Country Variation in Household Access to Financial Services'. *Journal of Banking & Finance*, 32(11): 2493–500. https://doi.org/10.1016/j.jbankfin.2008.05.004.

Idris, I. (2018a). 'Barriers to Women's Economic Inclusion in Tanzania'. K4D Helpdesk Report. Brighton: Institute of Development Studies.

Idris, I. (2018b). 'Mapping Women's Economic Exclusion in Tanzania'. K4D Helpdesk Report. Brighton: Institute of Development Studies.

ILO (2018). 'World Employment and Social Outlook: Trends 2018'. Geneva: ILO.

Kabubo-Mariara, J. (2003). 'Wage Determination and the Gender Wage Gap in Kenya: Any Evidence of Gender Discrimination?' Research Paper 132. Nairobi: AERC.

King, R. G., and R. Levine (1993). 'Finance, Entrepreneurship, and Growth: Theory and Evidence'. *Journal of Monetary Economics*, 32(3): 513–42. https://doi.org/10.1016/0304-3932(93)90028-E.

Levine, R. (2005). 'Finance and Growth: Theory and Evidence'. Working Paper 10766. Cambridge, MA: NBER. https://doi.org/10.3386/w10766.

Lotto, J. (2018). 'Examination of the Status of Financial Inclusion and its Determinants in Tanzania'. *Sustainability*, 10(8): 2873. https://doi.org/10.3390/su10082873

Maina, J. (2018). *Mobile Money Policy and Regulatory Handbook*. London: GSMA.

McKinnon, R.I. (1973). *Money and Capital in Economic Development*. Washington, DC: Brookings Institute.

Mndolwa, F. D., and A. L. Alhassan (2020). 'Gender Disparities in Financial Inclusion: Insights from Tanzania'. *African Development Review*, 32(4): 578–90. https://doi.org/10.1111/1467-8268.12462.

Naidoo, S., and A. Hilton (2006). *Access to Finance for Women Entrepreneurs in South Africa*. Washington, DC: World Bank.

Ndanshau, M.O.A., and F.E. Njau (2021). 'Empirical Investigation into Demand-Side Determinants of Financial Inclusion in Tanzania'. *African Journal of Economic Review*, 9(1): 172–90.

Nguena, C.L. (2019). 'Mobile Financial and Banking Services Development in Africa'. Working Paper Series 323. Abidjan: African Development Bank.

OECD (2018). *Bridging the Digital Gender Divide: Include, Upskill, Innovate*. Paris: OECD.

OECD (2020). *Advancing the Digital Financial Inclusion of Youth*. Paris: OECD.

Ouma, S.A., T.M. Odongo, and M. Were (2017). 'Mobile Financial Services and Financial Inclusion: Is It a Boon for Savings Mobilization?' *Review of Development Finance*, 7(1): 29–35. https://doi.org/10.1016/j.rdf.2017.01.001.

Pande, R., S. Cole, A. Sivasankaran, G. Bastian, and K. Durlacher (2012). 'Does Poor People's Access to Formal Banking Services Raise their Incomes?' London: Institute of Education.

Pazarbasioglu, C., A. G. Mora, M. Uttamchandani, H. Natarajan, E. Feyen, and M. Saal (2020). *Digital Financial Services*. Washington, DC: World Bank.

Sahay, R., U. Eriksson von Allmen, A. Lahreche, P. Khera, S. Ogawa, M. Bazarbash, and K. Beaton (2020). 'The Promise of Fintech: Financial Inclusion in the Post COVID-19 Era'. Departmental Paper 20/09. Washington, DC: IMF.

Were, M., Odongo, M. T. and Israel, C. (2021). 'Gender Disparities in Financial Inclusion in Tanzania'. WIDER Working Paper 2021/97. Helsinki: UNU-WIDER.

World Bank (2008). 'Finance for All? Policies and Pitfalls in Expanding Access'. World Bank Policy Research Report. Washington, DC: World Bank.

World Bank (2014). 'Global Financial Development Report 2014: Financial Inclusion'. Washington, DC: World Bank.

World Bank (2015). 'Empowering Women through Financial Inclusion'. Available at: www.worldbank.org/en/news/feature/2015/08/05/empowering-women-through-financial-inclusion (accessed 11 May 2021).

World Bank (2020a). 'Digital Financial Services'. Washington, DC: World Bank.

World Bank (2020b). 'Tanzania Economic Update: Addressing the Impact of Covid-19 Pandemic'. Washington, DC: World Bank.

10

Implications for making the achievements sustainable

Oliver Morrissey, Joseph Semboja, and Maureen Were

10.1 Introduction

This chapter draws together the lessons from the studies for addressing the challenges (constraints that need to be overcome) and leveraging opportunities (to facilitate change) to ensure the sustainability of development in Tanzania, particularly given the effects of the COVID-19 pandemic and other emerging global challenges. The analyses of firms highlight the importance of technology, innovation, market access and developing linkages—through networks, clusters, export diversification, and value chains—to support the competitiveness and sustainable growth of firms. Other contributions identify the importance of income diversification and financial inclusion for the sustainable development of households. Cross-cutting themes emerge on the need for modern technology and infrastructure to increase the productivity and employment of firms, investment in human capital to reduce gender inequalities and upgrade or equip workers as well entrepreneurs with relevant skills, and access to resources for innovation. Section 10.2 draws out these implications.

The emergence of the COVID-19 pandemic in early 2020 represented a large shock that would test the ability of firms and households to manage crises and sustain themselves. The apparent incidence of COVID-19 was low in Tanzania compared to neighbours, primarily because the government didn't report information, especially during the period May 2020 to May 2021. Between January 2020 and July 2022, Tanzania only reported just over 36,000 confirmed cases (compared to 336,000 in Kenya and just over 168,000 in Uganda), with peaks in September and December 2021, and January and May 2022. Tanzania recorded only 850 confirmed deaths (compared to over 5,600 in Kenya and 3,600 in Uganda), with peaks in October 2021 and January 2022. In contrast to Kenya and Uganda that had various restrictions in place from 2020 through 2021, Tanzania imposed no extensive workplace closures or stay-at-home requirements.[1] Although at the outset of

---

[1] Data on COVID-19 incidence, certainly underestimates for Tanzania, and lockdown indicators are from https://ourworldindata.org/coronavirus (accessed 12 July 2022).

Oliver Morrissey, Joseph Semboja, and Maureen Were, *Implications for making the achievements sustainable*.
In: *Sustaining Tanzania's Economic Development*. Edited by: Oliver Morrissey, Joseph Semboja, and Maureen Were,
Oxford University Press. © UNU-WIDER (2024). DOI: 10.1093/oso/9780192885746.003.0010

the pandemic in March 2020 the government undertook some basic containment measures such as restricting most mass gatherings and access to international flights and the temporary closure of schools, these were short-lived and lasted only a few months. When President Samia Suluhu Hassan assumed power following the death of President Magufuli in March 2021, some measures were put in place, such as recommending the use of masks in public and a vaccination campaign, but the government avoided restrictions that would significantly disrupt economic activity (Aikaeli et al. 2021: 1886).

While COVID-19 restrictions were not as severe as in neighbouring countries, the regional and global effects of the pandemic had a devastating effect on the hospitality sector (the collapse of tourism and lower domestic use of hotels and restaurants, many of which closed for periods), a direct impact on trade and an indirect effect on households. There were adverse effects on various sectors, especially MSMEs, and vulnerable groups including women. Most MSMEs depend on imported goods from countries that imposed travel bans and restrictions on industries, including closure of some firms, and exports were severely limited leading to reduced volumes of imported goods (Alliance for Financial Inclusion 2021). The adverse impact of the pandemic on tourism was felt in other domestic sectors such as transport, hotel and accommodation, food and beverages, and the retail trade, given their interlinkages with the tourism industry (Henseler et al. 2022). As a result, household incomes declined. Real GDP growth fell by about two-thirds to 2 per cent in 2020,[2] and per capita GDP declined; sales of SMEs declined by one third on average; about 140,000 formal jobs were lost in 2020 and incomes fell for most of the more than two million non-agricultural informal workers; poverty rose and over half a million people may have been pushed below the poverty line (World Bank 2021: 11–12). Section 10.3 considers how firms and households can address and recover from the COVID-19 shock and build resilience to cope with other future crises or shocks, while Section 10.4 provides final comments.

10.2 Lessons from the studies

Engagement in international trade offers a clear route to sustained growth for firms in manufacturing sectors but is not a guarantee without concerted efforts towards innovation, adopting (modern) technology, diversification and developing support linkages with other firms, including through integration in value chains (VCs), from which one can learn. Although international trade and regional integration potentially provide a wider market and support linkages and learning, SMEs in Tanzania have limited involvement in regional and global value chains.

---

[2] Based on data from Tanzania's National Bureau of Statistics, real GDP growth is estimated to have fallen moderately to 4.8 per cent in 2020.

While this provides some protection from global shocks, it also undermines firms' ability to grow, become competitive and sustain the growth. Moreover, the COVID-19 pandemic has further demonstrated the importance of building resilience through export diversification, which can be explained through a portfolio effect (absorbing shocks and reducing volatility) and a dynamic effect of learning from the introduction of new products (UNCTAD 2022).

Backward and forward linkages are key to enhancing industrial growth and market access. Chapter 2 by Kweka and Sooi considers the importance of firm linkages, especially between large and small firms through international trade—exporting (including access to VCs), importing inputs, and technology sharing are all ways that firm networks can be beneficial. The analysis confirms that firms that develop foreign linkages through trade (mostly manufacturing) tend to grow more. However, very few SMEs are engaged in international trade, while firms in service sectors are constrained in their ability to achieve sustained growth because they are small and local without structures to learn from more successful firms. While linkages with large firms can enhance the performance of SMEs, the level of such linkages is low in Tanzania. This is because SMEs have limited production capacity, low engagement in training and exporting, and appear not to benefit from technology partnerships (in part because so few have any foreign ownership) or industry associations (also noted in Chapter 4). Industrial policy to promote SMEs should encourage and support linkages with larger firms, especially for identifying and adopting appropriate technology, product, and process innovations. The evidence suggests that SMEs can improve productivity through competition with and learning from larger firms.

The analysis by Boys and Andreoni in Chapter 3 shows that national (NVC), regional (RVC) and global (GVC) value chains are associated with different opportunities for product, process, and market upgrading. GVCs offer the least potential for upgrading as firms are restricted to a narrow range of low-value activities (mostly apparel assembly), whereas RVCs and NVCs permit vertical integration and upgrading into higher-value activities and facilitate subsequent entry into more lucrative (in terms of revenue potential) GVCs. Preferential market access is important for regional and global VCs but features of trade agreements, such as rules of origin limiting where imports can be sourced from, affect incentives and limit the benefits of market access. Competition from cheap clothing imports and second-hand clothes (*mitumba*) has undermined the sustainability of some local firms. Those firms active in RVCs and NVCs are more resilient because they diversify into higher-value activities or through vertical integration into textile manufacture, whereas firms in GVCs appear less able to diversify.

Regional and international market access, such as duty-free arrangements in SADC, EAC, and AGOA, are a clear benefit for RVC and GVC firms as long as rules of origin are favourable. Uncertainty surrounding the future nature of agreements with the United States (AGOA) and the European Union discourages investment in GVC firms, although RVC firms can benefit from further opportunities within Africa such as the EAC or African Continental Free Trade Area (AfCFTA). Industrial policy can support the sustainable growth of apparel and textiles firms by recognizing how opportunities and needs differ between different value chains and ensuring that this is reflected in trade agreements. Leveraging the opportunities accorded by the AfCFTA will, besides providing access to a wider market of over 1.3 billion people, be instrumental in strengthening existing RVCs and developing new ones. Tanzania's parliament ratified the agreement in September 2021.[3]

The ability to increase productive capacity depends on the availability of inputs and technology. Linkages and trade are central to increasing access to intermediate goods and modern technology to boost productivity for sustainable growth. Saha, Bueno Rezende de Castro, Carreras, and Guariso (Chapter 4) show the importance of using imported technology to increase productivity for textiles and apparel firms to integrate with global markets; weak local networks and shortages of skilled labour are major constraints to absorptive capacity, given the importance of hiring labour with appropriate skills and learning from others how to incorporate these skills when adopting new technology to ensure full gains in productivity are realized. Upgrading of processes, especially adopting new technology, and products, into higher-value-added lines, are vital for firms to build resilience and sustain growth. Limited absorptive capacity is suggested as the reason why firms that introduced new products or processes were adopting what already existed in the domestic market—the products and processes were only new to the firm so there was no general sector upgrading. Firms reported inadequate access to technology and constrained ability to increase production capacity because of costly and cumbersome customs and procedures to avail of tax incentives for the importation of machinery and inputs, given limited availability and the low quality of local inputs and raw materials. Local firm networks, prevalent in the southern region of Tanzania but absent in the northern region, are associated with more productive firms, while firms in both regions derive few real benefits from membership of sectoral and industry associations.

Engagement in value chains and networks of firms, combined with innovation and access to technology, promote export diversification and competitiveness that support sustained growth. Misati and Ngoka in Chapter 5 show the association of participation in GVCs with sustainable growth of manufacturing exports, noting that manufacturing exports are mostly in low-technology sectors and engagement in GVCs is largely limited to textiles, garments, and footwear. Analysis of determinants indicate that FDI, tariffs in export markets, and inflation (capturing domestic economic conditions) are associated with low export competitiveness while total investment, labour productivity, infrastructure, and

---

[3] Launched in July 2019, the AfCFTA was expected to become operational in January 2021.

institutions (all measured at the national level) are associated with manufacturing export growth and improved competitiveness. Trade policies and deeper regional integration can benefit competitiveness by reducing tariffs and other barriers faced by exporters. The negative effect of FDI may be because it is largely in resource sectors rather than manufacturing, while the positive effect of total investment is consistent with benefits of improved infrastructure. A remaining constraint is that levels of technology-intensive and skilled-labour-intensive manufactures are low, while high tariffs on imports discourage the use of imported intermediate inputs that could increase productivity. Although GVC participation is associated with improved export performance and competitiveness, it remains limited beyond apparel, textiles, and footwear—further regional integration offers potential benefits.

All of these chapters show the importance of market access and technology adoption for increasing productivity and achieving sustainable growth. That notwithstanding, the role of gender equality in promoting sustainable development is widely acknowledged. Chapter 6 by Barasa addresses gender differences in innovation, noting that male-owned firms engage in more innovation and this appears to be because they have higher endowments, especially higher levels of investment (implying easier access to credit) and a lower skills gap (suggesting better ability to recruit suitable workers). However, despite having less favourable endowments, female entrepreneurs are found to use their resources more effectively (the coefficients are higher for female-owned firms); indeed, experienced females are more likely to innovate than males. Therefore, measures to increase the endowments of female entrepreneurs, such as supporting access to credit and management training and reducing skill gaps, would reduce innovation gender gaps, promote female entrepreneurship and improve competitiveness (given the importance of innovation and technology). Innovation in male-owned enterprises could be increased by hiring experienced female managers (implying that it is not the number of female managers but their skills and experience that matters).

The remaining chapters addressed experiences of households. Employment growth in manufacturing and increasing the value added of firms as part of structural transformation is essential to increase the wage share in labour income to support higher household incomes and achieve sustainable livelihoods. In Chapter 7, Khan and Morrissey show that increasing diversification into non-agricultural wage activities (which accounted for an increasing share of employment) and self-employment is associated with higher welfare (in terms of household consumption) whereas farming and agricultural wage employment (a source of increased employment for rural females) are associated with lower household welfare. The findings are consistent with evidence on the importance of off-farm employment for rural households and shows the importance of non-agricultural wage employment (growth of which requires a dynamic firm sector) for urban households.

The analysis reveals significant gender differences. Agricultural wage employment has been the main activity for increased female employment, especially in rural areas, but is characterized by low skills and earnings. Such employment may be the only option for less-educated females, chosen to meet household income needs rather than as a strategy to support sustained increases in welfare. Increasing productivity in agriculture is required to increase rural incomes and will benefit females. Although the most promising employment for all genders, males benefited most from the growth in non-agricultural wage employment, largely because they are likely to be more educated and able to meet the demand for skills by firms. Increasing educational attainment while reducing gender gaps will support growth in household welfare as long as employment opportunities for skilled workers increases (which requires sustained growth in firms and the services sector). Irrespective of gender, non-agricultural self-employment is associated with improved welfare, but employment growth has been slow.

Chapter 8 by Dimova, Halvorsen, Nyyssölä, and Sen explores the drivers of livelihood diversification and supports the accumulation hypothesis whereby richer households engage in more income diversification than poorer households. The greater diversification capacity of better-off households observed in the 1990s—attributable to access to credit, electricity, postal and telephone services, and migration—persisted in 2004. Nevertheless, diversification of poor households improved to the extent there were opportunities to move into off-farm self-employment activities. Rural households are willing to use income from agriculture to diversify into non-agricultural activities, and this can be facilitated by improving transport and market access.

These two chapters highlight the importance of increasing the availability of better jobs (with higher earnings) for sustained household development. Availing of these opportunities requires workers with education and skills and the ability to access credit (to invest in education, business, or farming). Several chapters indicate gender inequalities in endowments, whether for employment or entrepreneurship, that undermine growth potential. Chapter 9 by Were, Odongo, and Israel adds to this concern, focusing on the gender gaps in financial inclusion. Although the advent of mobile money services has greatly enhanced financial inclusion, women are less likely to access formal financial services (mobile phone and bank-based financial services which are the main forms of formal inclusion) and less likely to save or borrow compared to men. Factors that influence access to formal financial services include education, income, employment, and mobile phone access. Given the heightened need to embrace a digital economy following the effects of the COVID-19 pandemic, reducing the gender gaps and increasing formal inclusion through access to and use of digital financial services is important to build household resilience and support sustained improvements in household welfare. Among other measures, this requires improving female education, financial literacy, and employment opportunities; promoting equal access to digital financial platforms such as smartphones, as well as being cognizant of the gender differences in preferences (for instance, women prefer saving clubs and are less likely to use banks for saving). Furthermore, the growth of financial technology and innovation provides new avenues of funding businesses and can help address the credit constraints faced by firms, especially MSMEs, and facilitate cross-border transactions. Enhancing the access of female entrepreneurs to credit can reduce gender innovation gaps.

10.3 The pandemic and sustainability

The research for the chapters was completed before the COVID-19 pandemic in early 2020. As the pandemic was a large shock affecting sustainability of firms and households, and there were severe economic effects associated with employment and income losses, such as loss of export revenue and tourist earnings and disruptions in the supply of imported inputs and lower consumer spending, the authors considered some implications for their analysis. This section combines and integrates these reflections to derive medium-term implications for recovery and future sustainability.

Survey evidence found that sales, especially for SMEs, fell by over a third in manufacturing and services sectors while sales in the agricultural sector fell by over a fifth (World Bank 2021: 29). Kweka and Sooi (Chapter 2) note the adverse effects on SMEs as many firms reduced or even halted operations and linkages, especially those associated with international trade, were weakened or suspended. As Tanzania recovers, SMEs will require assistance such as reducing trade costs to facilitate re-establishing international linkages and reducing business costs due to statutory requirements and government regulations, including labour laws that constrain the ability of firms to adjust to economic downturns. The pandemic is likely to have had greater adverse effects on female entrepreneurs given their greater caring and family responsibilities (Barasa: Chapter 6).

In many respects exports held up well; although total exports fell by almost 10 per cent in 2020, this was almost entirely due to declines in services exports (especially tourism, which lost almost 80 per cent of revenue and had accounted for about 17 per cent of GDP in 2019) with a small (2 per cent) decline in traditional exports; manufacturing exports increased, and gold increased by a third. However, capital and intermediate imports fell by 15–20 per cent (World Bank 2021: 30). Given the importance of access to imported inputs and technology for firm performance and productivity, this could exacerbate the negative effects on SMEs and slow their ability to recover fully. The expectation is that over the medium term trade flows should be restored, although this will be constrained by the weakness of the global economy.

Apparel exports were affected by the global pandemic as global trade in ready-made garments and footwear was severely affected by the lockdown in developed countries. The closure of retail outlets was associated with an estimated 90 per cent decline in sales in the United States and European Union in April 2020, only slightly offset by online trade, although by the end of the year sales were only about 10 per cent below the normal level (Castañeda-Navarrete et al. 2021). The cancellation of orders by global buyers combined with the severe disruptions to global supply chains that has persisted beyond 2021 meant that the textiles and apparel sector in Tanzania is likely to have been severely affected. This undermined the achievements, documented in Chapters 3 and 4, of firms integrating into GVCs and availing of technology and upgrading. RVCs have the potential to recover faster and may prove more resilient in the future. The Tanzanian government implemented some measures to support the sector, such as encouraging local production of face masks, sanitary materials, and other personal protective equipment. Firms requested more support to reduce taxes and operating costs, including labour and debt servicing, and restricting imports of second-hand clothing (Chapter 4).

Given the household characteristics associated with vulnerability to poverty—low education, employment in agriculture, large households, and living in rural areas (Aikaeli et al. 2021: 1872)—inferences can be drawn on the sustainability of welfare improvements due to diversification since 2020. The impact of COVID-19 appears to have been less severe in rural areas so farming households and agricultural wage workers (many of them female) may have suffered a lower loss of income, although these were initially the lower-income households. However, the extent of rural–urban linkages (e.g. most burials take place in rural areas) and income transfers imply that the social and economic implications could be more pronounced and lasting for the rural sector. The non-agricultural employment sector experienced the greatest income losses during COVID-19, especially in urban areas (with higher deaths and health costs), but was arguably, sufficiently flexible to bounce back after the economy began to recover. Females were disadvantaged in non-agricultural employment as they worked fewer hours and were more likely to be in temporary or informal employment, and hence, suffered more from downturns in economic activity. An unintended consequence of avoiding lockdowns is that Tanzania gained less experience than other countries in adapting to online work and education and developing online systems.

10.4 Prospects for the future

As recounted in Chapter 1, Tanzania implemented a range of economic reforms from the late 1980s, especially in areas of trade policy and macroeconomic management, that helped establish the conditions for good economic growth performance and poverty reduction since the 1990s. While contributions in Adam et al. (2017) address reforms and performance from macroeconomic and sector perspectives, the chapters in this volume provide an assessment from firm and household perspectives. There have been improvements in firm performance, especially for those globally integrated through value chains and trade. The benefit is not simply through exports as global integration also supports technology upgrading, through imported inputs and networks, and competitiveness that supports a more dynamic domestic sector. The analysis of households highlights the importance of sustainable growth in firms to generate increased wage employment (associated with increasing household welfare). Enhanced financial inclusion with lower gender gaps is instrumental in providing access to credit for entrepreneurs (financing innovation), to support household investment (in education, agriculture, or business), and to make it easier for households to cope with income shocks.

The achievements are limited: export diversification in manufacturing is largely in low-technology products; participation in GVCs and RVCs is predominantly only apparel and textiles; levels of innovation and firm networks are low; growth in non-agricultural wage employment needs to increase, both to reduce the skills gaps of firms and to increase the availability of better-earning jobs for workers (for sustained increases in household welfare); and productivity, hence earnings, in agriculture remains low. One of the major constraints on sustainable firm growth has been low productivity, especially of labour, while low human capital has meant many workers were not prepared for higher-skilled work that would increase earnings. These constraints have to be addressed to support recovery from the effects of the pandemic and establish the foundations for sustainable firm growth. 'Meeting the dual challenge of investment and productivity growth will require a consistent focus on human capital formation, including skills training and job matching, supported by a favourable climate for technology transfer and innovation, and a proactive trade and investment policy that continually seeks new opportunities' (World Bank 2021: 77). The contributions in this volume show that these efforts can be effective in supporting sustainable growth of firms and an associated growth of non-agricultural employment improves the prospects for increasing household welfare.

Many chapters highlight the importance of education, to provide skills for firms, innovative entrepreneurs, and enable households to access higher-earning labour activities. While more needs to be done, access to education has improved and there is evidence for Tanzania that returns to education in terms of higher incomes are significant. Delesalle (2021) estimates that the UPE programme of 1974–78 increased consumption in 2002 of household heads exposed to 1974–78 programmes by 6 per cent. Serneels et al. (2017) estimated that returns for a year of post-primary school ranged between zero and 20 per cent for men and between 30 per cent and 50 per cent for women, although Belghith et al. (2020: 8), while recognizing that education is positively associated with earnings and household welfare, note that by 2018 there were minimal income gains from primary education. Barasa (Chapter 6) concluded that improving the quality of the labour force and encouraging female participation in STEM subjects promotes entrepreneurial activity by providing technical knowledge and computing and numeracy skills. Employers also value inter-personal and communication skills, soft skills that can be provided through on-the-job training and work experience.

Although, as noted, the COVID-19 pandemic had adverse effects on firms and households, especially through the loss of tourism and export earnings, and declining sales for many firms, the impact was less than for most countries because restrictions were relatively few and temporary. For example, Tanzania only required widespread school closures from the end of March to June 2020, although access to schooling may have been restricted for some schools or regions throughout 2021 (often closure was recommended even if not required), so the potential cost of lost education is relatively mild. Angrist et al. (2021) estimate that learning losses were lower in Tanzania compared with Kenya and Uganda which had longer school closures (with some variation, general school closures were in place in Kenya for March to December 2020 and April to August 2021, and in Uganda from March 2020 to the end of 2021). It will be easier for children to make up lost ground in education, mitigating adverse effects on human capital in the medium term so skilled labour will be available as firms recover.

The next few years will be challenging for Tanzania given the precarious state of the global economy. The global recovery from the pandemic has been derailed by the impact of Russia's invasion of Ukraine on energy and food supply and prices. Sustained high temperatures and drought due to climate change in many countries exacerbated these pressures, especially regarding food supply. The global environment remains highly uncertain, considering the prolonged monetary policy tightening in advanced economies, heightened geopolitical tensions and the slow economic recovery. The immediate implications for Tanzania are slow growth of exports, high food prices and increasing interest rates (with associated challenges for debt management). Countries have to prepare for a period of retrenchment with increasing poverty (or at least vulnerability). The optimism that Tanzania could have had for much of its performance by 2018 has to be tempered, but the gains made by firms and households since 2000 need not be lost. The analysis in this volume identifies some of the growth drivers to build on, such as financial inclusion and engagement in regional trade and integration, and constraints to continue addressing to increase the resilience of firms and households.

References

Adam, C., P. Collier, and B. Ndulu (eds) (2017). *Tanzania: The Path to Prosperity*. Oxford: Oxford University Press. https://doi.org/10.1093/acprof:oso/9780198704812.001.0001.

Aikaeli, J., D. Garcés-Urzainqui, and K. Mdadila (2021). 'Understanding Poverty Dynamics and Vulnerability in Tanzania: 2012–2018', *Review of Development Economics*, 25: 1869–94. https://doi.org/10.1111/rode.12829.

Alliance for Financial Inclusion (2021). *Mitigating the Impact of COVID-19 on Gains in Financial Inclusion: Early Lessons from Regulators and Policymakers*. Kuala Lumpur: Alliance for Financial Inclusion.

Angrist, N., A. de Barros, R. Bhula, S. Chakera, C. Cummiskey, J. DeStefano, J. Floretta, M. Kaffenberger, B. Piper, and J. Stern (2021). 'Building Back Better to Avert a Learning Catastrophe: Estimating Learning Loss from COVID-19 School Shutdowns in Africa and Facilitating Short-term and Long-term Learning Recovery'. *International Journal of Educational Development*, 84. Available at: https://doi.org/10.1016/j.ijedudev.2021.102397.

Belghith, N. B. H., W. Karamba, E. Talbert, P. de Boisseson (2020). *Tanzania Mainland Poverty Assessment: Tanzania's Path to Poverty Reduction and Pro-Poor Growth*. Washington, DC: World Bank. http://documents.worldbank.org/curated/en/254411585030305188/pdf/Part-1-Path-to-Poverty-Reduction-and-Pro-Poor-Growth.pdf.

Castañeda-Navarrete, J., J. Hauge, and C. López-Gómez (2021). 'Covid-19's Impacts on Global Value Chains, as Seen in the Apparel Industry'. *Development Policy Review*, 39(6): 953–70.

Delesalle, E. (2021). 'The Effect of the Universal Primary Education Program on Consumption and on the Employment Sector: Evidence from Tanzania'. *World Development*, 142: 105345. https://doi.org/10.1016/j.worlddev.2020.105345.

Henseler, M., H. Maisonnave, and A. Maskaeva (2022). 'Economic Impacts of COVID-19 on the Tourism Sector in Tanzania'. *Annals of Tourism Research Empirical Insights*, 3(1): 1–12. https://doi.org/10.1016/j.annale.2022.100042.

Serneels, P., K. Beegle, and A. Dillon (2017). 'Do Returns to Education Depend on How and Whom You Ask?' *Economics of Education Review*, 60: 5–19. https://doi.org/10.1016/j.econedurev.2017.07.010.

UNCTAD (2022). 'The Economic Development in Africa Report 2022: Rethinking the Foundations of Export Diversification in Africa—The Catalytic Role of Business and Financial Services'. Geneva: United Nations Conference on Trade and Development (UNCTAD).

World Bank (2021). 'Tanzania Economic Update February 2021: Raising the Bar: Achieving Tanzania's Development Vision'. Washington, DC: World Bank. https://documents.worldbank.org/en/publication/documents-reports/documentdetail/803171614697018449/tanzania-economic-update-raising-the-bar-achieving-tanzania-s-development-vision.

Index

For the benefit of digital users, indexed terms that span two pages (e.g., 52–53) may, on occasion, appear on only one of those pages.